# ALASKANS

# ALASKANS

## LIFE ON THE LAST FRONTIER

### RON STRICKLAND

## STACKPOLE
## BOOKS

Published by
STACKPOLE BOOKS
Cameron and Kelker Streets
P.O. Box 1831
Harrisburg, PA 17105

Printed in the United States of America

Cover photos, top to bottom, © Jeff Schultz, Jeff Schultz, Clark Mishler, Jeff Schultz, and Jeff Schultz, all of Alaska Stock Images.
Cover design by Mark Olszewski.

First Edition

10 9 8 7 6 5 4 3 2 1

Portions of *Alaskans* are reprinted with permission from the following sources:

Alaska Native Language Center. *Walter Northway.* Fairbanks: University of Alaska, 1987.
Bahovic, Fred. *The First Hundred Years.* 1989.
Blackman, Margaret B. *Sadie Brower Neakok: An Iñupiaq Woman.* Seattle: University of Washington Press, 1989.
Brookman, Al, Sr. *Sitka Man.* Anchorage: Alaska Northwest Publishing Company, 1984.
Madison, Curt, and Yvonne Yarber. *Josephine Roberts: A Biography.* Yukon-Koyukuk School District Biography Series. Fairbanks: Spirit Mountain Press, 1983.
Shields, Mary. *Sled Dog Trails.* Fairbanks, Pyrola Publishing, 1984.
Ulen, Tishu. As told to Shirley English. "Tishu's World" *Alaska Geographic* 10 (4): 19–24 (1983).

**Library of Congress Cataloging-in-Publication Data**

Alaskans : life on the last frontier / Ron Strickland. — 1st ed.
    p.    cm.
    Includes index.
    ISBN 0-8117-1865-4 : $24.95
    1. Alaska—Social life and customs.    2. Interviews—Alaska.
  I. Strickland, Ron.
  F910.5.A37    1992
  979.8—dc20                        92-14706
                                                   CIP

*To the next generation
of Alaska's writers and storytellers*

# Contents

# Acknowledgments

Bush traditions of cooperation predate recorded history. In telling me of Eskimo ways at Point Hope, where arctic conditions make hospitality synonymous with survival, Pigooruk St. Germaine said:

> Guests stayed for days and days, just like relatives. My grandparents or anyone else just welcomed the visitors and fed them and if their clothing needed fixing, the women fixed it up for them. My mom's great uncle used to tell me, "If a stranger comes to the village, give him a smile and invite him for a drink of water or hot tea because when you grow up you never know when you're going to need that smile from the strangers to make you feel good."

The making of this book has been full of those smiles. My long interviewing tours in 1989 and 1990 would not have been possible without generous assistance from people everywhere along the way. Amtrak provided assistance in the Lower 48, and the Alaska Marine Highway System helped greatly in Southeast Alaska. I am also greatly indebted to the White Pass & Yukon Route of Skagway; Alaskon (bus); Westours/Holland America Lines of Seattle; Yutana Barge Lines of Nenana; BP of Anchorage; and Kenai Fjords Tours of Seward. In addition, photographer Sheila Foster of Wilmington, Delaware, loaned me her faithful *Delawagon* van and contributed many portraits to this book.

This project was so underfunded that I only managed to survive by housesitting and by "homestays." My saviors included Keith Clark and Toni Diedrich of Anchorage; Barbara and Sam Davidson of Mercer Island, Washington; Bob and Nina Randolph of Seattle; David and Carol De Voe and Drenda Tigner of Fairbanks; Steve and Gayla Hites of Skagway; David Job of Juneau; Ted and Stephanie Hitzroth of Bellevue, Washington; Pat and Angie Skinner of North Pole; Connie Taylor of Cordova; Ron and Pat Welsh of Sitka; Connie Graffis and Rick Huff of Anchorage; Ruby and Robert Ackert of Waterville, Vermont; and Jack and Roo Slagle of Belvidere, Vermont.

I wish especially to recognize my travel partners: Kelly Bangham of Seattle; Joan Sias of Seattle; Bernie Zauner of Neuravensburg, Germany;

Loes Van Langen of Amsterdam, Holland; Kevin Paulus of Fairbanks; Sheila Foster of Wilmington, Delaware; and Jill "Tundra Tula" Sternberg of Brooklyn, New York. Tundra Tula distinguished herself by cheerily coping with two and a half months of often difficult travel and by weaning me from baked goods.

This project is supported in part by a grant from the Alaska Humanities Forum and the National Endowment for the Humanities, a federal agency.

Among the many additional people who helped, I want to mention Margaret Considine of Akron, Ohio; Mr. and Mrs. Kenneth Eckhardt of Newark, Delaware; Rick Hockley of Dillon, Montana; Orrie Bell of Petersburg; Claude Demientieff, Chris Butcher, and Cherie Gojenola of Anchorage; bike mechanic Dave Hawkins of Bellevue, Washington; Elisabeth Hakkinen and Rebecca Nelson, the Sheldon Museum, Leo Land, John and Sharon Svenson, and Ray and Vivian Menaker of Haines; Kim Turley and Richard Meeker of Juneau; Andy Pauken of St. Marys; Rep. Robin Taylor of Wrangell; Gov. Wally Hickel of Anchorage; Paul Brewster of Ketchikan; Donna MacAlpine of Anvik; and U.S. Park Service ranger Chris Kounkel of Spokane. I am especially grateful to oral history maven Bill Schneider for his experience and good sense; I recommend him to anyone who needs advice or inspiration concerning oral history interviewing in Alaska. (Oral History Program, Rasmuson Library, University of Alaska, Fairbanks, Alaska, 99775-1005).

Thank you *all!* Your smiles saw me through the hard times and made the good times even better.

# Introduction

Five dozen Alaskans have recorded their feelings and memories for this statewide self-portrait.

In selecting these stories I have been searching for the essence of Alaskan-ness, a quality sometimes as elusive as the northern lights and often as emotion charged as the call of a wolf across the tundra. Alaska is so vast that generalizing about it is risky. The coastal forests of Metlakatla have little relation to the arctic barrens of Barrow. North Slope wildlife has little similarity to that of the Aleutian chain. And the human history of one area is likely to be very different from that of even a relatively nearby district. Nevertheless, I hope that you will come away from *Alaskans* with an impression of both diversity and shared identity.

This book is the newest volume in a continuing series of oral history portraits of America's regions. It is also the fulfillment of a long-ago dream. I had wanted to go to the North ever since my boyhood correspondence from Pennsylvania with the postmaster of Allakaket, an Athabaskan village on the Koyukuk River. I had written to inquire about homesteading in the Interior, my noggin full of wilderness adventure, northern lights, Robert Service, and Sergeant Preston of the Yukon. Allakaket's postmaster wrote a gracious letter to adolescent me and that was the end of that. Temporarily! Thirty years later, in 1989, I tried again. But just going to Alaska the modern way, by jetliner, would have been too easy. I had to approach the North in a way reminiscent of the generations of other cheechakos, especially those of 1898. So I sailed north to Skagway, gold rush port for the Klondike. There rubberneckers from five cruise ships thronged the quaint streets, just as gold seekers had at the turn of the century. And like many of the old-timers, I took the White Pass & Yukon Route narrow gauge railway, switchbacking from sea level to 2,915 feet above it at White Pass. Once in the Coast Mountains at the British Columbia border I planned to enter interior Alaska under my own steam via the route of '98. So I bicycled from White Pass north across B.C. and the Yukon Territory, seven hundred kilometers to Dawson City. This month-long adventure (plus a side trip to Inuvik near the Beaufort Sea) was a quick glimpse of the peoples, wildlife, geography, and weather of the North, and it was all even better than I had dared to hope! Today I remain thankful to have seen Alaska first through the traditional door of the Yukon, to have lived on daily terms with the distances, horizons, and sunsets.

Some stampeders arrived in the Klondike by bicycle, and my experience pedaling north across the province revealed a landscape that retained stirring echoes of the gold rush past. By contrast, Alaska was a country at first difficult to differentiate from the rest of American life. Unlike the Yukon's outdoor historical museum atmosphere, Alaska seemed to have a permanent boom mentality. Only gradually did I learn how to pan for my own kind of riches. Amid all the Seattle brand names and Lower 48 appurtenances I hitched, bicycled, flew, and tugboated in search of the real Alaska. I interviewed in kitchens, village streets, boats, corporate headquarters, anywhere where there was a good story about people's feelings about themselves as Alaskans.

If I have done my job right, the sum of these chapters will be much greater than the individual stories. A reader will become immersed in a stream of Alaskan thoughts and experiences. That creek becomes a river and then a flood. The voices blend into a sea of sensation and memory called Alaska.

My definition of an Alaskan is someone whose self-identity is bound up with the state of Alaska. Being an Alaskan is often a conscious decision because of the hardships of climate and distance.

Am I creating Alaskan-ness in the very act of searching for it? Perhaps, but in exploring people's relationships to the land and its history I have restricted myself to how Natives, cheechakos, and sourdoughs have actually lived.

Remember, of course, that these storytellers did not usually see themselves as speaking about Alaskan-ness but about history. Their tales were offered to me as chronologies of real events. That they have become dots in a pointillist painting of Alaskan-ness will please and mystify them.

Alaska is still a very young state. I met many people (especially in Southeast) who had actively fought statehood during the 1950s. Alaska's population is transient, its economy still closely linked to volatile market forces and to government spending. The political and social impact of subsistence living and Native integration continue to evolve. Under such circumstances the Alaskan-ness of today may well seem quaintly old-fashioned in fifty years. I offer this book as a focus of debate about the future.

One way that I tried to get at the heart of the Alaskan story was to ask former cheechakos about their arrival experiences. Even now that becoming an Alaskan is as easy as boarding a 747, the process of "coming into the country" is still symbolic. Instead of a long sea voyage, a dogsled adventure, or perhaps a walk from Valdez to Fairbanks, the 1990's cheechako comes in relative luxury but in a state of great uncertainty.

Another way I sought Alaskans' sense of place was to ask about mentors and heroes. "Who most inspired you in your life?" I would ask, hoping that the answer would illumine what it meant to grow up in, move to, or develop in Alaska. The responses about parents, uncles, aunts, grandparents, friends, teachers, and other mentors were always interesting and often revealing.

I also gauged Alaskans' sense of place by how they have reacted to their environment's exploitation and preservation. This was a hot subject everywhere I went. For instance, Lanore Gunderson, then Wrangell's town clerk, said that the one thing all Alaskans agree upon is their dislike of the Sierra Club.

*I'm not an environmentalist. I'm highly resentful of the Sierra Club. I'm tired of Outsiders trying to tell us how to run this country. I mean the average Outsider doesn't know a blasted, blooming thing about Alaska! The average person coming into the state now is basically running away from something. They say they are trying to get back to nature. But they get up here and the first thing they want to do is set up all the rules and regulations by which they want to live.*

Unfortunately for everyone who wants to return to the good old days, the environment is an issue which will not go away. That was especially apparent beginning in March 1989, when Alaska's epic *Exxon Valdez* oil spill dominated national and international news. The megadisaster in Prince William Sound crystallized worldwide concern about the rapidity of man-made environmental change and showed that many Alaskans did care deeply about their natural heritage. Views expressed in this book range from Governor Wally Hickel's confident assertion that Alaska and America will never run out of resources to environmentalist Debbie Miller's feeling that North Slope oil development amounts to a "rape" of the land.

Another theme is dog mushing as a symbol of people's changing relationship to their land. Sled dogs have served their masters in the North for many generations, but in the 1950s and 1960s their work largely switched from hauling freight, water, and firewood to recreational racing. So, too, have many Native communities switched from total dependence on the land and its resources to a partial or seasonal subsistence lifestyle. Within living memory dogsleds have gone from being the Mack trucks of the North to primarily a form of entertainment.

Alaskan cultures and lifestyles vary from region to region, tribe to tribe, north to south, and east to west. I have tried, however, to emphasize some similarities. Noted dog musher Mary Shields says, "It's respected here and almost encouraged to try to find a different life and to live that way. I think you have to be tuned in to find the encouragement, but if you are tuned in, it's definitely there." Especially in the Bush, the possibilities still do exist to break away from Lower 48 ways.

Various Native Alaskans have contributed generously to this book. They do not speak with one voice, but their perspective is longer than that of most relative newcomers. Willie Hensley, originally of Kotzebue, speaks of the necessity of retaining a sense of traditional values and moral strengths. Other Natives all across the state told me of their personal and family struggles with alcohol and drug abuse. I have seen Interior streets lively at midnight with drunken villagers. But the same thing occurs across racial and geographic lines; Native inebriates are merely more noticeable. Social issues, such as addiction, racism, and regional rivalry crop up in this book not as analyses but in conversations, much as they would if you were jawing with someone in a wheelhouse, bunkhouse, mill floor, fishing pier, or steam bath.

One of the subjects that kept coming up during my travels in Alaska was the role of women in northern society. The state and the territory before it have long been known for a relative scarcity of women. Traditionally white men did not bring mates along when they came to work the gold fields, fishing grounds, or forests. Fred Elvsaas says, "When I grew up, there were a lot of people my age that were just like myself, with Native mothers and grandmothers and grandfathers and non-Native fathers. My father came from Norway. There were a lot of Scandinavians here and a lot of mixed blood from the Russians."

Although the role of women leaned toward child rearing and domestic activities in both Native and white cultures, the pioneer lifestyle of bush women usually offered a blurring of gender roles. For instance, eighty-six-year-old Anna Nick of Pilot Station says, "I was mostly an outdoors girl, going out with my dad, hunting, fishing, trapping. The first thing he taught me how to do was when the dog team stopped and he put the anchor down, I held the sled for him."

Here again, dog mushing is an interesting barometer of Alaskan life. Mary Hansen ran a trap line and competed in dogsled races in the 1930s. Mary Shields notes that today in the Fairbanks area more than half of all recreational mushers are women. Mary continues to use her large huskies for hauling wood and water to her wilderness cabin. I asked her once what she hopes for in a good camp at the end of a long spring day, mushing across the still-frozen wilderness. Her answer reveals some of the absolutes of the "real" Alaska:

*Out of the wind in a nice grove of spruce so I feel like I am nestled in the trees.*

*Near a little overflow or a hole in the ice so I don't have to melt snow but can get water out of the creek.*

*A place where I know I am going to get the sun in the morning to warm the tent up and wake me up early.*

*Maybe an uphill to start out with the next morning because the dogs will be frisky when we first take off. A nice grade going up so that I have a lot of control rather than a treacherous, icy downhill.*

*A lot of dead firewood around so it will be easy to get firewood in.*

Many people told me that it is easier to go to Alaska than it is to return from there. Former Nebraskan Bill Spear says, "You just develop a different way of looking at things in Alaska, a sense of adventure and independence. You become a much less formal person, unwilling to put up with people's bullshit. There's no way I could return down south and sell IBM machines or fit into a law firm or go play golf somewhere."

Other people told me about Alaska's spiritual values. "To struggle in wilderness," said Debbie Miller, "is to better know myself and to better appreciate what is left of our remarkable natural world." At the other end of the spectrum, centenarian Fred Bahovic told me, "You never questioned a man about his reasons for coming to Alaska; some men told you but most of them didn't. There was money to be made here and that was enough to know." Alaska for people like Fred meant excitement in the air. Grace Ford settled near Fairbanks after World War II.

*And so when my future husband proposed to go to Alaska, I thought, gee that sounds like an adventure! And, oh, it was wonderful. I loved it. Of course, these were the immediate postwar years and housing was at a premium. I mean people were living in chicken coops and dog kennels, for goodness sake. And my Lord, I got $1.29 an hour working at the general delivery window at the post office. Whoever heard of pay like that? Then to find the homestead at North Pole and come out here and live on it. I wouldn't take a million for the experience of homesteading! Then the birth of a town. Then the birth of a state. I was in on all these exciting happenings. I was just thrilled being here, meeting new people, having new experiences. Fairbanks was full of exciting-looking people. And when my child was born, I used to wheel her down Cushman Street and the old miners would throw nuggets or silver dollars in on the baby. You would never have heard of such a thing in the staid farming community where I was raised in central California. Just exciting times!*

Alaska more than most places is a state of mind, an allure. I don't know if the original hunter-gatherers felt that way, but the various groups of European immigrants certainly did, from the eighteenth- and nineteenth-century Russian fur traders to the Scandinavian fishermen to the prospectors and miners of every nation. Most people today probably cannot understand the gut-level lure of the North that drove so many to stampede into the country at the turn of the century, but hints of the old feeling remain in American popular culture. The amazing popularity in the Lower 48 of the magazine *AlaskanMen* is one sign. Another is the crowds of cruise ship tourists thronging Southeast's ports looking for an echo of the glory days of '98. And who in Philadelphia or Houston or Los Angeles can watch TV reportage of the Iditarod dogsled race without a twinge of envy?

No, the call of the North is alive and well. Listen for it when Sharon Butcher finds true love at the Talkeetna Bachelors Ball, Jeff Coghill rides the Tanana River, Gretchen Schmidt dances out the pipeline boom on Two Street, Mary Hansen freights into the Kantishna, Willie Hensley hunts to survive, Wally Hickel builds on the fault zone, Sandy Kogl patrols Denali by dogsled, and Joe and Vi Redington mush the Iditarod Trail.

The North attracts us with its friendships, freedom, riches, and wilderness. My challenge in *Alaskans* has been to portray that appeal through the state's rich legacy of storytelling.

Come with me and meet five dozen Alaskans who have each carved out a niche in the Great Land.

# Roy Ahmaogak

*Bowhead Whale Hunter*
*Barrow*
*b. 1960*

*Of all the Alaskan subsistence lifestyles, perhaps the most exotic to people Outside is that of the bowhead whale hunter. Roy Ahmaogak comes from untold generations of Inuit whale hunters, but despite a great technological advantage over his forebears, he still feels their same relief when he helps to satisfy everyone's food needs in the spring hunt.*

**M**Y GRANDFATHER'S brothers are still whaling. My father is a whaling captain, and I started from the bottom on his crew when I was about ten years old making coffee, washing dishes, and keeping the stove going all night. From there I've become a co-captain of my father's crew.

We live out on the ice whaling for three to four weeks with tents and Coleman stoves. We have two groups—the day shift and the night shift—and we're constantly on alert.

In my great-grandfather's time it was a lot harder to land the whales. Now, for instance, we have motorized snow machines instead of his dog teams. But for the spring hunt there's no difference. We still use the same skin boats like they had and we still paddle out to find and harpoon our bowhead. Only now we have a projectile that we put in the harpoon gun to slow down the whale. Last fall we used three bombs to land our forty-five footer.

We get so close to the whale that sometimes we almost bump into it. For an amateur that would be dangerous, but from my point of view there's not a whole lot of danger. Certainly not! No, I've never been afraid landing bowhead whales.

We have been taught that the whale we are going to catch just comes up and gives itself to our people. I've experienced that myself. After the whale has given itself, our emotions are very strong. We know for a fact that we will not go hungry for that season. We will have food to eat and food to share.

We do respect the bowhead whale. For us to survive as a culture we must understand the lifestyles and the movements of all animals. We have a prayer of thanks before we cut up the whale. We butcher it up and distribute it to the other crews that are on the ice, like a crew share, and they distribute it to their crew members. The successful crew that landed the whale takes a portion and sets it aside for the community to come and eat. And a portion is set aside for Christmas and Thanksgiving. In June we have a feast. It's like a giant picnic outside where we do distribute part of the whale. We do not waste one bit of the whale. The only part we leave back on the ice is the whale bones, the liver, and the lungs. Everything else is taken with us.

The bowhead whale will never be wiped out by the Native people of Alaska. But I wish that no oil exploration out on the sea ice will ever take the whales away from us.

Hunting bowheads is always remarkable. I can't separate one bowhead, such as the one I caught last year, from the one I'm maybe going to catch this spring. Landing a bowhead is always a happy moment.

# Katie Arriola

*An Empty Barrel Waiting to Be Filled*
*Ketchikan*
*b. 1953*

*Katie Arriola was a young Southeast Native whose bitterness about her stymied hopes reinforced her desire for an education. "Whether I did anything with it or not, I wanted to say, 'I actually have a degree that I earned on my own.'"*

*Divorced at age twenty-three and the mother of a two-year-old, she needed a well-paying job. In 1977 she joined a work force of five hundred men and a handful of women at the Ketchikan pulp mill. Denied the opportunity to earn the pay of a heavy equipment operator, she brought a sex discrimination grievance against the company and won. Despite her diminutive size, she then operated cranes and dump trucks until she was fired in 1985. She says that she was railroaded out of her job because as a union activist, she had been pressing health and safety issues at the plant. One and a half years later the state attorney general's office obtained restoration of her job and full back pay. To get rid of her once and for all, the company bought her resignation.*

*This high school failure went on to earn a political science degree at Oregon State because she was "deeply hungry" for education. Having succeeded there, she hopes to inspire her thirty-eight nieces and nephews along the same path.*

THERE IS no easy job in a pulp mill! You have to put up with all the different tasks. The men and women both suffer equally from the physical stress and pressure of producing the pulp, and everybody has to work together because it's so dangerous. Everybody has to look out for everybody else. It's no fun, you know, seeing people get hurt and not being able to work. You just have to depend on each other and help each other out wherever you can.

Probably the most dangerous thing from day to day is that they mix like six different chemicals to cook the chips and turn them into paper pulp. And there was always the high risk of being exposed to sulfur dioxide ($SO_2$). We had to constantly wear slobber boxes, a mouth respirator. It's just a very temporary emergency-escape apparatus. You know, you can be riding down the elevator and you can get in pockets of $SO_2$ gas. And you're instantly blinded, it burns your eyes. So you just have to be prepared to throw that slobber box in your mouth long enough to escape out of that area because at any time any of these pipes could break and your life be gone in thick acid mist. The two main buildings that process the chemicals are *always* dangerous because the gas is possibly leaking from broken lines where the acid has eaten away the pipes.

During the ten years I was there, they had two major mill evacuations and numerous, numerous times when people couldn't leave at quitting time through the exit until gas had cleared.

I started out there working when I was twenty-three. I was a single parent and I had a two-year-old son to support and raise. And it was quite intimidating. I knew the mill was there, and my then-husband was working there. When we divorced, I needed a source of income and decided to apply. I didn't really know what I was getting into. So I got hired on in the spring of 1977 as a general laborer in what they called the labor pool, where they dispatch you out wherever they're short-handed in the mill. And your jobs could change from one day to the next, depending on which departments were short-handed. It was straight days. So it was really convenient for me. At that time, there were probably five women including myself that were working down inside the mill among five hundred men.

After about six months of sweeping and cleaning metal shavings and stuff, our department was short on heavy-equipment operators, and I was the next senior person to be broke in. I didn't even have a driver's license, but they told me it was my turn and I, at first, told them no because I didn't know how to drive. And they said you either learn or we have to terminate you. So they just put me in a garbage truck, what they called a pack rat, just like a city garbage truck, and sent me out in the back yard to practice learning how to operate a clutch vehicle. I was scared to death, but after about eight hours of bouncing back and forth across the yard, they cut me loose and I progressed from there. I trained on different kinds of dump trucks and never went outside the mill. I gained so much confidence that that was the turning point for me.

It was difficult at first because the men resented me. They didn't feel that women should be out there in the first place. But the longer

I stayed, the more I became just one of the working class in the mill. However, I had to file a grievance against my department supervisor because any chance he got he would just refuse to put me on certain pieces of equipment. And when I started verbally complaining about it, they put me on shift work, swinging graveyard. I felt it was unfair they were not giving me the opportunity to earn higher pay—fourteen dollars an hour versus seven. I knew I could do the job if I were given the opportunity. So I filed a grievance through the union, and I won it within a thirty-day period and got back to day shift, where I should have been. There was just no question I was being denied the opportunity to operate the equipment. And after that was smoothed out, I was able to perform the job and show them I could do just as well as any of the guys in the department. So it was easier after that and most of the guys felt I should be given every opportunity to do the same jobs that they were.

What was most difficult about my entire stay at the pulp mill is that it was all outdoor work, year-round, and the weather conditions were treacherous a lot of the time, working out in the cold and pouring-down rain. But that was a sacrifice that I decided to choose because I was on straight-day shift and I was making twice the amount of money that I would have been making anywhere else.

My dad worked for a cold storage in this community for forty-five years. The exact same job for forty-five years! And I was very impressed with the troubles that he went through. He influenced me tremendously because I had so much sympathy for him because he loved his job and you couldn't persuade him to do anything different. He loved the fishing industry. And he actually made a name for our family. We have fourteen kids in our family and our family is well known in the community.

I just have the greatest respect for my father that he endured such a miserable job. We shared a lot in common, and later on he looked up to me a lot because I was knowledgeable about labor contracts, primarily due to my experience out at the pulp mill. And so, he would come to me—he didn't have much of an education—to ask me to interpret. "What does this mean?" and "How should I vote when it comes time to vote for the contract?" So it was kind of a special relationship that he and I had. Even when I was going to college, I always kept that feeling and thought close to mind that I was doing a lot of what I'm doing now more in his memory and out of respect for him. And I hope that I can represent people that come from his background, people who have no education and who do not know how to defend themselves against the employer.

My father is Mexican American. He came up from Los Angeles on a boat during the Depression when he was eighteen or nineteen years old. There was a big ad in the *Los Angeles Times* saying, "Workers Needed" to go to Alaska, all expenses paid. And he felt that he wanted to relieve his father of one mouth to feed, so he got on the boat.

My father and mother split up when I was six years old, and we were all placed in foster homes here in Ketchikan. And we stayed wards of the state till we turned eighteen. At that time, I think under the old welfare system, they were very strict on their policies with family units. We were forced to live in foster homes. And I think because our family was so huge, they would pair us up in twos and threes. I was the only one that was placed in a foster home by myself with other foster kids that were not members of my family. And I think it's because of that type of emotional trauma that none of us really had any role models, including parents. But we were always very aware that my father was here in town. And through the years we did establish a relationship with him: unlike what normal families have, but we all grew to love him. Even though all of us kids grew up in the same community, we're not a close, close family. We all recognize each other and respect each other, but we were not the close family unit that we should have been.

I think that I try so hard because I want to do something with my life and take control of my life instead of having somebody else tell me what I should be doing. I have brothers and sisters that can't get past that barrier. They limit themselves. I think I was lucky because the people I was originally placed with were old-fashioned and very strict.

Because we were such a large family somebody in the welfare department issued out an order that we were not to see each other, we were not to call, we were not to visit at all. They didn't want any problems. So I didn't see any of my brothers and sisters until I was twelve years old. We just happened to be walking downtown one day, and I saw the two sisters that are a year and two years apart from me, and we were across the street from each other. We thought we recognized each other, and then I realized that those were my sisters. We all three came running together, pulled away from our foster parents and just hugged and cried and didn't want to leave, once we saw each other.

When we were going through the school system, it just became impossible to keep us apart. We just took things into our own hands and started making our own arrangements and visiting and calling. It was always really hard. We'd take turns spending the night with each other. It was just really difficult. We'd cry miserably because we didn't want to go back to the other home and leave the home we were staying in. It was so hard. Very difficult. And I think all of us that have children now, we all try to avoid breakups of homes. And even if our families did break up, it's never going to be the devastation that we went through. At least our kids are going to have one parent and they won't be separated.

Our story repeated on an individual scale the problems of Native Americans everywhere with alcoholism. For instance, when I was growing up, I always had dreams that I'd find my mother. And I was always crying in my dream when I found her. By the time I turned eighteen it was my number one goal to find my mother and take care of her. I was never going to let her go again.

The last time I saw her was when I was age six. I did not see her again until I was twenty-one. My son was two months old, and three of us sisters went to Seattle to find her. And we found her and we were all disappointed because she turned out to be a chronic alcoholic. She was in real bad shape when we found her. And that's the way she is. She's rarely been back here to Alaska. She never got over having so many children and she doesn't know any of us. She'll never know any of her grandchildren. It is a tragedy.

Even when I met her when I was twenty-one, I didn't care about the condition she was in as long as she wanted to establish a relationship and we could start all over. And I offered on many occasions to send her a round-trip ticket and bring her home so she could meet the rest of the family. And we were just total strangers! No matter how many times I went to see her, there was just no acknowledgement. She couldn't tell us girls apart, she didn't know our names. Even when she did come back one time, several years ago, she couldn't identify who we were and she didn't know any of the grandchildren or what set of kids belonged to what daughter.

It was just a tragedy. I had to be satisfied that I had knocked against the wall more than one time and accept that this was the way it was going to be the rest of my life. I don't have a mother and it's really sad.

I think what I'm doing now in my life is trying to fill those voids as far as having some family ties. I see a lot of my brothers and sisters trying to do the same thing, but we all do it differently. I did it with my books, through learning about my mother's Tsimshian tribe. Because we have a lot of relatives in Ketchikan that we were never close to, but we always thought of her when we met one of them. So my way of coping with the breakup of our family and with my lack of a mother-daughter relationship was to do a five-year study on our tribe until I started to feel some sense of identity with it.

I got really heavy-duty into it, read up a lot, and got into designing my own dance blanket. One other sister is into it, too, and is one of the dance leaders in one of the dance groups in town. So it gave us a sense of belonging, that we're not just Alaska Natives. We actually know who we are and where we came from. That's been exciting to the two of us.

I still don't understand alcoholism, since I have never wanted to drink. But for my parents it was really difficult for both of them. It's just incredible, the life that they had. My mother and father came from totally different cultural backgrounds, his being Mexican American and hers Tsimshian.

My mother's parents died when she was just a teenager. She had a rough life. And when you come from an unstable background to begin with, there's a great chance that you're not going to have a stable home when you do marry. And because my dad was only making three dollars an hour we went through a lot of domestic tragedies, having our utilities shut off in the winter and having to ration out food for fourteen kids. It was really difficult. So I feel that maybe the breakup of the family was the best thing that ever happened to us kids. At least we had a chance at growing up. Maybe not like we would've preferred, but nonetheless we had people who were paid to take care of us. That was one of the things that I was bitter about all my life, growing up in these foster homes, is that the foster parents never let you forget that they're getting a fee for your head. And they tell you how much they're getting, what they're going to buy, that they're saving up the money they're getting to take care of you to buy a car or buy this, buy that.

So I was depressed a lot and did poorly in school because of that and because nobody cared what I was doing. They put me in a special education program in junior high school when the program was first offered here in Ketchikan. I just got nothing but Ds and Fs all the way through school because I found out I was never going to get punished. Nobody cared, so eventually I didn't care. And they put me in this program and left me there. And when I got into high school, I was still in the same program. We were not allowed to participate in the mainstream student environment. We were isolated in the back of the gym, and we were not allowed to have all the basic curriculum. We had our own special little math problems. It was all redundancy. And I finally gave up in my sophomore year because I realized that I was being cheated out of an education. That I knew what was happening and I wanted an education. But they said, "No, you've got some special disabilities and you can't compete."

When the Ketchikan High School decided to do an on-the-job training program, we special ed. kids became the guinea pigs. They told us, "We have to find a way to help integrate you into society. You're never going to be able to go to college. You'll be lucky if you can get through high school. So we've made an agreement with some businesses, and how would you like to get paid instead of coming to school? And you can still get high school credits and walk in the high school graduation ceremony."

So I didn't go to high school my junior and senior year. They paid me five hundred dollars a month to work in a state day care. They just said, "You can walk in the ceremony and get your diploma."

And that was the extent of my education.

Even with all those odds against me I still had a burning feeling that I hadn't gotten an education. During the next twelve years I hungered for a degree, so I decided to see what I could do at the junior-college level. And then at Oregon State. I felt that there was something better out there for me other than what I had been offered when I was growing up. I was never satisfied. I was just an empty barrel waiting to be filled!

# The Rev. Peter Askoar

*Russian Mission Priest #9*
*Russian Mission*
*b. 1948*

*Peter Askoar was born in the Yup'ik village of Russian Mission in 1948 and grew up subsistence fishing. To make ends meet he still dries his own catch for winter use, but nowadays he is a fisher of men. As the village's ninth priest, Father Peter receives no salary from his two hundred and fifty–plus congregation except impromptu donations of food and money. He is an example of the tenacity with which the old faith is hanging on in western Alaska. Russian Orthodox congregations have successfully recruited new priests, including Father Peter's two brothers, Father David at Newhalen and Father Alexie at New Stuyahok. They conduct their ancient services in Yup'ik, English, and Church Slavonic.*

*Father Peter lives in a modern house atop the bluff at Russian Mission. He loves to watch college football on TV, and he dreams of the day when he can visit the Mother Church across the Bering and Chukchi Seas.*

MY TWO brothers, Father David and Father Alexie, and I, we went to Kodiak to St. Herman's Seminary. It took me nine years to do the four years, and there were times that I said, "This is too hard."

My wife is the one that pushed all these years. Without her I don't think I would be a priest today. She often said, "You want this? Go for it! With God's help, we'll get by."

My parents were members of the church, and they were quite strict about the Orthodox faith. They continued pushing us when we were altar boys. But it was my grandfather, Father Vasily Changsak, who had the greatest influence on me. He continually pushed me into being an altar boy. Making sure that I got up in the morning. Especially wintertime, when services usually start around seven A.M. He was the one who pushed me to come to the church before school. I had just enough time to run over to the school.

He was a very loving person. Not very tall. Very gentle but firm. There were a few instances in the church when another boy and I got caught messing around in the church and got reprimanded for it. That I can never forget right to this day! Firm but very gentle.

I take after him, especially in the House of God. There are times that the altar boys feel the way I felt when Father Vasily reprimanded us in church. I know now that he did have a purpose in doing that.

This is the Orthodox church. We believe that it was founded by Christ Himself. We like to say that we are unique from any other beliefs that surround us here, especially concerning Christ and the Mother of God. We believe that the *Theotokos*, the Virgin Mary, is a God bearer. And at each service, however small our numbers, the singing and the readings are tied directly to particular parts of the Scriptures.

But lately people are more likely to get together to watch TV. I can remember gathering fifteen years ago at the house in the lower village that had the only TV. But now practically everyone has a set of their own and knows what is happening on the other side of the world, not just here on the Yukon.

This is my third year here. Before Father Gabriel passed away last spring, he mentioned a couple of times that because of television and VCR movies people do not have enough time to attend our church services. Unfortunately they have TV now as an excuse, but all they have to do is turn it off and walk over. Evidently that is too much work. Now we have a new idol, television. Rather than placing all our faith in God and doing His service in the church, we are giving our attention to that little box.

The elderly here believe that the animals have souls, but our church teaches that the animals do not have souls as we do. Yet because God created them I really can't say animals have no souls. If God wants them back, He'll have them back. It is not mine to say if they have a soul.

I try to set people's minds on the right goal, and that is to worship God alone and not TV or spirits or alcohol.

About four or five years ago the city council, through the prompting of the clergy, made Russian Mission a dry village. Since then the liquor problem has by no means gone away, but there is a greater sense of unity. People are more interested now in brotherhood and living together, as it used to be many years ago before alcohol was a problem.

# George Attla

*The Huslia Hustler, Still Hustling to Win*
*North Pole*
*b. 1933*

*As a boy, Huslia's George Attla began working with dogs on his family's subsistence trap line. He lived in a tent much of the winter and now has no desire to exchange today's comforts for any romantic ideas of the North. But ironically George himself has long been part of that romance as the winningest sprint musher of all times. He is a ten-time world champion and won the Anchorage World Championship Sled Dog Race twice in a row, in 1981 and 1982. His fight back from crippling tuberculosis in his childhood is the subject of the inspirational movie* Spirit Of The Wind.*

*George says that his dogs have been his best friends. And, he adds, there are only two kinds of dogs, slow and fast ones!*

**W**HAT ELSE is there besides winning? I enjoy running dogs, but I only do it for one purpose, and that's to win. I learned early in life what I wanted to do and I started doing it the best I could. If I got too old to win, I'd fold it up.

There aren't many people that understand dogs and can get performance out of them. To be able to understand the animal is a gift. I can hook up a dog and tell you if that dog has the mental makeup of a champion. I take him for a run and I can read the way he thinks, the way he works.

The same with my competitors. I usually figure out their weaknesses, too. I've raced for over thirty years and I've never won a sportsmanship trophy, so you know I'm there for one purpose.

It takes quite a commitment to be a dog musher. You've got to enjoy what you're doing because mushing is a very physical sport. They're very hyper animals. I mean they go crazy, chewing on lines, doing everything they can, they want to run so bad. They are jerking in every direction, and some of them are strong enough to move you the way they want. Just hooking 'em up is a chore. Like I ran thirty of them today. Thirty dogs—and that's handling and being jerked by each dog two times. But I would rather do this than anything else. I've done just about every kind of work you can imagine, and I have not enjoyed anything as I do my dog team. It's a lifestyle. I grew up with it.

When I was a kid, really the only thing we played at was trapping, running dogs, and running riverboats. My dad was my biggest hero then. He was a very forceful person. When he said something, I listened. It just didn't go in one ear and out the other because he'd remind me that what he said was important. Not by spanking me, but when he said something, he meant it. Like my dogs: I demand the best of them. They understand my way of expressing myself.

I enjoy running my dogs and training them and feeding them—the whole works—because a dog is a very special animal. He can read your thoughts and feelings probably better than your fellow human being can. Even if you don't win with a dog team, if your dog team gave you the best that they have, you couldn't ask for no more than that. So usually I'm satisfied with whatever they are able to accomplish. Most of the time when they lose, it's really my fault.

My favorite leader is a dog called Lingo. He's twelve years old now. I've got him boarded out in Rampart training pups. Lingo did not win as much as some of my other leaders, but he was the best. He is a dog that just gives you everything he has. Every race he ran, the team dogs just couldn't go fast enough for him. Usually a leader in sprint racing is getting too much pressure from his teammates. A lot of leaders get depressed running out in the front. But Lingo was never depressed. I've got some young ones now that look as promising as he was. But the super athlete is so hard to find!

Purebreds are much smarter than Alaskan huskies, but the Alaskan husky has a stronger will than most breeds of dogs. They don't crack under the pressure of running as fast as they can for as far as they can. They don't say, "This is too hard, I give up." They have been bred to pull a dogsled and run as fast as they can. They are born with the desire to do this.

I don't think that dogs have wills as strong now as when I first started racing. They are getting just like people. Compared to what I grew up with life is very easy right now. My father and I had to go out and catch what we were going to eat, but now I can go down to the grocery store and buy what I need. Today a lot of sled dogs can't make it over the finish line and have to be loaded in the sled basket. Well, when I first started in 1958, we were loading dogs, too, but the dogs we loaded were completely passed out from trying to run. These dogs now are maybe faster dogs, but if you see one in the basket crossing the finish line, usually that dog is sitting in the basket looking around. He didn't run until he passed out. I mean he had some more left when he quit.

Now they are quitting rather than saying, "I can do this."

It's not how strong you are. Winning is a state of mind. It's as simple as that. Anybody can win in anything they set their minds to do.

# Bob Atwood

*Beating The Drums For Anchorage*
*Anchorage*
*b. 1907*

*When Bob Atwood was a young reporter in Springfield, Illinois, he met a social worker named Evangeline Rasmuson, whom he married in 1932. Evangeline had grown up in Alaska, a territory Bob had been hearing about from his two adventurous uncles. It wasn't long before Edward A. Rasmuson, president of the Bank Of Alaska and Evangeline's father, offered Bob credit to buy a newspaper called the* Anchorage Times, *with a circulation of six hundred. Bob and his wife said that they would give the adventure five years. They were ready for a change. In Alaska's totally different lifestyle, however, "everything was a challenge," Bob said, and a dynamic person could quickly put his mark on a town that was only twenty years old. Under Atwood the* Times *welcomed new residents and actively lobbied new and old federal agencies to locate in Anchorage. The town's gains were everywhere else's losses. "Fairbanks was sound asleep," says Bob happily.*

I CAN COUNT five men through my life, at different stages, who were the key people. My father—he always thought I was wasting my time in my newspaper work—and then his brother, my uncle. And Chief Davies, who was a minister in the church I grew up in. My father-in-law, whom I got very close to. And Governor Ernest Gruening.

I started out hating Gruening. He was appointed to come to Alaska as governor as successor to an Alaskan who had been governor, and even though the Alaskan had been an alcoholic and not much of a governor, at least he was an Alaskan (who was thrown out to make way for this New York guy, a buddy of Ickes and Roosevelt.)

At first I wrote editorials against everything he did and everything he said. I even disapproved of his being here. Yep. Then when he came out here to Anchorage for his first visit as governor, Army commander General Buckner put on a big reception for him and invited everybody. As I came down the line to meet the governor, Gruening said, "Are you Atwood of the *Times?*" "Yeah." He said, "I want to talk to you about that editorial you wrote about me." And I said, "Which one?"

Oh, we got along correctly, socially, and all that, but we were at odds. He was a bad guy in my book, and I didn't want to be near him for fear he'd contaminate me. My father-in-law was a republican national committeeman, and I was a stiff-necked GOP true believer.

Once when I had to stay overnight in Juneau on my way to Skagway, darned if my hotel phone didn't ring, and here was the governor on the line wanting me to go up there for dinner. I had an awful time getting out of that, but later he was after me for something else. I figured, "This guy is just trying to seduce me into something bad." I didn't know what, but I didn't want anything to do with him.

The next time I was in Juneau, I was covering a session of the legislature. And it was horrible. What they were doing was just ridiculous. I found a book in the library called *A History of Alaska Under American Rule,* written by Jeannette Paddock Nichols as her thesis for a master's degree. It really told how the political forces worked and especially about the canned salmon industry. It made me realize that these were the bad guys who were controlling Alaska. The Outside canneries owners—all they wanted to do was come up here, catch our fish, and get out, leaving as little money as possible. They weren't interested in our having population or growth because that would mean schools, sewer systems, roads, and *taxes.* And they didn't want any taxes. Alaska had done without taxes for years!

So the fisheries people were always against anything for Alaska. And they did business with all the little merchants who supplied their canneries. The merchants were beholden to them, and they reflected the same thoughts. Southeast Alaska was all against statehood because the canneries didn't want it. Under statehood, we would take control of the fisheries away from the federal government and that would be the worst thing that could happen from the viewpoint of those Seattle guys.

I read that book, and all of a sudden I realized that what Gruening had been saying made sense. I could see the forces at work in the daytime in the legislature, and then at night I'd read that book and I could see it in history. So I started going to Gruening and talking to him about this. He responded, yes, that's what he had been saying all along. And all of a sudden we were buddies, fighting this issue. From then on our cooperation extended into other areas.

I liked his vision, his brashness, his courage. He wasn't daunted by anything. You might call him my leader, my motivator.

Another one was my father-in-law, Mr. Rasmuson, who had come up here as a missionary schoolteacher. When I got here myself in 1935 as a cheechako, I had already bought the local newspaper, and it had a very strong town loyalty. Many Alaskans saw me as a bigshot from the East who bought their paper and thought he was going to tell them how to run this country. They looked down their noses at me: "Who the hell do you think you are?" I couldn't say anything without having them challenge me, but Mr. Rasmuson was a great help, telling me the ways of Alaskans so I could understand what was going on. I think I got along pretty well because of him. In the first year or two I didn't take strong stands in editorials. I had to write neutral things that people would not get ruffled about. Because I was a cheechako and I didn't count.

Then after I'd been here a year or two, I could start in saying that this isn't so good, we'd better do something about it, and they'd agree.

I was one of the first for statehood, and I got bruised by Alaskans for it. During the war we had learned a lot of things about lobbying and how the federal government works. We had been lectured by the military about the importance of Alaska. We had lived with it all those years and we started this move for statehood. Governor Gruening was one of the first people for statehood. And the *Anchorage Times* was the first medium that went for statehood. All the other newspapers, radio, TV were opposed. Virtually all the business interests were opposed. The fisheries were opposed. Our main industry was opposed. The political structure was opposed. And here I was beating the drums for statehood.

I was a maverick. In the 1950s, the conservative people around Anchorage called me a Communist because I was in favor of things like statehood. But from the beginning I was a rebel, a Young Turk. The seed of that was planted in the 1930s. After World War II I got with a bunch here and we revolutionized things! It led to building Anchorage into a city.

From 1867, when Alaska was purchased, until 1940 very few things of national note happened in Alaska. Mainly the gold rush but that's all. My wife and I came here at the tail end of this period and when the territory's total population was only sixty thousand. We had no voting representation in Congress. No airmail and no long distance telephones. No road that went anywhere outside of Anchorage. We couldn't even drive to Palmer, our neighboring community forty-five miles away. We were just an isolated little knot of people here. All the towns were little isolated knots, islands surrounded by a sea of tundra.

That was the period when Congress didn't know what to do with

Alaska. They just left it here and didn't even defend it. We came into the war period in 1940 with only two hundred troops in Alaska.

We were here for the transition, when Uncle Sam decided he had to do something about Alaska. He spent a billion dollars building defenses and that brought an enormous, revolutionary change in the way we lived. At the newspaper I was at the middle of it all.

I was the editor through this crash program, when our whole town was converted into a throbbing service center for the biggest military establishment in Alaska. It was a sweeping change with pain and anguish as well as dynamic economic growth. It was a mixture. Some bad people came in here as well as good people. We had everything from hangers on and camp followers to good constructive people during that short era.

Then the Japanese invaded the Aleutian Islands in January of '42 and that made us an active war front, which brought another change. Not many Americans know what it means to be in an active war front. The military was the ruler of this place. We didn't have any state government or sovereignty. As a territory, we were a ward of the federal government. When they put the military up here, the commanding general had the power to exclude anybody from Alaska by written order. You couldn't travel without his permission or ship anything. He was the bossman.

That's a different way of living. Top generals are usually intelligent guys with some sensitivity about what they do. But a general can't do everything himself, so he delegates his authority to majors and captains and even enlisted men. In the lower echelons there are some stubborn dimwits who read an order and won't use any discretion. They cause trouble. And we lived with that.

We had air raids, blackouts, supply shortages, and personal restrictions. When we went to Seattle, instead of going into the terminal like other American citizens, we were directed into a plywood cattle chute that led to the U.S. Immigration Service, where we had to be identified. Our travel card was stamped "admitted" to the United States. That was part of the travel controls. We didn't like it.

Coming home, we had to have certain approvals or we couldn't get back. It was no way to live. And our mail was censored. Newspapers and magazines that came from Outside came with holes where the censors had cut stuff out. That was obnoxious. We tolerated all sorts of nonsense. My newspaper had five levels of censorship here in the military establishment. And sometimes a story had to be OK'd by all five levels. This was the so-called voluntary censorship of World War II. And that was an unforgettable experience. I don't know any other U.S. editor who lived in an active war front and put out a newspaper under the conditions we had in Alaska. It was so messed up. First of all they drafted all my printers into the Army, and I was having trouble publishing the newspaper. I finally went out to the general and told him that he had drafted all these guys and I was getting down to nothing. There were no printers available Outside because they had all been drafted, too. So I said, "If you want a newspaper in this town, you'd better send those guys back to me." He pondered that for a while and he assigned them back to put out that paper in uniform. They were my men but they were all in uniform, putting out the paper.

I went up to the general once and said, "I can't get newsprint because you are shipping so much military cargo there is no civilian space left and my newsprint is sitting on the dock in Seattle." I figured out the date when I would run out. I said, "If you want a newspaper after that date, you've got to see that that newsprint gets up here." Later he showed me a wire he sent to General DeWitt in the Presidio, the big boss at San Francisco, asking for this newsprint to be allocated space. I remember the last sentence of that wire, "Continued publication of this newspaper *highly essential* to the war effort in Alaska." Gee, that made me feel good!

# Fred Bahovic

*Rowboat Trapper*
*Hot Springs Cove, Baranof Island*
*1889–1990*

*The popular image of an Alaskan trapper is of a fur-clad sourdough mushing his dog team through the winter landscape to check his trap line for marten and mink. Centenarian Fred "Mirko" Bahovic was an authentic Alaskan trapper, but Fred trapped by rowboat. That's because his territory was the shoreline of Baranof Island. His haul in an average season was anywhere from twenty to fifty pelts, all retrieved by oar power.*

*Fred rowed forward instead of backward both to be alert for dangerous rocks and to locate his traps, unmarked for fear of trap rustlers. Only cheechakos row backward, laughed Fred.*

*Fred, of course, was a cheechako once, too. When he arrived in the North from Yugoslavia via Chicago, his first job was piling lumber in a sawmill near Wrangell. But he soon became a hand troller and then learned trapping from an old sourdough named John.*

*In 1987 Fred Bahovic made the national news when he and his wife failed to return from a day of rock hounding. The motor on their thirteen-foot Boston Whaler had conked out because the tank had been filled with stove oil instead of gasoline. Because Fred was then ninety-seven and had no survival gear, he and his wife were given up for lost.*

*Imagine everyone's amazement when the pair showed up that evening, Fred having rowed ten miles through tricky tides and currents. His only problem, he said, was that he was very hungry.*

**W**E WERE at least ten miles or more from home when I started rowing. The worst of it was that the current was against me. So I had to keep on rowing even if I had to row all night! Well, everybody thought that we were lost. They were all waiting for us at the float, figuring that I could never make it because I was ninety-seven years old.

But I am used to rowing. Ten miles was nothing to me. Why, when I used to hand troll for salmon, we did nothing but rowing! You know, these hand trollers nowadays, they got an engine and a gurdy and they call themselves hand trollers—which they are not. Hand trolling is when you have oars as your mode of propulsion and nothing else. You have your line in your hands, and when you push your oars forward, it gives motion to the spoon at the end of your line.

*The following account of Sourdough John originally appeared in Fred's self-published* The First Hundred Years.

When I came to Alaska in 1912, they had just started hand trolling. There was no such thing then as power trolling.

When I was trapping, I'd row about twenty miles a day, all through Warm Springs Bay on both sides. Then down south and up north for a mile or so. And I set traps as I went. I always tried to get home before night. That's where you learn how to row [laughter] because you don't want to be sleeping out in the woods in the wintertime.

That never happened to me. I always made it home.

But you really have to get on your oars to get ahead of the currents and tides. It's not easy. You've got to know how to row in rough water. Don't lift your oars up too high because the waves will throw your oars out of position. Or even throw 'em out of the boat.

Back in 1925, when I was new to Alaska, the best thing that ever happened to me was joining up with an old sourdough trapper named John. He was seventy-six when I met him, and I can't recall his ever saying how many of those years he'd spent in Alaska or even why he'd come there in the first place. You never questioned a man about his reasons for coming to Alaska; some men told you, but most of them didn't. There was money to be made here and that was enough to know.

John made the best old-fashioned sourdough hot cakes I ever ate. But, more important, he knew when it was time to trap mink. Mink skins were black and not prime until late November. John could tell from the state of the first mink how many weeks we should wait before setting traps in earnest. He knew how to stock supplies to see us through a six-month winter of trapping. He was firm about not wasting game.

We shot what we needed to eat and not a deer more. In those days, there were no fixed hunting seasons.

It was John who taught me how to tan a trap to get rid of the human odor, boiling the trap with hemlock bark. He taught me how to skin mink and stretch the skins. Then he assigned all the skinning and stretching to me. He was fair, though. He chopped and sawed all the wood, and he made the sourdough hot cake breakfasts that made life worth living.

The first winter together, we set out from Wrangell in October after waiting for days for the weather to calm enough to put the boat back in the water. We were mighty proud of that boat. It was the *Evolution,* a new gas boat I had built in Seattle and named after Darwin's principle. The gas engine was new to Alaska and seemed pretty special.

We set out to explore for new trapping grounds and decided to head for Admiralty Island, about one hundred miles away. It took us a couple of weeks to get there, what with one thing and another. And then we had quite a time deciding on the best bay in which to anchor the boat for the winter. Finally we settled on Eliza Harbor, a well-protected bay, sheltered from all the winds by a very narrow bar that jutted out about six miles. The signs of mink were good and we could see deer and ducks for game. Fresh water was easily found, and soon I had felled two trees for our fires—a yellow cedar for kindling and a large spruce for firewood. The camp prepared, we set about tanning the traps and planning. John would take one side of the bay and leave the other to me. We set out the next day, each in our own rowboat, pulling away from each other like men in a duel.

I was pretty slow in those days, and by the time I had set my most distant traps and was heading back to the anchored gas boat, it had begun to grow dark. The southeast wind picked up in about an hour, blowing hard toward the head of the bay, where a river fed into it, running through large, grassy flats. I rowed with the wind, stopping only now and then to set an additional mink or otter trap. As I approached the river flats the air was alive with mallard ducks. Back of the flats, mountain peaks rose three thousand feet high without a break or pass through their steep sides. The ducks, panicked by my approach, had taken off into a sixty-mile-an-hour headwind. They made no headway at all. The wind tossed them higher and higher until I saw the flock clear the top of the mountains and blow over, out of sight. Since I had no gun with me, their whole frightened flight was without cause.

Now it was my turn to work against the wind. I rowed toward the *Evolution* between the gusts. Against them, no progress was possible.

Several hours later, darkness had settled over the bay and the last point was still ahead. Exhausted, my mind had begun to conjure a strange and terrifying world of its own.

Suddenly out of the woods, I heard a voice cry my name: "Mirko, Mirko! Who-oo, who-oo." Somebody needed help!

"Hallo!" I cried. "Who is it?"

No answer.

I rowed on. Finally I could see the anchored gas boat. As I approached it there came another, "Who-oo, who-oo!"

I pulled up close to the boat and shouted to John, "Somebody is calling from the woods. Is it another trapper warning us off?" Trappers don't like uninvited guests, and a warning was worth attending.

John looked at me for a long moment. Finally he said, "Haven't you ever heard an owl?"

# Buster Benson

## A Wanted Man
## Haines
## b. 1925

*Everyone in Haines calls the town sawyer "Buster," and I doubt if many folks who depend on him for wood know his real name. If you need chipped wood waste for horse bedding, posts for jacking up your house, or dimension lumber for a construction project, Buster is your man. Buster Benson is such a local fixture after twenty years up from Oregon that his customers and friends banded together in autumn 1989 to help him. A retired carpenter named Dick Aukerman saw him working out in the rain one day and said, "You're too old to be doing that. We're going to put you up a shed!" He and seven other friends and neighbors did just that.*

JUST A little bit of everybody was here as soon as I got my mill all set. I had it set up earlier once, but the wind was blowing all the sawdust in my face and into the saw motor and I had to keep blowing that off every day to keep the motor cool. So I had to change the mill around. I'm glad I didn't put up a building before I found out which way the wind was blowing.

Sawmilling is hard work, sometimes seven days a week—fourteen, fifteen hours a day if I have to go haul logs up on the Klehini River above Porcupine. It's whatever the daylight lets ya. You gotta make hay while the sun shines up here in Southeast. The wintertime, you don't have much daylight. Only about seven hours.

I work all winter except when it gets extremely cold. When it's so cold that the lights won't come on, I stay home.

Oh yeah, I like the weather! It's *good* weather here. It don't get overly hot. And right in this area it don't get overly cold. It gets down to zero but not too much below. You've got to go up the road a ways to get down to twenty or twenty-five below.

I just like the people. They're real people. Everybody knows ya and they try to help one another as much as they can. That's like where I was born and raised in the little town of Jewell, Oregon, way out in the country.

I worked in the woods in Oregon since I was about fifteen years old. When I was young, I worked on the rigging a lot on the high lead logging. Then I operated my own logging outfit down south there for about fifteen years. In 1969 I came to Alaska for the challenge and the new country. Since then I've only been out of here twice in twenty years.

I was over at the old Alaska Forest Products site out on Sawmill Road, but they sold the property and I had to move over here. This is not a big paying proposition but you can make a living at it. It's slow but I cut good, full-dimension lumber, and I always have a market for it.

This is a little different than a big sawmill. This carriage runs on a track, and the log stays stationary. You go across the top to square off the top, then start down on the side to get whatever dimension you can get out of it. Like I'm going to cut two-by-fours out of that. Two rows of two-by-fours on edge. And the rest will be flat.

Everybody knows me. They all come to get wood from me. In fact, Scott Cary has been inviting me out to his house on Mud Bay. His house is all built out of my lumber in a post and beam style. It's kind of unique the way he done it, too.

Somebody wants a board, they can get it directly from me. They don't have to wait two or three weeks to get it from down south. They can come here to me and get a board and take it and put it up.

They really depend on me. It's surprising how much they depend on me! If they need timbers to jack up a building with, I can cut 'em today, not tomorrow. Today! That helps a lot.

Yep, everybody wanted to come and help me put up a building. So you know that if you get volunteers to do that, it means that they want you here!

# Porky Bickar

*Falling for Gags*
*Sitka*
*b. 1923*

*Mount Edgecumbe dominates the Pacific skyline of Sitka, Alaska, the way a sow bear with cubs dominates a river bar. Like the Pacific Rim volcanoes St. Helens and Redoubt, it is a time bomb waiting to go off. In 1974 no one realized that better than Porky Bickar, a jack-of-all-trades, one-time champion logger, and perpetrator of some of Southeast's most infamous practical jokes. To Porky, also known for organizing the annual All-Alaska Logging Championships, every day is a potential April Fool's Day.*

APRIL FOOL'S Day of 1974 I woke up, and it was a nice clear sky and I could see for a hundred miles. I saw Mount Edgecumbe over there in her glory, capped with snow. I got up and told my wife, "I'm going to do it!"

The first thing she said was, "Don't make an ass of yourself!"

I tried all over to get a helicopter outfit. Finally about eight o'clock [A.M.] I got a hold of Earl Walker in Petersburg with Temsco choppers, and things started to churn.

Earl Walker said that just as soon as he could see two telephone poles there in Petersburg he would be over to Sitka. Because he liked the idea. In about an hour, here he pulled in with a chopper. So we slung one set of old tires and I put a pile of oily rags and a bunch of smoke bombs and everything that would make a good fire. We took off in the chopper and he dumped me off. I even had four or five cans of spray paint. And I stamped a big April Fool in the snow and painted it with black paint. These letters were fifty foot high in the snow.

Then when Earl came over with the rest of the tires—we had about seventy-five altogether—I stacked the tires in a circle and waited for him to go back for the other tires.

We filled the smoke bombs in around the tires and touched it off with gasoline and Sterno and headed for home.

It was quite a feat! If that fire had lasted a little longer, I could probably have bought some cheap property in town 'cause it stirred up quite a few people.

Just think of big billows of smoke coming out of the crater! People in Sitka could see it just as plain! It got them stirring around like ants. They called the Coast Guard, and the Coast Guard sent a whaleboat over to the volcano and even pulled a chopper down from Gustavus.

Finally the radio station let it out of the bag and said, "I wonder what Porky's doing now?"

It was a lot of fun, but we had a few repercussions. The Sierra Club didn't like the idea of desecrating the area. Those spoilsports are the worst anyway as far as I'm concerned. They try to stop everything—even a person having fun!

I felled timber for many years. That's why I came up to Sitka in 1960, a long time before some of these do-gooders even knew what a tree was like. They don't even realize that some of the timber here is way overripe. It cleans the air, it cleans everything when you get new-growing timber! It gives the country a whole new aspect.

Timber is not like oil, where when you pump the oil out of the ground, you have nothing left. We've got some of the most beautiful second growth coming up here that you ever saw in your life.

I was born and raised around Brooklyn, Washington, out of Aberdeen. A real timber country. Right now Weyerhaeuser is logging where I helped log when I was a kid. Some of those trees are thirty inches through and nice beautiful timber down there.

Oh, I've had some good gags played on me! Some dandies.

One time I was having dinner with a friend named Dave, and his sister was up here from California. I had just been down to the cannery, and this Bob Wyman runs the cannery, and I told Dave, "Let's go down and get some crab. They've got thirty thousand pounds of it down there. We can send some to San Francisco with your sister tomorrow." Good thinking. My wife insisted that I call up Wyman and ask him for permission to do it instead of just going to get 'em like I always do. I called and got his permission and then when I had just put ten or twelve nice crab in my sack, here the police come and they said, "What are you doing?" And I said, "I'm stealing crab like I always do." And they said,

"Well, we're going to go down to the jail." I said, "OK, I'll follow you down." "No, we'll follow you," they said.

So we got down to the police station and I said, "Hey, I've been playing with you guys. Why don't you call up Wyman and ask him about it." So they called him and said, "Did you give Porky permission to go in and get crab?" Wyman said, "Porky who?"

So he turned the tables on me.

I was on the police commission at that time, and I got the chief of police to come down there, and he told the men it was a joke. We pull everything like that.

When we only had two thousand five hundred people in Sitka instead of eight thousand, I used to know every person in town, and we had a lot of fun.

In the woods, too, if you work for a good outfit, it kinda seems like a family. It was Barton and Renyvann from Hoquiam, two individuals who, when they were coming up to Sitka in 1960, they wanted to know if I wanted to come up and work, and I said sure. So I came up with 'em, fallin' timber right up at Katlian Bay on the Tongass National Forest. A lot of overripe out there but a lot of nice timber, too. . . .

Down in Washington they build a road out, and they have trucks go haul the timber out. Up here, men live out at camp; I rode a boat in every day from Sitka. It was twelve miles up to where we were logging. We put in twelve-hour days working on a per-thousand basis. Busheling. Piecework.

I was supposed to have been one of the good fallers in the country. In 1962 I was in the Guinness permanent records for falling, limbing, and bucking ten million three hundred thousand feet in one year! And I don't think that ever will be beat because that was beautiful timber.

I like falling. It's good work. It's whatever you want to make it. If you work hard, you make lots of money. If you want to sit around and loaf, you just make what an ordinary person makes.

I'll grant you it's dangerous, but if a person watches his p's and q's . . . I got hurt a few times but it wasn't that bad. Widow makers fell on me and hit me in the head and knocked all my teeth out and everything like that. Getting hit in the shoulders and the back and logs rolling over me and stuff.

It's safe enough if you watch yourself, but a person gets caught up with it. After you have worked so long in the woods, you're going to get caught. You're bound to get hurt. Here we have a lot steeper ground to work on than they do down below in America there, where they often have nice big flats where you could ride a bicycle. Up here, you start going up those hills and it is tough going. Hauling your saw and tools and then getting out of the way when you fall a tree.

Sierra Clubbers don't have any idea of any aspect of what it all entails. They don't realize how many thousands of people would be destitute without these jobs. And it would entail many lawsuits if the government broke its contracts to the pulp mills. Sitka would lose at least thirty percent of its economy. It would affect the schools, businesses, welfare, and relief.

I like to work in the woods. It was a job, but it was a job I liked. I don't know. Just the principle of going out there and making a living for yourself and the harder you worked, the more you made. It's the American way of living. A person that's industrious can do it. And I felt good about it 'cause I figured I was industrious enough.

And I liked the open air out in the woods. There's nothing better than to tackle one of these mountains and walk around. People chastise me so much for cutting timber, but I'm just as good an ecologist as any one of those Sierra Clubbers!

# Al Brookman, Sr.

*From Cheechako to Old Salt*
*Sitka*
*1906–1989*

*At the southeast end of Alaska, far from Roy Ahmaogak and Barrow but equally dependent on the sea, is the old Russian capital of Sitka. In 1926 Al Brookman and his father were beginning to think of Sitka as home, having come into the country recently from Outside. As cheechakos, however, they still had a few things to learn. "Dad and I were so inexperienced that we didn't know even the simplest rules of survival in that big, wild seacoast land," said Al. "We went from one jackpot (predicament) to another, learning by trial and error—mostly error." When his father got a job at the powerhouse, Al shipped out aboard a thirty-six-foot fishing boat called the* Hecla. *Captain Adolf Thomsen, a Norwegian from the old country, became Al's mentor in the arduous and dangerous work of long-line halibut fishing.*

*Alaska has long led the nation in the tonnage and value of its fishing catch. But the harvest in Al's story is how an apprentice learns the ropes and how a cheechako becomes an old salt. The following account of this growth is taken from Al's book,* Sitka Man.

THE HALIBUT season opened February 15 in 1927. A fifty-mile-per-hour northerly gale howled and the skates [lines with attached hooks] were all frozen solid.

We had to hang the skates overboard to thaw before we could bait up. We wore cotton gloves that got wet immediately, and my hands were soon numb. I had always considered myself as tough as the next guy but this misery seemed beyond human endurance.

Adolf lectured me about being cheerful, no matter how trying the conditions were. His advice helped later when I had to work with a crew of strangers, and every man was an expert while I was still a novice.

The weather was so bad that we were forced to fish inside waters where we caught few halibut. The best fishing was in the open ocean. About mid-June, Adolf decided to rig for salmon trolling and no longer needed a deckhand, so I was without a job.

The halibut schooner *Portlock* was tied at the Booth Fisheries dock to take on ice and bait. I had heard that one of her fishermen had gotten ill and they needed a replacement. I asked for the job and told the skipper I was green but that I could bait gear without making snarls and I could coil the gear neatly behind the gurdy. There were eight men on the boat and they held a meeting on deck to decide about hiring me.

The skipper asked two questions: Had I ever steered a seventy-foot boat? Did I get seasick? I told him I had learned to steer by compass on the tender *Mutual* and that I had never been seasick and wouldn't expect any pay if I wasn't able to work. I was hired and went after my sea bag; each man furnished his own gloves, tobacco, boots, rain gear, and blankets.

As soon as we let go the lines and got underway it was like being in a different world. Martin Selenas was captain, and, as on all ocean-going vessels, his word was law. He never gave an order unless it was necessary, but a man was expected to comply as fast as possible and without complaining.

I was the only one aboard who wasn't Norwegian. Most spoke with an accent, but used English at all times unless singing a song or telling a joke that didn't make sense in English.

Each fisherman stood a two-hour watch when in outside waters, with ten hours off. I drew the midnight to two o'clock shift, and when my first turn at the wheel came we were about eight hours out of Salisbury Sound with a fifty-knot southeast gale blowing from the stern quarter. We had a large foresail up with the sheet slacked some to keep it full, making it very hard to steer a straight course. The terrible pressure on the sail made the ship crowd hard to port.

When I walked into the wheelhouse, a fisherman named Black Jack was steering. He said, "Yust hold her nor'west by west three quarters west," and stepped out of the wheelhouse. The wheel started spinning to port and the ship started to broach from the pressure on the sail from that fifty-knot gale.

I hung on to the wheel and tried to stop the spinning compass, but I had to steer by the wind for about ten minutes before I got the *Portlock* back on course. I am sure that Martin was lying in his bunk snickering to himself, ready to take over if I couldn't handle it.

It was always a contest trying to beat the other guys to the work, and on several occasions I felt like a complete fool because the other guys had beaten me to the work. Men old enough to be my father were working rings around me, so I had to force myself to speed up.

I was careful about baiting. Carelessly placed bait on the skate will cause a baited hook to slip toward the bottom of the coiled gear, and when setting, the whole coil will go out at once in a bad snarl.

I was careful to watch where I placed the skates that I baited, so I could see if any of mine snarled. Being the only greenhorn aboard, I expected to be blamed for a snarl whether I was guilty or not.

Sure enough, as soon as the first bad snarl went over the stern, one of the crew said, "That's what we get for having a greenhorn aboard."

I called him a liar and pointed to the skates that I had baited, and not one caused a snarl. After that if a snarl went out, the crew just shrugged their shoulders and said nothing.

Martin set the gear in one hundred twenty fathoms of water, making it very hard to heave the gear back. At night we had lights on the flagpoles that floated above each buoy line. I was on the night watch, and these lights indicated the buoy positions were okay, so we could haul the gear back and reset it after taking the fish off.

The watches were divided so we could fish around the clock. We averaged four to five hours sleep every eighteen hours. When we weren't sleeping we worked at top speed, with just enough time off to eat.

We fished the entire trip on Portlock Bank, offshore from Seward and close to the continental shelf. For a time we averaged one hundred pounds to a skate, which was poor.

One fair-weather day Martin told my partner to let me take the roller. The roller man has to unhook the fish without stopping the gurdy—if he can. I had done the coiling behind the gurdy, a job I could do well, and my partner was an expert roller man.

The roller control lever was tricky—a two-speed affair, with full speed one way and half speed the other, and neutral or stop in the middle—the trick was that it was very hard to find neutral. I narrowly escaped pulling the skate anchor off when I came to the end of the buoy line, and to my amazement there was a fifty- to sixty-pound halibut on every hook as far down the line as I could see. I couldn't stop the gurdy, or power winch, so I had to take the fish off as they came aboard, gaffing the wildly fighting halibut, letting the hook tear free, and throwing the fish into the checker on deck, then get ready for the next fish.

The whole crew watched my crazy performance, laughing wildly.

And, of course, they were elated that we had at last struck heavy fishing. Martin danced in the wheelhouse and sang a Norwegian song.

I asked Ingvald, my partner, what Martin was singing about, and he said it was an old country fisherman's song, something about "every time you get a greenhorn at the roller you run into heavy fishing."

We had everything but the hatch coaming full by the time we ran out of bait and started for port. We had been fishing so hard that I was ill from lack of sleep, and it was my bad luck to have the first turn at the wheel. I opened all the wheelhouse windows for fresh air, and somehow managed to keep awake until my watch ended. I then slept the full ten hours until it was my watch again.

The crew voted to go to Prince Rupert, British Columbia, to sell. I was bitterly disappointed because I had long before made up my mind that I had had my fill of this kind of fishing and was ready to leave the *Portlock*.

We sold forty-four thousand pounds of halibut in Prince Rupert for five and a half cents and eleven cents a pound when the price was almost the same in Sitka.

Sitka had nothing to offer for recreation because of Prohibition. Prince Rupert offered legal liquor sales and more than fifty ladies of the evening on a line, supervised by the police. Martin allowed us to draw twenty dollars each, giving us permission to bring booze aboard if it was well hidden and if we were all sober when we docked in Ketchikan.

The chief engineer and I pooled our money and bought six quarts of bonded liquor and hid it behind a fuel tank. We wanted something to celebrate the Fourth of July in Ketchikan, where we expected to arrive on July 3. When we arrived there the customs man came aboard to look for contraband. None was in sight, so he had a cup of coffee and a piece of pie, then went aft to the engine room where the chief was fussing with the engine. "Is there any booze aboard?" he asked.

"Not a drop, sir," the chief lied, and the inspector left.

After the Fourth of July celebration, I took passage on the SS *Queen* back to Sitka and was happy to be home.

I have owned two long-line halibut boats since, and the things I learned from those schooner fishermen have helped greatly. They were the true professionals and the best sailors in the world. It was a valuable experience for a young man just starting a lifetime of owning and operating fishing vessels.

# Sharon Butcher

*Ten Men for Every Woman!*
*Talkeetna*
*b. 1952*

*Marriage-minded women Outside often look to Alaska with the same wistfulness
as did the 1898 gold rush stampeders. Alaska's single women often deny any
local advantage, however, because such urban centers as Anchorage, Fairbanks,
and Juneau have the same men-to-women ratio as cities Outside and because,
they say, rural Alaskan males are likely to be woodsy, penniless, and alcoholic.*

*Yet the image of handsome, available "real men" persists. In 1986 Texas nurse
Sharon Butcher tested that myth by searching for Mr. Right at the Talkeetna
Bachelor's Ball.*

IN DECEMBER 1986 I had only been in Alaska three weeks and didn't
know anybody. I read an ad in the *Daily News* that invited single
women to come party for the weekend at Talkeetna's wild-game barbe-
cue, dogsled rides, and bachelor auction. I thought it might be a good
way to meet people, so I went and wore my cute little wool herringbone
knickers, gray Icelandic sweater, glacier glasses. I mean I looked like
such a cheechako.

When I first got to Talkeetna, the town was full of scraggly, burly
guys, all of whom wanted me to buy them drinks. They were all looking for women with a job because most guys in Talkeetna only work in
the summer and need a woman to support 'em through the winter. I
was pretty overwhelmed. I felt like a pile of raw meat in front of a bunch
of hungry dogs. So I tried to keep to myself all day.

The first guy that started to hit me up to buy him drinks, he had
offered to buy me a drink first. He placed the order, and the bartender

said, "Where's your money?" He said, "I don't have any. Put it on my tab." The bartender said, "You don't have a tab." So I wound up having to buy the drinks.

Later I picked a cute guy named Chris Butcher out of the catalog of the bachelors to be auctioned that night. He had a heavy beard, but he was not as scraggly as some of the others, like Grog, a Neanderthal guy with long, scraggly blond hair and a thick beard who hadn't taken a bath in several months. You couldn't get near the guy. In fact, as a joke, some of his friends had taken up a collection and had rented him a tuxedo. So I had seen him all scruffy looking, but then they took him in a back room and washed him up and dusted him off and put him in a tux and out he came. I mean it was just an unbelievable transformation.

All day long they had been having events like the wilderness-woman race, where women had to snowshoe through an obstacle course, run down Main Street carrying empty buckets and run back with them full of water, and then chop some wood. The last thing was to drive a dog team over a mile-long course and cross the finish line with a guy in the basket and then open a beer and give it to him. I mean it was just this ultra, ultra sexist contest that only local women could ever win because it is so difficult.

That night at eight o'clock at the Fairview roadhouse, where the walls are plastered with pictures of famous McKinley climbers like Ray Genet, the place got packed with Talkeetna guides and guys who lived in the woods. There were maybe fifty women who had come up from Anchorage on a chartered train. I had driven up by myself because I didn't know what to expect. I wanted to be able to get away if I had to!

The band started playing at eight o'clock, and about every fifteen minutes another bachelor went up to be auctioned. Of course, people were getting so inebriated that it all started to unravel at about ten o'clock. It started off kind of official and then got to be just a free-for-all. Fortunately Chris was one of the earlier ones because they were still sober enough to auction him off.

Chris went pretty high, for thirty something. Then girls went wild for a seventy-year-old man because he was a fun guy. The highest bid, about fifty dollars, was either for him or for that guy who was in the paper the next day for dropping his pants to get a higher bid.

In my opinion Chris was the best looking, but I didn't have enough cash left to bid enough for him after buying drinks for those scraggly guys. So after Chris went to someone else, I thought, "Well, shoot, that's too bad." But I happened to be standing by one of Chris's good friends. I struck up a conversation with him, and as we were talking

Chris walked up and told about how his dog, Doobie, was usually real faithful and just sat and watched Chris through the window but had disappeared from outside the building. So Chris was going to go out looking for Doobie on his new snow machine. I quickly said that I had never been on a snow machine—which was true.

And it was fortunate I had never been on a snow machine because Chris was about three sheets to the wind and kept dumping me off. We were in the snow about half the time because Chris hadn't learned how to drive this tippy new machine yet.

We wound up sticking together the rest of the evening. The party went on all night. I think Chris barely did his duty by the woman who had bought him.

I didn't think I would see Chris again after the Bachelor's Ball, but a month later when he came to Anchorage for supplies, he called me and we went out for a date. He asked if I would like to come up to his cabin the next weekend. That sounded pretty neat to me because one of the reasons I was interested in him was that the auctioneer had said that Chris was building a real neat cabin. In fact, he had lived in a tent for three winters, hauling and milling his own logs. He worked in Anchorage during the summers to earn money for building supplies—after his first grubstake had been wiped out by hospital bills after a grizzly attack!

But the next weekend at Talkeetna, there was Chris in his Carhart overalls with a big pistol strapped to his hip. You have to carry a pistol when you ride a snow machine out there to scare off moose on the trail. I thought to myself, now here I am going out in the middle of the Alaskan wilderness, eleven miles from the nearest road, in December, not knowing a soul or where I am. This guy has got a gun. I thought, "I've lost my mind!"

But I went anyway. And I'll never forget that ride. It was snowing as we zoomed through the dark woods. The trees were full of hanging "grandfather's beard," which looks like Spanish moss and which glowed an eerie green color. Snow was coming down in beautiful, thick flakes like something that somebody from the south only dreams about.

And I was riding on the back of a snow machine behind this guy who's got this pistol. It was wild. It was real romantic.

Well, when I got to the cabin, it was just beautiful. The bottom story had a wood stove beside a huge bay window. And the upstairs sleeping area had a dormer window. I remember the next morning getting up and sitting in front of the dormer window and watching the sunrise on Denali, starting at the top, turning the glaciers rose colored and then gold. Chris was downstairs cooking a really nice breakfast on the wood stove. I thought to myself, "Golly, this is like in the movies!"

Later I never gave Chris much serious thought because he was going to be living in Talkeetna and I in Anchorage. But he was pretty persistent. The next thing I knew he had moved to Anchorage. We kept dating two years. It took a while for him to reel me in. We decided to get married because we both wanted to start a family and exactly three years after I met Chris, Meryl was born on bachelor auction day.

In Dallas the female to male ratio was awful, six to one. In Alaska it was definitely true that the ratio went the other way, but a lot of the Alaskan men were kind of like Grog. Maybe a little too rugged. The country men sometimes had too much wilderness in them. They wanted to live out in a cabin and let you haul water, chop wood, and that sort of thing. And in Anchorage most of the men were married, and it didn't seem a whole lot different than Dallas except that the single men were more outdoorsy.

So, girls, I recommend going to the Talkeetna Bachelors' Ball. Really! Just to get a taste of it. I wouldn't expect to score there. I certainly didn't go there intending to. But it's pretty entertaining.

# Charlie Champaine and Roxy Wright Champaine

*Leaders*
*Salcha*
*b. 1949, 1950*

*Many mushers say that good lead dogs are born, not made, and that all the trainer can do is channel the leader's natural intelligence and desire to run. But does that born-not-made argument apply to the mushers themselves? Consider the case of Roxy Wright Champaine of Salcha, Alaska. Her grandfather was a guide to pioneer missionaries; Roxy's father, Gareth Wright, is one of the most famous Alaskan sprint racers. Roxy was the first woman to win both major sprint races, the Anchorage Fur Rendezvous and the North American in 1989. In addition, she has also won Europe's most prestigious race, the Alpirod.*

*Roxy's husband, Charlie Champaine, keeps the family winning with first places at the Fur Rondy in 1984, 1988, 1990, and 1991 and the North American in 1990.*

*Dog food, however, costs twelve hundred dollars a month, so Charlie and Roxy have to keep scheming to succeed. They sell pups, charter their boat on Prince William Sound, and win races. That they are longtime leaders in a quintessentially Alaskan sport cannot disguise the sheer joy that they still find in mushing as hard and fast as they can.*

**C**HARLIE: TO me the thrill of mushing is having a team of sixteen to twenty dogs when they are right at the peak of performance for the season. That's a tremendous amount of power on a twenty-five-pound sled with waxed runners. It's the one-runner-around-the-corner ride! I come to a big hill and I speak to them real quietly and I can feel them accelerate. Everybody is well trained and into it and having a good time. I like that a lot!

They have the power to take total control of me if they so choose. The fact that they don't and only get better and stronger at what we trained them to do is very rewarding.

For years both Roxy and myself were very low on money, so we had to be very critical about which dogs were kept and which dogs were gotten rid of. After years and years of doing that we reduced the gene pool to a pretty high standard. On top of all their other abilities our sled dogs must have sheer speed. For example, the team that Roxy won the Alpirod with last year, virtually no dog in that team could have made our main team which remained here in Alaska. They were all good guys but they weren't the best of the best.

And that's how we race.

We breed for speed, endurance, and more importantly a very strong desire to race and continue to race. They're extremely athletic. They're running twenty-five miles at an eighteen- or nineteen-mile-an-hour average speed, three days in a row. They are well-balanced guys.

**Roxy:** There are four or five other kennels with the quality of dogs we have. But you can only go as fast as the leaders in your team, and we have been very fortunate in producing some good leaders. Sometimes that's luck. Or a combination of breeding, training, our ability, and everything put together. I have had lots of favorites. All my leaders are my favorites. They are all special and individual. I've had some that were better than others, but I love 'em all.

Let me tell you about my first leader. He was the biggest character I've ever had. He was very independent. If he was loose and I wanted to catch him, I had to pretend I wasn't going to catch him because otherwise he'd run away from me.

When he was about five years old, he decided he didn't want other dog teams passing him. And this was a dog that a little kid could crawl on and take his food away and not be hurt. But soon he was biting the musher of the team passing me because he knew he was not supposed to fight with other dogs. So he decided, "Well, I'll bite the person!"

Anytime anybody took this dog to use for a leader other than myself, he'd always check them out to see if they were going to be the boss because if they weren't, he'd stop and lift a leg on snow or stop and come back and sit in the sled and lick their face. This guy was just a character!

His name was Sam, and he was my leader when I was sixteen and began racing. First I had to harness break him, but he was such a hyperactive dog that he wouldn't hold still. I had to sit on Sam for about ten minutes just to get him harnessed.

My dad, Gareth Wright, was racing dogs before I was ever even born, so naturally I grew up around them. I loved the dogs and working with them. As a little girl, I said that when I grew up, I wanted to be a dog musher. I started racing when I was sixteen and have been racing now for twenty-four years.

My dad is a very interesting person, a very fun person to be around. Dogs take a lot of time and money and effort to be competitive and he has been competitive in the sled dog world for over forty years. He worked on developing a major breed of sled dogs which he called Aurora huskies, and almost all the top teams throughout the state have some of the Aurora husky bloodline in them. What I most admire about my dad is that in spite of having been involved for forty years, every year he is still very excited about having the fastest, the best puppies ever seen. It's just neat that he can stay so enthusiastic about something that takes so much effort. He still feels that mushing is new and fun.

So imagine how excited he was in 1990 when Charlie and I let him drive our championship team in the Tok race at the end of the season. That team's leaders, Rex and Pluto, were then the best sprint leaders in the world, and Rex had originally been my dad's dog. In 1989 that team had won every race I ran. So at the North American banquet Charlie asked my dad if he'd like to drive the team in Tok. My dad said, "Are you kidding?"

Those two leaders had been in front of our team for the last two years. It's hard to get two fantastic leaders, and it is very impressive running them in front of a team.

That was a pretty special race because my dad has done a lot over the years to help me and Charlie both. And it was a special payback to let him drive the best dog team in the whole world.

**Charlie:** After the first day Gareth was in fourth place. The Tok race is two twenty-mile heats, paralleling the Alaska Highway, so the majority of it you can drive along in a car and watch. So it's great for spectator excitement. We were timing Gareth from our car whenever he was visible, and it was quite the road rally with all those spectator cars dodging in and out. Of course, the race had been a last-minute decision for Gareth. He and I had driven the team together on Thursday before the event but they had needed a rest after the North American. So Gareth had only been on the team once before the race and that was with me. So the first day he ran cautiously and he came in fourth. The second day the team won by almost two minutes overall!

**Roxy:** It was fun, a lot of enthusiasm. Dad really enjoyed that race. And he came in first!

# Henry Chapman

The Anvik Mission
Asheville, North Carolina
b. 1895

*In 1887 at Anvik, site of an early Yukon River trading post, two priests, John Chapman and Octavius Parker, established the first Alaskan mission of the American Episcopal Church. The people there were still living in traditional underground houses and following age-old customs and beliefs. The Reverend Chapman, who taught himself Ingalik, the local language, tutored students from neighboring villages in rudimentary Bible and English classes and dispensed medical help to a Native population severely hit by European-introduced diseases. In 1898 John Chapman became postmaster of the village's first post office (receiving winter mail over the Iditarod Trail from Seward). In 1923 he introduced electricity and a short-wave radio to link the mission to other settlements. In little more than two decades the Anvik people went from the Stone Age to long-distance electronic communications.*

*Henry Chapman was born at the mission in 1895, his parents' first child. He attended his father's mission school and grew up to minister to new generations of Anvik natives after his father retired to New York City in 1930. Henry Chapman continued the mission's work until 1948.*

**M**Y FATHER went to Alaska in 1887 in response to an appeal from Commander Stockton of the U.S. revenue cutter *Bear*. Stockton was moved to compassion by the plight of the Eskimos on the Arctic coast who had been exploited and abused by the crews of whaling ships. Himself an Episcopalian, he appealed to the Episcopal Church to send missionaries. It had been just twenty years since the United States had purchased Alaska from the Russians. During those twenty years the

Russian Orthodox Church, the Lutherans, the Moravians, and the Pres-
byterians had sent missionaries to Alaska while the Episcopal Church
did nothing. My father felt that it was high time for the Episcopal
Church to do something.

My father's personal example was the main factor in my decision to
become a priest. I was inspired by his sterling character and by his complete devotion to his work. Following his example just came naturally to
me, and I became a candidate for the ministry in 1917, when I was a
junior at Middlebury College.

I was born in 1895 and made my first trip to the Lower 48 when I
was four years old. My mother was going home to Middlebury, Vermont, to have her next child. My father stayed behind at the mission,
and we went down the Yukon River on the little steamboat *Margaret*
about four hundred fifty miles to St. Michael's, which at that time was
the only port of entry to the whole Yukon Valley. Before we got there in
early October, ice was forming in the Yukon River and there was a
question whether we could make it out. Fortunately we did because
there was no doctor within hundreds of miles of Anvik.

That was my first trip Outside, but I later graduated from high
school and college in Middlebury, Vermont, and in 1921 from the General Theological Seminary in New York. I returned to Anvik in 1922 to
assist my father with his ministry.

Some of the pioneer missionaries to Alaska deserve the bad press
they have received because they tended to patronize the Native culture.
It is true that my father was more confrontational than cooperative toward local shamans, but he didn't downgrade the Indian culture as other
missionaries did. With the help of [several Natives], he collected a number of Indian folklore stories and published them under the title *Tena
Texts and Tales.*

One of the most admirable traits in the Indians is their respect for
the land and its resources. I remember an instance of that. When I was a
boy in Anvik, I used to go swimming with the Indian boys of the mission. One day when we were on our way home from the swimming
hole, we noticed a group of Indians gathered around a fire. We stopped
to see what was going on. One of the Indians had shot a black bear, and
the people were eating the boiled meat. True to the Indian tradition of
hospitality, they invited us to join them. As I was eating the meat one of
the mission boys said, "Eat it nicely so that Robert will have good luck
the next time he kills a bear." Back of that admonition was the traditional respect for the spirit of the bear that had been killed.

Only men were allowed to eat bear meat, through which they

might acquire some of the strength of the bear. They didn't want their women to become that strong!

Like other tribes of Alaska, they believed that it was bad luck for a person to hear a hoot owl. Those owls make such an eerie sound that it is easy to see how that superstition originated.

During my father's early years in Alaska, he was asked to write an article for *The Churchman* on "The Attitude of a Missionary toward His Parishioners." The editors took themselves very seriously. My father was more lighthearted, so he wrote back that in Anvik the attitude of the missionary toward his parishioners was usually on his hands and knees— referring to the fact that when he made his pastoral calls in winter, he had to crawl through a tunnel to get inside the underground huts.

I, too, did some things that are not normally done by most priests and pastors. I succeeded my father not only as priest in charge of the mission but also as our fourth-class postmaster. And I was a licensed radiotelephone operator and had a regular schedule with the U.S. Army Signal Corps operator in Flat, ninety miles east of Anvik. Each morning and evening I gave him the weather report for the benefit of the pilots who carried the mail.

Because there was no dentist anywhere near Anvik, people who had the toothache came to me to have the tooth pulled. The only preparation I had had was watching my father do it! Fortunately, during my first furlough in Asheville, North Carolina, my dentist showed me how to inject Novocaine—which made it easier for both my patients and me.

Of course, my goal as a missionary was to preach the Christian faith. I measured my success by how many people were influenced to accept Jesus Christ as their Lord and Savior. But the influence of the mission went beyond that because I came into contact with everybody in the community, whites and Indians.

In the Bush, missionary wives had a great influence, too. My wife accepted the isolation and the long, cold winters without complaining and was of inestimable help to me in my ministry. For instance, sometimes we had no registered nurse and my wife had to deliver the babies and care for the sick. That was when her ten weeks of nursing training at the Episcopal Hospital in Philadelphia really came in handy!

The mission's influence was also spread by its parishioners. I particularly remember two of them. One was an elderly woman who was the first to be baptized and confirmed after my father had been working for several years. She was known to me only as "Simon's mother." I remember her as a gentle, kindly person who was widely respected in the community. The other was Isaac Fisher, one of my father's first students. After he grew to manhood, he became my father's interpreter and traveling companion. I remember my mother telling me that when I was of preschool age, a friend in the Lower 48 sent me a set of building blocks with the letters of the alphabet on them. Isaac taught me my ABCs from those building blocks. When I succeeded my father, Isaac interpreted for me and taught me the ABCs of taking care of myself on the trail.

# Jeff "Coggie" Coghill

*Pilot, Tanana and Yukon Rivers*
*Nenana*
*b. 1959*

*Jeff Coghill grew up in the village of Nenana under the spell of two great influences—his father and the Tanana River. His father is Lieutenant Governor Jack Coghill, an archconservative whose family fuel business spun off from his English father's general store. When Jeff used to complain to his dad that other kids made fun of him because he always smelled like fuel oil, the response was, "Son, that's the smell of money." Jeff says he didn't get along with his father until he quit working for him at the age of twenty-one. A stint of work Outside did not suit him either: the population and the competition "made it difficult to be an individual." Returning to Alaska, Jeff worked his way up at Yutana Barge Lines, from swabbing decks and cleaning toilets to piloting for the Tanana, a one-hundred-twenty-foot flat-bottomed tugboat. Doing so reunited him with the second great influence in his life, the Tanana River. Jeff averages ten to fifteen summer trips downstream as far as St. Marys, eight hundred thirty miles from Nenana. As pilot he oversees the freight, spells the captain at the wheel, and motors out ahead of the tugboat in the pilot boat to find the deepest channels in the braided, unpredictable river.*

**M**Y JOB is to find the edge between the shallow water and the deepest water. Pushing downstream we need four and a half feet minimum draft, and sometimes I measure that with a stick instead of my depth finder because accuracy is so vital. We pilots say, "The stick never lies."

Piloting all comes down to reading the water, the boils, wind streaks, and current streaks. You'll see a glassy, smooth area and then maybe a dark line with ripples on it that could be an edge where it might drop off from two feet into the deep water. Or a bottom hole will cause a disturbance on the surface. Deep-water boils have a tendency to be voluminous and violent where a shallow-water boil might just kind of bloop up in what the map people call a dune.

The Tanana River is constantly moving, and its silt is of facial-powder fineness. With my stick I can feel the softness of a moving bar telling me that it might shift. A hard bottom—probably frozen, it ain't going to go nowhere.

The Tanana River is narrow, shallow, and probably the fastest-navigated water in all of the United States. What makes it special is the changing silts, the channels moving back and forth, and the bars moving in, moving out.

Finding the channel in my sounding boat is my greatest responsibility. How far out I go from the tugboat depends on how bad a crossing is and how exact I have to be. If I have a good wide, deep crossing, I can run out three quarters, a half a mile ahead provided the captain doesn't mind. Some captains like you to work closer. Some like you to work farther away. I can afford to be a little sloppy on the wide crossings.

On a bad crossing, say the Squaw Crossing at the confluence of the Yukon and Tanana rivers, the channels are constantly changing and I work about three hundred feet in front of the barge with my electronic depth finder. But even being very careful, everybody gets stuck on the Tanana River. Even the best have done it. And when I'm out in my sounding boat and the captain is following me, if I run him aground, it's automatically my fault. Therefore, it's a humiliating experience. And there's a lot of peer pressure, too. The other pilots and captains will find out about it and rag me pretty bad. (I can give it out as well as I can take it.)

My first time running aground, I busted up the tow, and I put a pretty good-sized dent in the side of the boat. But that grounding was not as bad as the second one, when I sat on a gravel bar down at the mouth for five days. There was a wind-blown tide, the wind changed, the tide went out, and in like fifteen minutes we lost two and a half feet of water. I had already been stuck, but by the time the tide went out, we were high and dry! In a couple of the pilots' chart books that place is now called Coghill's Bar.

There's several bars that are commonly called by pilots' and captains' names. There's Captain Brown's Bar, Brian's Bar, Teddy's Crossing.

Captain Teddy Diedrich was one of my mentors. He and David Walker were a team that ran the MV *Yukon,* which was the twin to this MV *Tanana.* And when I was a child between the ages of eight and twelve, I periodically took a week-long ride with them on the boat to see Galena. Teddy was a close friend of the family. And that's where I got to know David Walker. Real fine people!

Teddy and David were what started me on loving river work. Them and the two big tugboats, the *Yukon* and its twin, the *Tanana,* which in those days they carried bigger crews. Captain Walker and Captain Diedrich were like in command. I admired them for being able to take those big boats down the rivers and stop at all these neat places.

When I visit Captain Walker now where he has retired at Holy Cross, he always wants to know about the Tanana River because, like I say, the Tanana is the challenge, the one that brings the best out in you. When I was working on the *Yukon* tugboat in 1978, the year before it burned, Dave Walker would come down the Tanana River and be smoking one cigarette right after the other, gripping the stick tightly, and drinking cup after cup of black coffee. But as soon as we would hit the Yukon River, Dave just kicked back in his chair, flipped his hat back, looked over at me and said, I can't emulate his voice, "Jeffry, get me a cup of Ovaltine!" He was just so relaxed! He sat back and enjoyed his cigarette.

Like him, I have been blessed because I honestly and truly enjoy my work. I am happiest when I am out on the river meeting the people and maneuvering the boat and the tow. I enjoy the challenge where every load and every trip is different. Each day I have the opportunity to learn new things. It's an adventure, not just a job.

Over a hundred sternwheelers used to run these rivers, and there is still a lot of romance here. Someday somebody will find a way to move the freight faster than we do, but I don't think the river will ever die as a form of transportation.

I like to think that I am a piece of history, too. I want to be like these guys that we meet on the beach who say, "Yeah, I used to work on the steamer *Nenana* and I used to cut firewood for 'em."

The Yukon can seem pretty boring sometimes, but if you turn your back on her, she will definitely grab you.

But the Tanana is the greatest challenge, sounding her out, trying to bring the captain through a bad crossing. Every pilot says he hates to go out in the sounding boat, that it's eighteen hours of pure hell. But even though in the summertime you curse it, in the wintertime you think about nothing else, waiting to get back on the river.

# Helmi Conatser

*Eagle Island Iditarod Checkpoint*
*Eagle Island, Yukon River*
*b. 1941*

*Although much of Alaskan employment falls to the single, transient, worker, it is the old-fashioned families, nuclear and extended, that cement isolated bush communities. After immigrating from Germany to Florida in 1959, Helmi Stange married machinist Ralph Conatser. Ralph had always wanted to live in the Alaskan Bush, and in 1965 he and Helmi moved to Sitka. They lived in a tent and fished the Alsek River. In 1975 the couple homesteaded on a Yukon River slough, or backwater, seventy miles upstream from Grayling. Starting from scratch, they and their youngest son, Steve, built comfortable dwellings and a lifestyle of raising huskies, trapping pelts, and fishing a fish wheel (a revolving trap). Every other March their isolated world is jolted by dozens of visitors: Iditarod mushers, pilots, spectators, judges, veterinarians, and ham radio operators. Helmi, a musher herself, mothers the mushers with fresh eggs and her trademark moosemeat stew.*

*Famed Iditarod champion Libby Riddles has described the Conatsers' semiannual welcome as "an example of the finest in Bush hospitality."*

CLINT AND Vanita Thurmond are our neighbors. They are twenty-five miles down the river at Blackburn [Mountain]. In early March I keep in touch with Vanita on the CB and the single sideband twice a day, waiting to see if any mushers have passed her house yet. Ralph and Steve and I are expecting to see the first one at the mouth of our slough. And, of course, we are wondering if it's going to be Susan Butcher or if it's a male. I or Steve usually go down there and check how many dogs they have and if they are going to drop any. I have to check that they have their mandatory promotional materials, ax, snowshoes, sleeping bag. They just open up their sled bag and show it all to me. I have to check each thing off or else they can't go on. All the mushers are very polite. It's just kind of a fun time because after being isolated all winter we suddenly meet racers and volunteers and spectators from all over Alaska, America, and other countries.

The mushers really like it here because they have a nice cabin to come up to off the ice. They can get warm and dry out all their clothes and dog booties. And I always cook them something special because out on the Yukon the wind chill might be seventy degrees below zero!

# Fred Elvsaas

*Aleut-Norwegian Making Things Happen*
*Seldovia*
*b. 1933*

*Greatly influenced by his tradition-oriented Aleut grandmother, commercial fisher-man Fred Elvsaas in 1972 became the president of the Seldovia Native Asso-ciation, one of two hundred Native corporations that grew out of the Alaska Native Claims Settlement Act. As a successful land company manager, Fred leases recreation areas, sells timber, and contracts for health and social programs. The Seldovia Na-tive Association even built a shrimp processing plant, which it leased to a Japan-ese firm. Fred's priorities are shareholder control and community service. Sel-dovia's joint program with Port Graham and English Bay to prevent young people from becoming addicted to drugs and alcohol has unified the three villages and made a real dent in an otherwise intractable problem. That spirit of coopera-tion typifies Seldovia, a village where Natives and non-Natives have worked well together even as far back as the Russian era.*

**W**HEN I was growing up, there were a lot of people my age that were just like myself. We had Native mothers and grandmothers and grandfathers but we had non-Native fathers. There were a lot of Scandi-navians here, Swedes and Danes, and a lot of mixed blood was already here in Alaska from the Russians.

My grandmother was a very firm believer that the non-Natives, es-pecially from the United States, were very weak people who could not survive without help from the Natives to get them through. She did not have much respect for non-Natives. She always thought that we would have been better off if they had left. But she liked my father. He came from Norway, not America, and that made a big difference. Those people from Seattle or from San Francisco were not really looked at as Alaskans by her.

So I grew up in this mixed atmosphere, but there were only a few instances that I can recall in the schools where the teachers didn't want to accept Natives as equal. Seldovia was a little bit different than the rest of Alaska because here the Native people made things happen. They made the biggest salmon catches. So we didn't have the high degree of discrimination, even though we always had the newcomers that thought that if they came from Texas, they must be God's gift to earth. Those are the very people that my grandmother was so convinced would never survive a winter without Native help. And I firmly believe she was right. Obviously they came here because their own home nest was so filthy they couldn't make it there, either.

It's unfortunate in this day and age that the real Alaskan is the guy that got here before the other guy that followed him. They really think that's how it should be.

The law now is that if you're here thirty days, you are an Alaskan and you can get the state Permanent Fund checks and state longevity money.

Today, for the most part, people are willing to work with the Native people and the Native people are willing to work with most everyone. But we always have somebody that thinks that the Natives got something for free in the Settlement Act. We had an incident a few months back where people wanted to build a road. They thought since it was Native land, there'd be no objection. We had quite a time making them understand that this is private property. They understood that their home was private property, but they didn't look at the corporation's land as private property. And that particular type of person will never accept that. We have to keep reminding them.

In turn, we've made a great effort to be a good corporate citizen. We've done a lot of things for the area. We sponsor Boy Scouts, Girl Scouts, school Christmas-stocking programs, senior hot lunches, all of the little things that need somebody as the gel to make it work. We do these things, but two thousand years from today there will be somebody with that same prejudice. It's unfortunate.

When I was young, for years Seldovia developed pretty much socially around a club system. They had the pinochle club, the library club, the women's club, Native Sisterhood, Native Brotherhood, and so forth, and they had plays and entertainment, and they did things throughout the town. And then the social life moved into the bars during the forties and the early days of the king crab fishery, when there was lots of money, and there were the bar-type activities and the school activities. There was a definite split between the school people and the local bar people. That has changed greatly now. There is very little social activity in the bars except for parties from time to time. The new school system under the new borough got to be more and more accepted. Schoolteachers are finally looked at as real citizens now. They are buying homes and staying more than one year and raising their families here.

We got away from the territorial school after statehood in 1959 into the Kenai Peninsula Borough School District. Don Gilman, who is now the Kenai borough mayor, started his career in Seldovia as the school principal. He got us very active into developing this new open-concept school system. Our school now is K through 12 and has a gymnasium and swimming pool. We had the first swimming pool in the Kenai school district. We have a hot lunch program. We have just as good a curriculum as any American school has. All the audiovisual programs. We have made great strides. That was a collective effort by everybody in Seldovia. The man-hours of the people were logged, and they ran into the thousands of hours because people recognized the need and they wanted that. And that made the school system much more accepted. Social life evolved into a different mode.

So now we have people that are active in the school and churches as well as those who hang out in the bars. It's not an us-versus-them attitude anymore. We made our improvements through social change and we succeeded in spite of the world. I really have to give Don Gilman a lot of credit for bringing our town together in a united effort.

Anybody that's willing to do something inspires me. What bothers me the most is when I see people waiting for somebody else to act. I've always been of the opinion that if you are only going to be on the earth a short while, you better do what you can while you are here 'cause you sure as hell can't do it after you're gone.

# Vernon Evan

*"I wanted an education."*
*Marshall*
*b. 1922*

*On the Yukon River the area from Russian Mission to Norton Sound is Yup'ik Eskimo country. Vernon Evan's village, Tuckchek, was decimated by introduced illnesses when he was a boy, and its houses and graves tumbled into the river. Vernon's hopes for an education also collapsed; he was thankful to get a job on the river's steamboats. But the boy whose chances at a formal education were short-changed eventually became a teacher, a dance instructor.*

I NEVER SAW English dancing down at Tuckchek. Our village just had plain Native people; we never saw any whites except Fathers. And we only had Eskimo dancing. But I used to skate the five miles from Tuckchek up here to Marshall all by myself, and I'd go watch a square dance over at the store. When I got old enough, I started thinking to myself, "Well, those white people are having fun and I don't see why I shouldn't, too. Dancing don't hurt anybody."

Eskimo dancing, they stopped it for quite some time after nobody was interested anymore. But when I moved to Marshall in 1938, my brother-in-law got the Eskimo dances going here. But he died. Then my first cousin handled it, but he died, too. So I took over. And twenty years ago I got the English dances going again because dancing is for everyone, mixed ages and whole families. They say Eskimos love to dance and it is true! I like to do both Eskimo and English dances.

During dog-racing time on the Yukon in spring, people call us from other villages like Takshak, St. Marys, Mountain Village, and Pilot Station to invite us to Eskimo dances and contests. Then we see which person from all the villages is the best dancer. It's a lot of fun when people come from all over for the dog team races in March. I used to be in those races, too, but I have retired from everything. But Eskimo dancing, I'll never retire!

The first thing I do to teach Eskimo dancing is to translate the song I am going to sing into English so that you can dance along with the story. By looking at the motions, an expert can tell what the song is about.

I used to sing only the other villages' songs. The other villagers came over here to hear me sing their songs. But then one night I was talking to a couple of the old guys from Pilot about how they had made their own songs. They told me that in their village it was very popular for them to make their own so that the people could hear what had been happening in the community. For instance, if a person goes out trapping all the time, he might make a song about it.

So I started writing my own songs. I was teaching Eskimo dancing up in Fairbanks for five weeks, and when we came back, my wife rode the railroad for the first time and I wrote a song about that.

I should write a song about *muktuk* [whale blubber] because I was raised exclusively on Native foods. Getting muktuk is not as difficult as people think. Food stamps are spoiling the people and few go out for muktuk anymore.

I grew up before airplanes. They used to have a mail run with dog teams changing from village to village. In the spring of 1930 that's how I went up to Holy Cross to school, with the last mail run by dog team.

It was the first time I met the mailman. We never got no mail down there in Tuckchek. I didn't even know what mail was like until I went to school. The Tuckchek people didn't get any kind of mail at all. No food stamps, you name it, they didn't get nothing! Only when the ATG, Alaska Territorial Guard, started did they begin to get letters.

I only stayed one year, when I was nine or ten years old, at the Catholic mission school at Holy Cross. After one year my uncle wanted me back. He'd adopted me when my father died. My uncle was strictly Native, living off the country. I don't know what he wanted me back for because when I came back, I had nothing to do. I even cried when I left the school. I wanted to have more education but my uncle said, "Come on home!"

That mission grade school was free, and there were all kinds of people from all up and down the river. Anybody was welcome to go to school there, and I was very glad to be getting out from my uncle's camp to go to a different place. When I started school, I felt more like I was at home. I had been mistreated by my uncle's wife. So I wasn't nervous a bit to go to school where the priests, brothers, and sisters treated us just like their own kids.

When I first went to the mission, I couldn't even say yes or no in English. I had to have an interpreter. But I learned quickly because I was so mischievous at the mission, especially trying to make girls cry, that I always had to sit in the corner facing away from the class. I was so mischievous that I had to work on my papers all the time, always in the corner. The more I stayed in the corner, the faster I learned. Even during the summer I went to school Saturdays and Sundays when the other kids were working out in the vegetable gardens. On the weekends I would be in school all by myself, still in the corner. That was my place.

After I came back to Tuckchek, I couldn't talk my language for four days. I had to have my uncle interpret when I came back. But after four days I had relearned my Native way of speaking.

# Doug Geeting

*Glacier Pilot*
*Talkeetna*
*b. 1953*

*Modern planes and navigational aids have revolutionized bush flying, and large commercial aircraft, air taxi services, and private aircraft are all part of an increasingly high-tech mix. Glacier pilot Doug Geeting routinely flies single-engine planes in the extreme conditions of Mount McKinley, North America's highest peak. "The mountain," as he calls it, is not only part of the often-violent storm patterns of Southcentral Alaska but also it makes its own weather. Rising from practically sea level to twenty thousand three hundred twenty feet, the mountain's ridges and buttresses are promontories across which break oceans of arctic air. To fly climbers and rubberneckers to the Great One, a pilot had better have learned the country well.*

*The new breed of Alaskan flyer flies less by the seat of his pants than by the preflight check list and the bottom line. Doug Geeting, indisputedly a bush pilot in the Alaskan tradition, tells me about some of his mentors who epitomized Alaskan flying.*

**B**UDDY WOODS was an incredible pilot. He was my mentor or hero, but he was one of those guys that you never really hear much about. He just did his job. He'd be headed Outside on some vacation and they'd jerk him out of the airliner to go do a rescue. He'd do the rescue and meet up with his wife in Hawaii or somewhere. That's the kind of guy he was. It was no big deal to him. He even landed on the summit of McKinley. I've flown cover for a lot of his rescues and he was an amazing pilot in PBYs and every other thing. About five years ago Buddy died in a crash over on the other side of the range. He was flying his

Caribou and from what I heard, the elevator cable broke. He was hauling fuel, so it burned when he crashed. But he could fly anything that there was around and he was also a mechanic who really understood machinery.

Kenny Holland was another good pilot. He had Holland Air Services, which is now K2 Aviation. Kenny was an old-timer who had worked up in the Arctic as a polar bear hunting guide. And I used to follow him around with Cubs when he hired me out as a pilot to help with his hunters. I learned a lot from some of those old bush pilots 'cause they really knew how to work their equipment.

Cliff Hudson is another extremely good pilot and the kind of guy that will say no to a client. And that's the attitude that I have developed in my three pilots now. I send them on a trip, but if they don't like what they see, it's their prerogative to turn around and come back.

Cliff was great at just sitting down and if you had a question about something, he wasn't an instructor, but he could get the point across to you pretty good. He'd been around for a long time flying and he had never really had any accidents.

He was my first boss up here, and I did pay attention to him. I learned a lot from him, just little things, taking care of an airplane, that make a difference down the road on how much you are going to spend at the end of each year to get your airplane back into shape.

In 1975 I flew up from California in a 1946 BC-12D Taylorcraft looking for work. My first experience of Alaska was Anchorage, and I don't mean to put Anchorage down, but I didn't like it and I didn't like what I was doing there. It just wasn't my idea of what Alaska was. So I returned to California. But that only lasted for a couple months before I loaded up my Taylorcraft and flew north again. I didn't know where I wanted to go. Maybe Canada, maybe back East. And that's the truth! I was sort of lost, trying to find myself. And then I ran out of money and I found myself real quick. Broke and sitting in Talkeetna.

I started working for Cliff Hudson because I had seen him sleeping in a waiting room at Merrill Field while getting an inspection done on his airplanes. He was just snoring there, but he looked like an interesting character, so I sat down and woke him up and asked him some questions about working. He said, "Well, I might be looking for a pilot maybe."

So I had put the hint out, but Cliff didn't hire me until I got to Talkeetna and hung around for a while.

As a private pilot, if you've got the guts to do it, you can land at fourteen thousand feet on the mountain. Legally you can go have a picnic at fourteen thousand if you want to do that. But as a commercial operator, if I did that, they'd shut me down.

The Ruth is a good place to go. I try to tell pilots that if they want to land on a glacier, the Ruth Amphitheater is safe, it's big and roomy, and there is not a lot of our traffic. The Kahiltna is a different story. The Kahiltna is a zoo during climbing season, in May and June. In fact, we get nine or ten 185s going in there every hour. And sometimes all at once. And it really gets messy if there are two or three airplanes parked on the glacier that are unknowns, people that don't monitor our frequencies. We usually monitor 1227. We've had some real close midairs in the last couple of years. Real close ones. When you see them go by, you keep thinking about your whole life going in front of you. Then you start thinking later that night about what happened in the Grand Canyon and the regulations now that they have that they are no longer allowed to fly below the rim. We don't want that to happen up here, so we are trying to keep it as organized as we can.

If something gets me, it may not be the one little thing but a combination of little things. Like if I screw up on a flight plan and wander off in the wrong direction and get into bad weather, they'll never find me.

Back in the sixties and the seventies, when I was pumping gas and washing planes for money in the southern Sierras, I didn't have a lot of money to spend for instruction, so I got books on aerobatics and soaring. I think that soaring has been my biggest asset. I learned an awful lot about weather that way, too. If you are used to flying a sailplane, you are constantly looking for ways to stay up. If you're not a glider pilot, you're looking at the weather as an enemy, but in a sailplane you look at the weather as a friend. That helps to build confidence for when you get up in the mountains and you get a little bit of turbulence. And that doesn't automatically mean that you should turn around and head for home because you can use winds and their lift to your advantage.

The biggest problem with pilots that fly up around the Denali area is lack of experience. Or maybe they are out to impress somebody in the airplane. Sometimes they come in to see what we recommend about flying into the Alaska Range. We'll tell 'em, "Stay at seven thousand feet and go on into the Ruth Amphitheater over the Ruth Glacier. It's a beautiful ride. Stay on the right-hand side going in. If you have a problem or if you don't like the weather or you hit a downdraft or whatever, you can always make a turn and go out. Stay high at all times so that you can escape to lower terrain if you have a problem." We tell them this all the time.

But what they'll do is get down right on the deck and start going up the glacier, and they'll find that the airplane cannot climb the glacier because it's rising terrain. Then they get to a point where they cannot make the turn and they've got to land. And they end up putting the airplane up on the glacier. I won't mention names, but I know that a couple of the flight schools in Anchorage did that a couple of times.

There's a lot of guys operating in this state that should not be operating, period. Too many of 'em have already had casualties. And not just broken wings. We're talking about fatalities. And I don't like to see that because it makes me look bad. It makes the whole business I'm in look bad.

Sometimes tourists ask, "How many accidents have you had?" That hurts because *I* haven't busted anything.

Sometimes air taxi pilots get pressured by their bosses or by the chief pilot, and there's the peer pressure on somebody that comes to town and gets a job working for an air taxi operator. But everyone just has to make up his own mind. If I look out my window and have to think about the weather very long, it's common sense to think that it's not good enough to go. There will always be better times to make the trip.

If I go to the range and there's a little turbulence, I can feel it as I go in and see little signs in the sky. I may see a little bit of snow drifting across one of the ridges and be able to anticipate which way the wind is blowing and whether it is sinking or rising. I try to anticipate the flow of the air around the peaks and through the passes just like you'd watch water flowing in a brook.

I used to make attempts to take people in, mostly climbers, just to save face. Climbers hear stories about going into fog banks and doing weird things on the mountain. And I have done some weird things that I never want to do again. Certainly not just to get somebody to some place. Now I say, "We'll just wait till the weather gets better and I can get you to the glacier safely so you can go climbing." Then they say, "Well, we think you can get in there right now."

My rule is that the airplane costs two hundred fifty bucks an hour, and if the weather gets bad and we don't get in, you owe me two hundred fifty bucks per hour, whatever that time was unless I have guaranteed to land you where you want to go, and then I pay for it because that was my mistake. But I will fly around all day long for two hundred fifty bucks an hour. I may not get anywhere except into your wallet, but I'll do it.

To me as a professional, saying no to a client is the hardest thing to do. I've got to work at it. If the weather is getting worse and a client is pushing, trying to get there, and there's three or four air taxi operators on the field, he's going to go around to each one of 'em and try to find somebody who's going to go. And those are the kind of climbers that I tend to back away from anymore because it's just a pressure thing. I can see the accident hovering out there in the future.

I guess the reason I stopped doing a lot of those things is that I'm not that hungry anymore, to be honest with you. Whereas there are guys out there starving flying airplanes and doing a lot of strange things with them to make a living. I just hope they reach the point where they can start saying no to some of that stuff, and then we'll see a lot fewer accidents.

Mistakes that *I've* made? Oh, man, I've made lots of them! Where do I start? I've been real lucky. Sometimes I have made it through things and wondered how and why. But I don't make those same mistakes again. It always seems to be the other mistakes that I never thought about that creep up on me. I've done some real dumb things and some things that I thought were necessary at the time. I'll just mention one.

I went down a few years ago out at a lake that I was going to buy some property on during a big open-entry thing where you stake out your land. Over-the-counter stuff. I thought, "Well, I'd better go get some of that." And I went out to this tiny, skinny lake. It was in January and had been like thirty below everywhere for two weeks, and I thought that there should be enough ice to hold an airplane.

I looked at the lake. I had my girlfriend with me. She was a schoolteacher. So we were flying around on a Sunday afternoon at two o'clock. The light was pretty good. Good enough for an hour or two anyway, and we went out there. I decided to stop, get out, and look around. Walk on this land I was going to get.

I touched down, looked back to see if there was any overflow. Perfect so I took off again and came around and landed again in the same tracks and continued my roll. I was going to make a turn at the upper end of the lake. When I got there and looked back behind, there was water coming up from the ski. Overflow! Oh, man, how could there be overflow here?

Then one ski went down below the ice, and plunk I was over on the wing tip and there we were.

We weren't going anywhere. There was no way that we could get the airplane unstuck. It was perfectly clear out there and it was *cold*.

I had a really elaborate survival kit with everything you could imagine in it, but I had it in my living room and I was going through it the night before—this is really the honest truth—just to see if everything was still in there. Checking out the latest food things, candles, how many books I wanted, bottles of whiskey, whatever, for when I'd go down, to have the comforts. So when I landed out at that lake and got stuck, it didn't bother me because, no problem, I had all this stuff. Man, I could get it out and start using it. But when I looked back, it was gone! Then I remembered that it was still in the living room. So I never got to use it. Next time it'll be there. I guarantee you that! So we ended up stuck there for four days and nights.

Shortly after that my girlfriend moved back to California.

# Timothy "Awilinga" Gologergen

*Yup'ik Reunion*
*St. Lawrence Island and Nome*
*b. 1919*

*The Cold War was a godsend for Alaska because massive defense spending built a base of economic well-being under an otherwise boom-or-bust natural resources economy. Socially, too, the military has changed Alaskan culture from the old sourdough and Native mix to a society much like Main Street America. But what is often forgotten, even in Alaska, is that the Cold War exacted a direct toll on that group of Alaskans for whom the Bering Strait was a link, not a barrier.*

*Tim "Awilinga" Gologergen grew up on St. Lawrence Island, using seal oil lamps and knowing nothing of electricity, timepieces, or even trees. St. Lawrence Island had been part of Russia until the Alaska purchase of 1867; his sense of place was focused more on Provideniya on the Chukotsk Peninsula than on any part of the North American mainland. But before long he was tapping out Morse code for the Army in the China, Burma, and India theaters of World War II. Later he helped to establish and maintain the first runway at Savoonga on St. Lawrence Island (where he also taught grammar school).*

*The Bering Sea border was shut in 1940, separating family and clan members. So imagine the excitement when on June 13, 1989, a planeload of Alaskans including Tim Gologergen and his wife Anna made the first "Friendship Flight" to Provideniya.*

WE GOT off the airplane not knowing what was going to happen. We were so excited the adrenalin was flowing all over the place. The white Russian border guards didn't smile. I just kept telling my wife, "Keep waving at them," as we went through the massive crowd at the airport. Most of the children were waving the American and Russian flags.

The border guards hadn't smiled yet but they kept following us around. The Yup'ik people we saw were the first we had seen since the border was closed in 1940. We just smiled at each other. I told my wife, "Go mingle with the crowd."

I saw a couple of Siberian Eskimo ladies and I asked them, "Do you speak Yup'ik language?" One of them said, "We sure do!" The other one started crying. We all embraced and started talking at the same time in Siberian Yup'ik. Everybody looked at us and were so happy that they cried, too.

We started talking at the same time. "Is old so-and-so still alive?" Most of the people we had known had died and the people we saw at Provideniya were the next generation that had been mostly named after their parents.

The sons and daughters of the people we used to know were there to greet us! At dinner my wife and I sat with a young lady and asked, "Do you know a schoolteacher that used to come down to St. Lawrence Island?" And the lady started crying. She said, "I'm his daughter." So by chance we had actually sat with the daughter of the fellow we were looking for. We all started crying and then we embraced. I looked around and people were in Yup'ik-speaking groups. Everybody was asking the same question, "Where is so-and-so?" The Siberians were asking the same questions of us. "Where is so-and-so that used to come up here to trade back and forth in the 1930s and 1920s?"

The time was really flying as we started getting acquainted. We asked them who their father and mother were. That's why we were in groups as we traced them. The minute we found a relative, they came over from other groups. Finally there were big groups here and big groups there.

We stayed there from morning till twelve midnight when we returned to Alaska. The time was really short but we got acquainted enough that later we phoned to invite them to come visit us. One lady we had met in Provideniya came over and stayed with us all summer. Her mother was of our clan—Qiiwaghmiit. Traditionally our clan had used slings for protection against raiders from Siberia and for hunting birds. So we were known as the people that liked to throw rocks. We were always a strong group that liked to help others and to work together as a team.

All through the summer people came and stayed with us. We learned that on the Russian side they had retained more of the hunting-gathering livelihood and everyday culture than we had. That got me interested in our traditional life-style. That's why I taped everything I saw when I was over there. We are losing it now since we have refrigerators and because we can buy food at the store instead of eating our seafood and the vegetation we picked on St. Lawrence Island. We used to eat a good diet because the seal, walrus, and the other seafood had a lot of iodine and the greens we picked had a lot of vitamins. Now we eat junk food.

My wife and I have made three trips over there. Last summer we stayed four weeks at a relative's house after she had stayed a month in Nome with us. Her husband's family name is Yaimisin. Our fathers were related closely but as the years went by our families had drifted apart.

We Siberian Yup'ik speakers give our children the names of our parents, aunts, and uncles because of our love for our elders. So certain names are traditional in one clan or family. For instance, my daughter June's Eskimo name, Yatgawen, is still over there. Her great uncle named her after her great aunt who had died in the U.S.S.R. And her son Derek's Yup'ik name is over there, with a girl named Uyghaggaq, meaning rock. My youngest boy's name is over there; she's an old lady, probably seventy-eight years old, and her clan name is Tikegghaghmi, meaning a point of land. My son Russell is about twenty-eight years old, so the traditional name survives.

I haven't been able to find any individuals I knew from the 1930s, just the names. The people I had known had died, especially the young fellow that used to be in the Russian Army over there. I was in the American Army when I made a 1941 furlough to St. Lawrence Island and met him as he was making a trip to Gambell by boat. He was looking for two white Russians that had defected to the United States. This was the last Siberian Native that we ever saw for forty years.

I feel sad about the many years of lost contact because that contributed a lot to our loss of traditional values and of our Siberian Yup'ik language. If we had not had that gap, we would have preserved our culture the way our relatives did on the Russian side.

When I go back next time, I want to make more tapes about our traditional style of living. When our relatives came over to Nome last summer, we went out looking at the vegetation and they told us what was edible. We have many things growing at Nome that we didn't realize were useful. Roots and things our Siberian cousins even use for medication. Each time I learn something like that I feel so happy to be videotaping this information before it is too late.

# Peter Hackett, M.D.

*The Mayor of 14,000 Feet*
*Anchorage*
*b. 1947*

*Peter Hackett came to Alaska from Chicago as a young medical doctor because of what he calls "a hormone problem." He was in love with a woman he had met at eighteen thousand feet on Mount Logan in the Yukon. After he spent five years with her in Alaska, she married his best friend, but Peter was hooked on Alaska's opportunities for outdoor adventure. (He regularly skis cross-country from his home in downtown Anchorage!)*

*Even among Alaska's outdoor fraternity Peter Hackett stands out as a hard-core mountaineer. During his first trip to Asia he hiked twelve hundred miles across the Himalayas. That midseventies experience made it hard for him to settle down again to a routine existence. His footloose lifestyle was reinforced in 1981, when he became the first American to solo on Mount Everest, a climb begun as a medical research trip to investigate the effects of altitude on the human body. The five-month team effort culminated when Peter fell just after reaching the summit. He was saved from death by catching his legs behind a rock as he was hurtling down the mountain. He felt "a profound feeling" that he must have been saved for something important in life.*

*In 1982 he returned to Alaska with a lot of ideas from the Everest expedition about setting up a medical research hut at fourteen thousand feet on Mount McKinley. Soon he and his colleagues were both rescuing climbers and using them as guinea pigs to advance medical knowledge about such oxygen deprivation diseases as emphysema.*

*Peter Hackett became the first physician to make a living out of high-altitude medicine, lecturing and publishing about his research. His camp is manned continuously in the peak climbing months of May and June. Supplies are brought in by army helicopter in early May, and the underground facilities are powered by solar, wind, and backup generator electricity. Peter and many of his fellow rescue doctors have suffered from frostbite and life-threatening situations. Denali is an unforgiving environment.*

THE COLD is extreme on that mountain. When we fly in in the first week of May, it's minus forty every night. And then in June it warms up to about minus twenty-five. There isn't much night in June, but there is a difference in temperature because the sun travels around the mountain. When we're in the shade, it's much cooler. So at night we are in the daylight but the sun isn't on the camp. It's around the other side of the mountain, and that's why the night temperature varies from minus forty in early May to minus twenty-five in June.

Yet for the climbers this mountain will always be popular. It's what the Park Service calls "an attractive nuisance." A legal term for maybe something in your backyard that attracts kids. It and Mount Logan are the highest arctic mountains in North America.

The reward is to be able to stand on the summit of the continent and to enjoy some of the raw beauty. It's a stark, lifeless beauty with no wildlife or vegetation—rock and ice. But to a lot of people the reward is in getting away for a few weeks from their normal lives and pitting themselves against the elements.

Weather pretty much determines everything. That's what makes the mountain such a challenge. Although it's not technically difficult—about half the people who try the mountain make it—it's always a survival experience. You have to know when to turn around, when to dig in, and not let the cold or the altitude get the better of you.

Digging in is an entirely necessary skill. You must always have with you a shovel, a stove, a sleeping bag, and some fuel and food so that if you have to dig in right away, just take off your pack, pull out your shovel, and start digging. And that is not an uncommon scenario.

On Denali there's very much of a local climbing style, which is low-tech, going slowly, and building snow caves and igloos to get out of the fierce conditions. Which is why Alaskans on Denali are generally a lot safer than the others. For example, Europeans come over with no experience of how to dig in during a storm. All they know how to do is put up tents, and they get blown away and quite often die. Whereas the Alaskan tradition is to go slower and take more time and dig under and not use tents so much. So when the big storms come, you're perfectly safe and cozy compared to a tent. When you get winds over thirty, forty miles an hour, there's just no way you can guy a tent down tightly enough to not make a lot of noise. So these snow shelters provide a lot of quiet and comfort unless they are hastily made in a survival situation. Once you get under, if you have the energy, you can make them almost palatial. Build in little niches and nooks and platforms. These days we put in windows by taking a frying pan and melting snow in it and letting it become ice. Then we take that see-through disk of ice and put it in the wall of the igloos and snow caves to make a skylight. It's pretty neat!

People think of Denali as the ultimate wilderness, and a lot of them act disappointed when they get there and find crowds of thirty, forty people camped at one place. But if they really wanted to get out and see the ultimate wilderness, all they would have to do is switch to a different route, where they won't see another soul.

They call me "the mayor of fourteen thousand feet." That's where the camp is, and it's a big staging area for all the climbers. It does turn into a little city up there sometimes. It's actually a lot of fun, but it is not a wilderness experience. It gets very crowded on that one route.

Climbers tend to stay there for two or three days to acclimatize before going higher. Japanese, Poles, Russians, French, Germans, Austrians, Swiss, Canadians, Americans all together there. I like it!

We screen every single climber that comes through the camp for their blood oxygen level with a machine that measures how pink the fingernail is. We don't have to draw any blood. And so the climbers come in and we make sure that they are acclimatizing okay to the altitude. So we meet everybody. Then we pick the ones that appear to be having problems and invite them to do some further studies. If someone's fingernails look a little dusky colored or grayish.

We researchers are so consumed by our work that we don't get to socialize much. But we do see the climbers coming through, and then if we have a night off, we invite climbers over to our camp. We have the only heated facility, and so especially in storms, we're very popular!

Our real purpose is research. The only reason we do rescue is 'cause we're there and we're acclimatized and we're mountaineers and we're physicians. We sort of owe it to the climbing community because they are nice enough to let us do research on them so we reciprocate. It's a quid pro quo. It works quite well.

But our primary purpose is to study the causes of altitude illness and devise methods of prevention and treatment. We have made a lot of useful discoveries, such as medications for treating high-altitude illness. We have made rather profound discoveries of drugs to treat brain edema, the swelling at altitude, as well as lung edema of altitude. We analyze the data and publish them in national medical journals for people around the world to benefit from the knowledge.

My mentor in this was a doctor by the name of Charlie Houston. He is about seventy-nine years old now and still going strong. He's very famous for having led the first American expedition to K2, the world's second highest mountain, in 1953. He was also on K2 in 1938. He also did the first ascent of Mount Foraker here in Alaska in 1937. And his dad was a mountaineer.

Anyhow, over the course of his life he has published extensively in the field of high-altitude medicine. When I was a trekking doctor in Nepal, I started seeing a lot of altitude illness and I noticed his name in the literature. I wrote to him saying that I had seen all these cases of altitude illness and asking him for advice on what to do with the data and whatnot, and he was very helpful and very open and he really helped to get my career launched. I just hope I have his kind of energy when I am his age.

Actually there are quite a few younger doctors in this field now, and it is fun for me to help direct and advise them on their careers and research projects. I look forward to getting more into that role in the future because I want to begin to see something besides winter. And I don't need to be up on the mountain full time anymore because I feel that I have succeeded in what I initially set out to do. Even though over a thousand people a year try to climb the mountain—a lot more than when we first started our research in 1982—our work has dramatically lessened the death rate, and that is very satisfying.

But being in the mountains has an even deeper satisfaction. For me every journey up a mountain or into a valley is as much an internal journey as an external one. Everyone has different motives, but for me what happens to me internally has always been a big part of it. For one thing, just getting out of the environment I usually operate in can be quite releasing and give me a new perspective and freshness. Another thing, the day-to-day challenges and the concentration you are able to put into what you're doing at the time without distractions promote a lot of personal growth.

Then you have the interaction with friends on the mountain. The camaraderie, the scenic beauty, and being outdoors all the time generally add up to a very worthwhile experience even if you don't reach your goal. Ideally a climber enjoys the trip whether he gets to the summit or not.

# Mary Lenzi Hansen

*Wide Open Spaces*
*Big Delta*
*b. 1905*

*Mary Hansen's Alaska is the North of opportunity, of wide open spaces and of "welcome, cheechakers." Trapping, mining, and mushing, Mary lived the life-style celebrated today in the Iditarod Race. She describes racing in the 1930s as "just for fun" because everyone knew that Leonhard Seppla was sure to win. In fact, Mary herself set a record in 1937 by being the first female mushing professional to compete in what is now called the North American Championship race.*

*Her dogs were large for trap line and placer mine freighting. From 1929 to 1933 Mary Hansen and her husband placer mined and trapped on Crooked Creek in the Kantishna District, now in Denali National Park and Preserve. A Seattle cheechako, Mary had taken immediately to bush life and especially to the dog mushing that was everyone's primary form of transportation.*

*Mary recently retired at eighty-five from her job as a school baker.*

NEW PEOPLE like me kept trickling in, and each spring cheechakers would be driving their dogs out to their placer claims or trap lines. My husband and I took seven mining claims on Crooked Creek in the Kantishna, and we mined right in the creek with sluice boxes. Between '29 and '33 we took out about four thousand dollars a year from a couple of months of summer mining.

We put in a dam in order to pick up a sluice head of water, and with it we washed off the overburden. When we got down to bedrock, we shoveled what little was left into the sluice boxes and washed it through with water. If we had gold, it was caught in the riffles of the sluice box. We brought all that equipment in on dogsleds. I used to outfit in Nenana in those days, and eighteen miles out there was a road-house called Knight's near where the McGrath road [trail] branched off toward the Iditarod. On long-distance trails there were stopping places, roadhouses. They weren't dine and dance, you know! A road-house was strictly a place that took care of dogs and horses and men, who-ever came by.

From Knight's Roadhouse we turned off on the Toklat River, freighting our staples from the Coghill store and the Northern Commercial store in Nenana. Staples like rice and flour and lard and dog feed, and then I freighted it out to where we were gold mining a hun-dred miles out at Kantishna.

We used as many as nine dogs for freighting our outfit to the mine. Then when we were trapping, why, we split the team, four or five apiece.

What I liked most about the old Alaska was the wide open spaces. You didn't have neighbors. My goodness, you could go for hundreds of miles and not encounter anybody. You might pass another dog team and you might not.

On the trail from Nenana to where I mined, I might pass the mail team or somebody like me freighting in his mining outfit. And the Natives 'cause there was a Native village at Knight's Roadhouse out of Nenana. I passed other people who were mining in there but that's about all.

Now they bring in thousands of tourists where then there was only one person now and then. Our old way of life is pretty hard to find ex-cept here and there. It's pretty well watered down. There are too many people!

And if I met another musher, he was going the other way as a rule. Or he might come behind and pass me if I wasn't fast enough for him. We might stop a few minutes and talk, but we had to be careful that our dogs did not fight. Usually about all you'd do on the trail was say hi and holler some little news as you passed. The places to visit with each other were the relief cabins, which the government provided with a stove and a frying pan and an axe so that you could get wood. You never left the place without leaving kindling and wood for at least one fire. Because somebody might freeze to death trying to get there. Or they might be half-frozen when they got there and just barely be able to light the fire. So you were pretty careful about that.

There wasn't food in those relief cabins; everyone brought his own, but I've stopped in those cabins sometimes in the spring when every-body was freighting their outfit out from town and there would be ten, fifteen teams, maybe not all going my way. That made a good trail.

You knew where everybody was in your district and they might visit at your cabin or you at theirs. Or if I went to cabins and the person was gone, I tied my dogs out and started the fire. Maybe they came home way late at night. Sometimes I visited there a couple of days. Generally you carried your dog feed with you. But I started supper and when they came back home, it was ready. We were all just one family. People were very much more friendly than today, perhaps because we were so few.

I worked out at mining camps, and anybody who came by, you fed 'em. I had twenty men to feed. If people came through looking for a job, I fed 'em. Oh, there were a few feuds over gold mining, but we got along a lot better in those days than we do today, when everybody is afraid that you are going to get something they've got.

In my time the Natives would welcome you, but today a lot of 'em won't. They don't even want you near what they call theirs. Think of the things the laws have taken away from the Natives. Naturally they aren't very happy and it's going to rub off on you.

In town a lot of people felt the Natives were dirty and ate different and smelled different, but if you met Natives out on the trail, there was no discrimination. Whenever I was coming out of Kantishna, I usually met Natives on the trail near Knight's Roadhouse. Sometimes I needed dog feed and I traded tea and a few things with them for wild meat like salmon, caribou, moose, rabbit, squirrel. You were allowed to then—except sheep meat. When the caribou went through in the migration, miners and trappers would kill a bunch, let it freeze, and cut it up later for the dogs. We all did that. It would be against the law today.

The dogs ate frozen salmon and frozen meat. Their teeth are that strong! I used to bring it in and thaw it some, but sometimes I just threw it to them and they'd eat on it frozen hard at forty, fifty below zero.

How fast I could travel depended on my load, dogs, and how cold it was. When I freighted my outfit in for the year about the last of March or early April, I figured on making about ten, fifteen miles a day. I traveled at night when everything froze because I had to be careful not to be on the ice when it was about to go out. I wanted to be off the ice about the fifteenth of April.

I've fallen in a few times, but I was lucky enough to get out and either get back to a cabin or change my clothes right there and go on.

In the spring traveling is very dangerous because the ice gets very mushy. So I traveled at night and rested my dogs most of the day and waited. I tried to go in loaded at night, rest, and come back and get the other loads during the daytime. By the first of March there is quite a bit of daylight, so as soon as it froze about seven or eight o'clock at night I would start in whether or not it was dark because my dogs would take me because they know the trail. And in the dark, my leader, Midget, could smell the trail and not get off it.

I never wore a headlamp, but a lot of times our moonlight was so bright that I could read the newspaper by it. And the northern lights were so beautiful! They were all colors and flashed all over the sky like sunbursts and ribbons.

When I first came in 1928, I took a cat with me trapping. Generally I had a canvas around the load on the sled and the last thing I did before starting out was to put that kitty in a box and tie that canvas down. And when I got anywhere, the first thing I'd unlash would be the kitty. A lot of cats are pretty smart and, of course, one of the first things you do when you get in like that—it's kind of cold so you go into the relief cabin and light the fire and put some water on for cooking or for tea or cooking dog feed. And that kitty of mine would walk down the towline. The dogs would be all laying down. They're tied and the leader can hold 'em out. And they're tired anyway. And she walked down the towline. She was a good friend of the leader and she'd give her a slap on the nose and walk over to where I was in the cabin. The kitty would do that all the time, and that was her downfall!

In those days we didn't have boarding kennels, and when I got into Nenana and kitty came in heat, she could go around my dogs. They'd all nose her and kind of look at her, "What's the matter with you?" But she went up to a strange dog and, of course, got killed.

Running dogs came natural to me. Nobody told me how. A lot of it I had to learn by myself, like hooking 'em up and saying gee and haw and whoa. Teaching 'em to stop. Mine would stop but, of course, if there was a moose or if they smelled game on the road, why, look out! I could be in trouble. Though they were pretty good and ran on the trail, as a rule. If they took off, I could be in trouble. And sometimes they did.

Midget was what I counted on. She would stay in the trail. Of course, she was awful small and eight dogs could pull her, but she was so smart that I could write a book about her that nobody would believe. She knew ice, water, trails. If I minded her, I didn't get into trouble, but if I didn't, look out!

I was lucky but I did see a lot of people in trouble with dog fights or their team being stampeded by a moose. If something like that happens, you have to figure out something fast. Stop your team. Of course, I always had a long rope in the back of my sled and I might be lucky enough to get that tied around a tree. Oh, yeah, I can have a lot of fun!

I never did believe in races. I always thought they were cruel because they are too hard on the animals. Racers had lost a lot of dogs and I didn't like it. But my husband, Bert, decided to enter the 1937 Fairbanks Winter Carnival race, three days of sprint racing, twenty miles each for two days and the last day thirty. It was my team, of course, because when Bert had met me I had had the team. He made me promise that if he couldn't go in—he was working as a cook—that I would take the team in. We didn't even think about the fact that there were no women in the races.

So it turned out that he couldn't get off work, so I went up to Judge Clegg, who was registering the entrants in his law office. It was a Sunday and he was surprised as all heck. Law offices aren't open on Sunday and he had his feet up on the desk and he was smoking. I'll never forget that! He was surprised to see me walk in. His feet came off of that desk! The pipe came out of his mouth. He was a gentleman. He said, "Hi, Mary." Of course, everybody knew everybody. "What are you doing here?"

"Is this where they register for the races?" I said. He said yes. "Well, I'd like to enter the races," I said. He said, "But women don't enter the races." I said, "Well, why not?" So then he called the head of the carnival, which was Bobby Sheldon that year. He called him and I could hear some of the conversation. The judge said, "I've got Mary Hansen here and she wants to register in the race. What'll I do?" And I could hear a little humming and hawing on the other end and finally I heard, "Well, let her!"

And that's the way that went. I crashed it!

Then when the men came to register, nobody talked to me. They all knew me from the restaurant where I cooked, but they didn't know what was happening. The judge was quiet about it. Pretty soon one of the old, old mushers, Leonhard Seppla, he knew what had happened. And he was at the top of the list, of course. So he came over and shook hands with me and he said, "I'm glad you came in, Mary." And I thanked him. That broke the ice and from then on everybody was family.

# Olaf Hansen and Jim Rhodes

*Boatwrights Having Fun*
*Wrangell*
*b. 1930, 1919*

*Alaska has represented opportunity and independence to generations of cheechakos. Olaf Hansen's father arrived in Wrangell in 1925 from Norway via Seattle. Though penniless in the old country, he soon built up a profitable boat construction and repair business serving Southeast fishermen and canneries. Jim Rhodes grew up in equally humble circumstances in Oregon and arrived in Alaska after World War II looking for a chance to build a new life.*

*Olaf Hansen began working in his father's shop at age sixteen, mostly using "Norwegian steam"—muscle power—to get the jobs done. Today he and his friend and employee, Jim, still love the delights of wood. A visit with them in their boat shop is rich in boat talk and pride in being Alaskan.*

**O**LAF HANSEN: My father's name was Olaf Hansen also. This boat shop had been started in 1916, and in 1928 Dad bought it with his brother Alf. It was a small boat shop with a shed on the side where we built all our boats until it burned down in 1982. That old shop, I swear it was colder inside than it was outside. I remember that when I was in high school I used to work in there steaming and bending frames for the new boats Dad was building. It was so cold. . . . I remember a December when we put all the frames in a forty-foot boat in one day. Four of us. I remember working our ass off! Excuse my French. Anyway, we got all done, it was about four thirty in the afternoon. Dad run uptown and come back with a case of beer. We're all sitting around there drinking, all sweaty. My mother come down. "Hey, you know what the temperature is?" "What is it?" "Eighteen degrees!" There we were sitting around drinking beer. It was so darned cold!

Usually we quit working at twenty above because if you have to wear gloves, your efficiency goes down. But here this new insulated building, we put heat in it in the wintertime. Sometimes we have a space heater going to break the chill and keep the temperature up to about forty degrees.

The first ten years after I bought this shop from Dad, I had all these old guys working for me. If a stranger came in and I was busy, he would invariably go to Jim or Arthur, "Are you the owner?" "No, the kid over there." They were all looking for the owner, not for a kid. Now it's too late and I'm the old guy.

**Jim Rhodes:** Oh, we had lots of fun. Boy, we sure got our noses wet on some of those launchings, too. I'll never forget when we launched a new boat and Gilbert slugged me and I passed out colder than a wedge. I didn't have many but . . .

**Olaf Hansen:** You went out like you did because Gil was spiking your drinks. I seen it. That was the day, too, that a sailboat named the *Williwaw* came because it had been rammed. The owner wanted us to look at it right away. I said, "Fella, come back tomorrow. Today we have a launching and we're all getting drunk!"

**Jim Rhodes:** This is a place that you're supposed to have fun. That's my outlook on life. And that's why I've enjoyed Alaska because I've had a lot of fun. And where else could a working man, working with his two hands, make enough money to travel the world the way I have? I would have been too poor anywhere else. I'd either have been out on strike half the time or I wouldn't have had any work half the time.

**Olaf Hansen:** And here if you want to moonlight on another boat on the weekend, that ain't no big deal to me. You'll be back Monday morning. I don't care. Up here you can do whatever you want because Alaskans are more laid back. Now it's getting a little worse, but until recently we did everything with a handshake. We didn't have to put a big contract out and you pay by the tenth of the month or pay eighteen percent interest.

The biggest change in Wrangell was after we got the ferry system in 1963, more people coming in here.

**Jim Rhodes:** All those birds have got to do is just buy a ferry ticket and the first place they hit is the food stamp office.

**Olaf Hansen:** I was on the city council from '67 to '70 and we'd give undesirables a blue ticket, a ferry ticket to Petersburg.

**Jim Rhodes:** That just aggravates Petersburg!

**Olaf Hansen:** Well, we had to aggravate somebody. And it only cost us three or four dollars to Petersburg.

**Jim Rhodes:** The first boat I ever helped build is right here in this harbor today. The *Marcele,* a seiner we built for a fella by the name of Nore. Later he sold it to a cannery. That boat has had three keels; it was built that solid. And it's yet today considered a damn fine boat even though it's had three keels in it and been rolled completely over twice because they had her lightly loaded and they pulled the seine and the seine skiff up on her and ran full bore into a following sea.

**Olaf Hansen:** She came up upside down.

**Jim Rhodes:** She has a fairly sharp, round bottom with a high bilge. Old Grandad Monk designed her in Seattle.

**Olaf Hansen:** We started building her in '47, when I was sixteen years old, and we launched her in the spring of 1948.

**Jim Rhodes:** Your job was creosoting the frames. Oh, boy, did you hate that!

**Olaf Hansen:** Around here, being a small shop, you've got to be able to do everything. You've got to creosote and know how to put timbers together, how to make planking, do cabinetwork, caulk, paint. Most yards have different people for each job.

**Jim Rhodes:** You've got to know how to fit in a new stem or a stern. Horn timbers and sternposts and other things.

**Olaf Hansen:** My uncle Alf liked to build new boats, but he didn't care for repair 'cause on a repair job someone else has built the boat and you've got to know how much you can tear out. Where to stop and start again and still make it look good. A lot of people haven't got that knack.

**Jim Rhodes:** No two boats will give you the same repair problems to solve. That's the beauty of working on repair. Then you think you've got it all solved and you'll tear something out and, "Oh shit!"

**Olaf Hansen:** My Dad *liked* repair. Right after World War I things got tough over in Norway, so Dad came over here and found a job as a shipwright at a cannery repairing boats. My dad moved up here in 1925 and got a job in a big boatyard in Wrangell in the winter. And him and one of the owners of the yard built a little troller, the *Norman*—I seen the hull of her up there in Tenakee once—and he trolled in the summertime and worked wintertimes in that Wrangell yard.

In the summer of 1928 he was out trolling west of here and the trollers went on strike because they were only getting two cents a pound for salmon and they wanted three cents. They were on strike for about six weeks. But one of the guys that kept on fishing, scabbing, was the guy that owned this boat shop. Linton kept on trolling. He didn't strike with the rest of 'em. He was a scabber. Anyway, in September when the guys came back into town after the strike, this guy didn't have any boats coming to have any work done so he put the place up for sale. My dad heard about it and he called his brother Alf in Seattle and they bought the place.

**Jim Rhodes:** In those days Wrangell was a Native town. The ANB [Alaska Native Brotherhood] used to have a big dance about New Year's here at their old hall that burned down. And that's where I broke my leg in a big Indian battle. Three days later I was back under a boat, caulking, letting the one leg hang down.

**Olaf Hansen:** That's all you can do. I can remember in the thirties and forties my Dad had four or five guys working in the winter. Later I had eight or nine guys, and that was too much 'cause some guys were sleeping on the job. When I put in that second ways is when I started to have a problem finding boatwrights. They aren't making 'em anymore. They're not learning and the ones who know are dead.

**Jim Rhodes:** There are very few old shipwrights for the very simple reason that you wear yourself out. Another thing is that you seldom see any very heavy ones. They're all pretty trim from jumping around and working like hell.

In 1947 I'd just got out of the service and I was so shaky from malaria, why, I didn't know whether I'd be able to hold a job or not. So I and the wife and the youngster come up here. And I had fifty dollars in my pocket when we crawled off the boat. I figured I'd hunt and fish, if nothing else, for groceries.

I came up from below, from Oregon, where I was born. I had fished all along the Oregon-California coast. Just before the war I was fishing for crab out of Eureka, California. . . . Up here I first went to work in the cold storage for about a year. Then I went to work for your dad the year he decided to take his wife to Norway. He paid me two and a half dollars an hour at first and two ninety when I left in 1954 to work at the lumber mill. Then I worked as a shipwright back in Maine because I figured they had real boatyards back there. But I found that when they had work, I worked, and when they didn't, I didn't, and the pay was poor, too. So I thought, "Well, hell's fire, this is no place for me! Kid, you better get your rear back to Alaska!"

This country has treated me well! Where else but Alaska could I arrive with only fifty bucks in my pocket and be worth what I am today? And do all the traveling I have done? I have traveled all over the world and I have never found any place I liked better than Alaska!

# Willie Hensley

*From the Narrow Path to the Wide Road*
*Kotzebue*
*b. 1941*

*"If you have lots of freedom," asks Willie Hensley, "what do you use as a guide-post for your life?" Willie grew up subsisting by hunting and fishing near Kotze-bue, where his Iñupiaq Eskimo culture stressed communal values. But when Willie went Outside, first to boarding school in Tennessee and then to George Washington University, he swam farther and farther into the mainstream of American life. As a student he floundered, trying to accommodate his bush iden-tity to unfamiliar ways.*

*Yet in 1966 at age twenty-four he was elected to the Alaska House of Rep-resentatives and in 1970 to the state senate. In 1990 he was the unsuccessful Democratic candidate for lieutenant governor against the Hickel-Coghill ticket. In between he was a founder and president of Nana Regional Corporation's Red Dog Mine, learned the reindeer business, and kept his hand in at seal hunting.*

*Willie Hensley from his twenties onward has been a distinguished Native leader. He is described by former U.S. planner David Hickok as having been the only Native spokesman who urged that subsistence fishing and hunting rights be retained in any agreement with U.S. government. Failure to follow that advice is still bedeviling Alaska Natives today.*

**W**E WERE hunters and fishermen and trappers and always had been. I was born in Kotzebue, but survival was more difficult there be-cause it was farther from the wildlife and driftwood. So we lived along the Little Noatak about fifteen miles from Kotzebue at a place called Itkatuq. We lived there because we had easy access to a variety of fish: sheefish, whitefish, grayling, pike, salmon. And to rabbits, ptarmigan, muskrats in the spring, caribou, and of course, we also got seal oil from seals along the coast. To this day I have seal oil in my house all the time. In fact, seal oil is an absolute necessity. I cannot eat an Eskimo meal without having seal oil. That would be like missing half the meal.

We did buy goods that we needed from Kotzebue, a good day's trip from Itkatuq by dog team on the ice. Or, in summer, by skin boat, kayak, or homemade wooden boat across the open water. Fifteen miles was a long way to row. By the late forties some outboards were moving in and a few people had larger boats with inboard engines. We hitched rides on those when we were heading up to the Little Noatak in the spring or summer. People moved around a lot after the game and fish and we didn't camp in one spot all the time. Snow machines made it possible to live in the village instead of out in the country. And that eliminated all the work of keeping dogs, too.

We spent most of our energy just trying to find food. It was hard work. We caught a lot of small game as a matter of course back then. And we still hunt beluga whales. (We don't have the large bowheads where we are.) We are also dependent on moose and caribou. A few springs ago my nephew and I and a couple of others went *oogruk* hunting, which is something we do in the spring when the ice is breaking up and the bearded seals are sunning themselves and it's time to replenish your supply of oil and meat, what we call *mipkuq*. And we got two walruses, out there on the ice about twenty-five miles from shore.

I was raised more traditional than most people in my generation in the sense that as I was growing up we lived in sod houses away from other people, at least three different ones that I can recall along the coast and upriver on the Little Noatak. The last one we lived in is still standing; the roof is caved in. So I feel that I was raised in the twilight of the Stone Age. We did not have any plywood or lumber to put on the floor. We used willows. We only had one window, at the top made of beluga gut skin. We had a metal stove that we built out of a fifty-gallon drum. We had Blazo cans to sit on. We had no beds.

The pressures of civilization generally are to look down on your own culture because your life isn't as adequate as the Western world's. But I have always respected my own heritage. It was a hard life and we had nothing, but that's the history of people from that area for the last eight or ten thousand years. We never had anything material to speak of because we just couldn't lug it around. It didn't make sense to have a lot of stuff. And if we had stuff, the culture said we should share what we had.

A black lady from Virginia named Virginia Powell helped me to get motivated in school in Kotzebue. And also, there is one teacher who is still alive; she was my first-grade teacher, Miss Logan. She is still living in Juneau. She is in her eighties.

Yes, and there was also a Baptist missionary in Kotzebue who helped me find the school in Tennessee. Richard Miller lives here in Anchorage just down the street from me. He's a retired schoolteacher now. He met me when I was about eleven or so, took an interest in me, saw some potential, and encouraged me along.

What do I think of the missionaries? Richard Miller, as a person, is a good guy. But with any introduction of new people or technologies, there's always good and bad. At least the missionaries generally had a positive side of life in mind, even though some of their ideas were destructive to our cultural survival. At least they were better than the boozemongers who were trying to peddle booze off the whaling ships. Or the gold prospectors who were simply after the gold and didn't care what happened to the people.

I was most affected by my mother, who actually wasn't my real mother but my mother's uncle's wife. And it was not unusual in our days to be adopted out to a grandparent or somebody else in the family. It often was the case that people couldn't possibly support another person. And so my sister and I were raised by my mother's uncle. So Priscilla was the greatest influence on my life. She was maybe in her early forties at the time that she took control of my life and tried to raise me right. So if there was anybody who imparted values to me, it was she. Values of several thousands of years that had enabled people to survive in that environment. Self-discipline. You had to be a hard worker. You had to be dependable. You had to be positive. In their own way the elders railed against negativism because when things got tough, you couldn't give up. And life was always hard.

There were things like humility because you weren't strong by yourself. You had to work with people and submerge your ego somewhat even though that goes against the Western way.

When I was growing up, traditional spirituality was not as strong as it had been, but there was a great belief in God. The Quaker church was the strongest church in my region. But the reality was that man was not a lot different than the animals in the sense that animals also had spirits. There was a great consciousness about the spiritual world, but there was also great concern because the *angatkut,* our priests or spirit people, were very powerful. Some of them as humans had evil aspects and used their power improperly. And so people were quite negative to the *angatkut,* the spirit leaders of the old world.

Those were some of the values back in those days. The idea of re-specting elders and helping people who were helpless was built into our consciousness. You had obligations to others to help them survive and a commitment to your own role as a hunter.

So, yes, I like many others have been through a lot of change. I am no exception in the sense that the generation before me, they had to go through their changes, too. But when I look back at their lives, a lot of them, I don't think they could see that it was possible to change the way that things were being introduced and the way institutions were being created.

In my generation, I felt that we needed to minimize the damage that was being done by the schools, the political institutions, the eco-nomic system. First of all I figured that we needed to have control of our space, our land. Otherwise we were being subjugated to changes that we had no control over.

I made the motion in the AFN to push for sixty million acres of land. Complete-control ownership. Of course, we also wanted to con-tinue to hunt and fish. People don't remember that the obstacles to securing land were almost impossible because the traditional American method of resolving these land disputes was to spend many, many years in court, as the Indians did, and then end up with only a few cents an acre. Indians never ended up with land. That was the history that we were fighting in the late sixties. Those who had the largest amount to say, that is, the senators and congressmen who chaired the committees, as well as the Interior Department, who was supposed to be our guardian, hell, they didn't want to give us anything. Maybe a million acres at the most, just a few acres around each village. They even wanted to—now you're really getting me agitated. Secretary Udall's first staffer, who eventually became head of Consolidated Edison, his idea was to allow us to go to court, but he was going to have the date of taking as of 1867, which meant that he wanted to give us seven and a half million dollars. So the early response to our search for land was that either we did not have any rights to ask for anything of any consequence or the idea was to try to pay us a few cents an acre. So it was an uphill battle all the way.

When we started the process, we weren't thinking about big finan-cial institutions or huge amounts of money. In my part of the world, what we wanted was to be left alone to make our own way into the twentieth century without all these pressures. And we had to have access to the fish and the game for our way of life.

Cultures are constantly changing as they adopt new ideas, new technologies from the neighbors. And it's been no exception up here.

Things had been changing long before I showed up in the forties. Those changes in our part of the world began a long, long time ago when we accepted a lot of goods from the Russians. Some of the steel, pots and pans, and tobacco we traded for with the Chukchis and the Eskimos in what is now called the Soviet Far East. When I was a boy, a lot of the names I thought were Eskimo were actually Russian. Like we call soap *miilaq*. In Russian it's *muuila*. Coffee is called *koffee* in Russian, *kufeak* in the Yup'ik-speaking areas, and *kupeak* by the time it comes to Kotzebue. Sugar is called *sakhar* in Russian and *sakhala* by the Yup'ik. So lots of things got to us through the Siberian trade before the British or American goods came.

But changes came rapidly because of the new communications in the late 1960s and early 1970s. Many of our cultural ways are still very much alive, but unfortunately with the missionaries and the government and the school systems and the different religions and technology and political institutions, there has been a lot of turmoil within the lives of the Native people in Alaska.

One of the reasons that we're having problems is that we're becoming more like you people. In the sense that we don't have as much self-discipline as we used to. There's a great tension between individual rights and group behavior. In my youth there was always a standard for our behavior and everyone was involved in the effort to raise children properly. But in American society there is a great concentration on individual rights. In our traditional world the path was narrow concerning what was right and what was wrong and how you were as a human being. But in American society the road is wide. And people even go beyond that and still don't get in trouble.

In the past we never had any umbilical cords to some federal or state agency for our survival. We had to survive by our own skill and strength and group effort. I think we need to steer away from dependence because if somebody knocks that prop out from under us, we will be in real trouble. The way I look at it, we have to begin to practice the values of right and wrong that we have lived by for hundreds, thousands of years. That is where we can find the necessary self-discipline to reject alcohol and drugs and antisocial behavior. There is a lot in our traditional society that can help us find a sense of personal responsibility.

I made my gigantic leap when I left Kotzebue and went to Tennessee to boarding school. I went really out into the stratosphere with that move. I went to the foothills of the Smokies for four years, straight out of Kotzebue. I was just barely fourteen and had to adjust to that environment. I left everybody.

I survived.

# Wally Hickel

*Building on the Fault Zone*
*Anchorage*
*b. 1919*

*Wally Hickel began life in Kansas, dirt poor and eager to escape a tenant farmer fate. In his youth he sold insurance, paid his way West by prizefighting, and traveled Depression America until in 1940 he fetched up in Alaska, the country that has shaped him (and vice versa) ever since. After World War II he quickly made a name for himself in residential and hotel construction. That name soon became synonymous with Alaska development and with Alaska Republicanism. Governor from December 1966 to January 1969, his ambitious winter haul road to the new North Slope oil fields was soon panned by environmentalists. Wally says, "To hell with the critics; how would they have built it any differently with only five hundred thousand dollars?"*

*As Richard Nixon's first secretary of the interior, from January 1969 to November 1970, Wally Hickel won environmentalists' grudging respect for his leadership on such issues as whale protection and international conservation. Fired by Nixon for sympathizing with rebellious antiwar youths, Wally Hickel returned to Alaska to two decades of entrepreneurial adventures. In 1979 he formed a citizens' group called Commonwealth North to study Alaska's public policy issues. By the late 1980s Hickel was gambling on creating a market in Japan and Korea for North Slope natural gas. Beginning with no market, no pipeline, and no permits, he was far into this new dream when fate at the polls sent him in another direction.*

*An ebullient go-getter, Wally Hickel had never been one to shy away from the limelight. In 1974, 1978, and 1986 he launched abortive campaigns to regain the governor's mansion. By mid-September 1990, written off as a Republican has-been at age seventy-one, he had not even entered the gubernatorial pri-*

*mary. Yet in a move that stunned Alaska and the nation, he bounded onto the ticket of the Independence Party and won the November election.*

I WAS BORN an entrepreneur. No one taught me.

The entrepreneurs that I've known were people that were taking care of unmet needs. In my case, after World War II everyone was leaving Alaska because there was no place to live. So I started building houses. I had never built a house in my life, but I got into housing because I saw a need.

When I saw that there wasn't a good hotel in town, I built the Traveler's Inn in 1953. The Traveler's Inn was probably the most modern motel in America before motels were popular. But I got into that because I saw a need for a first-class deal. Most of the motels in those days were just little one-story things with no restaurants, no nothing. In fact, the Traveler's Inn in Fairbanks is still the major hotel up there, and I built that in '55.

I helped bring the first natural gas into Anchorage in 1959. There wasn't anything here, and I saw an opportunity. Today that company is Enstar, and it supplies Anchorage with all its natural gas. That's one reason why in 1982 I started YukonPacific, the world's biggest project, to bring Alaska's vast reserves of natural gas to market. Natural gas is the world's cleanest fuel. And in a world dependent on fossil fuels, it makes sense to use this fuel in the interests of the environment.

Anyhow, entrepreneurs see things that have to be done. They're not professionals. I never knew what a gas line was, but I could put it together. That's the way I feel about Alaska, too. The challenge has been to create our own country. Thirty or forty years ago we didn't have a vehicle to become a country. We were a territory and the next step was statehood. And so we took that step. Today independence could work, but it would be quite difficult because if Oklahoma wants something, Kansas doesn't fight it maliciously. They are together. But when Alaska wants something, every son of a bitch out there thinks he owns Alaska and you can't get anything done!

Mankind enhances, not destroys, this world. The truth is that we haven't scratched the surface of the earth yet. I've written a major article in *Reader's Digest* on the fact that we've only just slid around the skin of the apple of this earth. We'll never run out of resources. The only thing we'll ever run out of is imagination.

When I arrived in Alaska in 1940, I started washing dishes. Very simple. It was a way to eat. And then I got a job at a dollar an hour burying the pole line when they were going to build the Fort Richardson military base. I just did whatever I had to do. There was always something to do.

I had to borrow to come to Alaska, so when I got here, I didn't have the option of going back home. I didn't have any money. So I didn't look in that direction. And when I took a job washing dishes, I didn't say, "Well, I have a degree, I'm going to look for something in a lawyer's office." I took the dish-washing job, found another job, and looked some more. The young today in many cases can have too many options. If you have too many options, you pass up a lot of opportunities waiting for something that you think might be right. I didn't know what was right. I just kept searching it out. I didn't have a goal to build a lot of houses when I got here. Or build a pipeline. I just moved forward, never looking back.

If you're too educated, you set your goals too low. If, after studying law, you become an attorney in a few years, you've reached your goal. I never had a specific goal. I never dreamt of going to Washington as secretary of the interior, but I went. And I never dreamt of building a pipeline, but I built it.

My goals have no limits. That's the truth!

For instance, I had just arrived in Tokyo the day our 1964 Good Friday earthquake happened [in Anchorage]. I said, "I'm going back and rebuild the town." When I saw the devastation, I said, "I'm going to build a hotel." The geologists were saying we should move the town toward the mountains to avoid the risk. I said, "Abandon Anchorage? No way!" Anchorage was *my* city and I was going to help it.

I always thought of Alaska as my country. Just like "She's *my* wife and those are my kids!" Very personal. I fight that way. Just to show you how I think, when I was asked to go on the National Space Board, it became *my* position, *my* space. I put everything into it! If you are just there filling a seat, that's all you are ever going to do. But it's got to be possessive. When I read the Bible, it is *my* God. And I am possessive about Alaska.

After World War II no one needed us Alaskans. And in order for a country or an individual to grow, someone has to need you. So we turned our attention to where people needed us. Though I had no personal economic interest in it, I started working with the Japanese in 1953, just to make Alaska prosper. The United States was our competition; they didn't need us. How could we get our wood products into Oklahoma and Kansas if we couldn't get them past Seattle and Portland, our competitors? But we could put them in Japan!

Conservation means appreciating something. It doesn't mean that you don't touch it and don't use it. The most precious thing on this earth is not a tree or a caribou. It's a human. Because the human is the only reasoning animal on earth. That's the way God made it. The fox can't take care of the caribou and the caribou can't take care of the alligator. But that being called man can take care of the total. He might make mistakes, but he has enhanced this world since the day he was on it.

The world was very hostile in prehistoric times, and it's been hostile ever since. They call this the delicate tundra up here. It's very, very tough and unforgiving. You can walk around on a beach in Hawaii and live nicely, but I can put you out fifty miles from Anchorage here where you can still see the city, and without some man-made device you won't survive. Mosquitoes would get you.

If Alaska were a separate country, our leaders would understand our unique situation. All the other states are in the temperate zone and share the same engineering. It won't fit here. The original North Slope pipeline engineers were the best in the world, but they didn't know a damn thing about burying a pipeline here in permafrost.

In 1967 I got a message inside of me about Prudhoe Bay. So in May of that year I told Harry Jamison, a young geologist, I said, "Drill, and I want that well in by Christmas!" He said, "Governor, what makes you so positive there's oil?" I said, "If it's not there, I'll think it there! Harry, there's forty billion barrels of oil there. Forty billion!"

That's what you call vision. You see things. Ten years later Harry Jamison came back and he said, "I'm here to confirm what Governor Hickel said ten years ago. There are forty billion barrels on the North Slope. We'll get twenty billion out."

I made that prediction public. I didn't just quietly think it. I told the world. You either believe or you don't believe! And that Little Guy inside doesn't lie to you.

Sure I have accomplished a lot, starting from nothing, but that Little Guy doesn't think it's so great. He keeps on giving me more things to do. The minute I stop and think it's that great, I'm through. I can't rest on my laurels.

Let me tell you something. There'll be frontiers two thousand years from now. There will be frontiers as long as there are children born and people dying. And the world ends when they die, and it starts when they are born. It doesn't matter when they're born, the frontiers will be there.

Frontiers are in the mind. They're no place else.

# David and Mark Hickok

*Divvying Up Alaska*
*Anchorage*
*b. 1924, 1922*

Congress passed legislation in the 1970s that was almost as significant for Alaska as the 1959 statehood act. The Alaska Native Claims Settlement Act (ANCSA) of 1971 and the Alaska National Interest Lands Conservation Act (ANILCA) of 1980 settled the issues of aboriginal rights and of federal retention and disposition of northern lands. Initially, with ANCSA, eighty-three million acres of federal real estate were withdrawn to be preserved as new parks, forests, wildlife refuges, and wild and scenic rivers. Later, Congress passed ANILCA, which dedicated one hundred three million acres for these purposes; President Jimmy Carter signed this act into law in the waning hours of his administration. A tumultuous era of map redrawing had ended.

Because Alaska's total population is only the size of Seattle's, anyone with a little gumption can soon be an effective agent for change. An Anchorage woman named Mark Ganopole channeled her environmentalist zeal into the seemingly obscure task of collecting data for a conservation resource map of Alaska. In the greatest coup in American conservation history, that map became the template for a vast kingdom of wildlife, wilderness, and "multiple use."

David Hickok was a key player in the 1970s, too, as the natural resources officer of the Federal Field Committee. It was the committee's 1968 report, *Alaska Natives and the Land*, which established the basis for federal compensation to Alaska Natives for their aboriginal domain. David and Mark were professional acquaintances at the time of the events in this chapter, but in 1971 they both attended a pipeline meeting, became bored, stepped out for coffee, and found that they had a lot of Alaskan history in common. Married since 1974, they still argue over the old battles, as veterans are wont to do.

**M**ARK: IT was called the Maps on the Living Room Floor and De-bating Society because there were never enough tables to put the maps on. Most of us were down on the floor as a result. At that time David and I were not married. My name then was Mark Ganopole, and I was one of the founders of the Alaska Sierra Club chapter, which we had started in 1968 because of the oil discovery at Prudhoe Bay. I had been a conservationist in California since I was eighteen. In fact, I had escaped to Alaska in '59 after watching what had happened to California. I was married to an oil man, Jerry Ganopole, also a founding member of the Alaska Sierra Club, and he asked to be transferred here because Alaska was a wonderful, clean new place that had not been despoiled as yet.

After we established the Sierra Club chapter in 1968, a member named Joseph Fitzgerald came to us and said that there needed to be a location and evaluation of the most significant Alaska federal lands for wildlife habitat, recreation, and outstanding scenic beauty. Joe was the chairman of the Federal Field Committee, a giant of a man intellectually, a Rhodes scholar. He had been chief economist for the Civil Aeronautics Board, been the president of Ozark Airlines, and had held a number of significant policymaking positions in government.

By that time there was a brand new umbrella organization for wilderness called the Alaska Wilderness Council, to which organizations such as the Sierra Club and the Alaska Conservation Society, the Wilderness Society, and the Isaac Walton League belonged. The Alaska Wilderness Council was statewide, with directors in different places. I was the South Central director and the one who coordinated all the statewide wilderness studies. But it was difficult for us here in South Central because we had little wilderness to work on except for the Chugach National Forest. Once we designed a wilderness for that, then where were we?

Anyway, we gathered five of us to start evaluating federal lands as Joe had suggested. I sent letters out through the Wilderness Council all over the state to ask people to evaluate their areas so that our little council could create an Alaska matrix map, including an early environmental impact statement analysis, which we would submit to the member organizations. We detailed each of our conservation proposals and their advantages and disadvantages of retaining the areas for future public interest. We showed on our maps areas of outstanding conservation value, and we analyzed how they might best be classified.

We had not quite finished by the time of the fall 1971 biennial

wilderness conference in D.C. By that time the leaders of the conservation organizations had persuaded Senator Alan Bible to prepare a pend-
ing amendment to the ANCSA legislation. This amendment was for
land use planning. I don't trust land use planning, especially when I
could see that there was a chance that we might actually get some of
these areas for parks and refuges. But we didn't label what they would
be. We merely evaluated what was in areas that we designated.

And so when Senator Bible's amendment failed to pass, the leaders
said, "Now this has failed. What shall we do next?" Well, I knew David
Hickok, my present husband, and I remembered his saying something
about how the secretary of the interior could withdraw lands and freeze
them. So I stood up and said, "Let the secretary withdraw lands for national parks and refuges" and they said, "But there are no resource stud
ies to show where those lands are." And I said, "Yes, there are. We have
almost completed our map, *with six overlays!*" And the leadership of the
biennial wilderness conference liked that so well that before that evening
was over it was agreed I should go back to Alaska to finish the study.

**David:** The irony of this was that in the Senate version of Native
land claims legislation there already was a section calling for a study for
the determination of new parks, refuges, and national forests in Alaska.
The conservation folks seemed not to have been aware of it.

By this time, the fall of 1971, the Senate had passed its version of
Native land claims legislation three times and the House had their bill
under consideration. Conservation leaders arranged a meeting with
House Interior chairman Mo Udall to discuss their acreage-withdrawal
concept and recommendations. At this time I was seconded to Scoop
Jackson's staff from the Federal Field Committee to assist with the Native land claims issue. My friend Harry Crandall of the Wilderness Society invited me to the meeting in Mo Udall's House office. So we go in
and Stu Brandborg of the Wilderness Society and a whole raft of fellas
were there. Anyway, I had known Mo Udall when I had had a fellow-
ship in the Congress. So this group walks in the door and Mo said,
"Dave, what are you doing here?" And I said, "I guess I'm some kind of
an expert witness."

So the dialogue started and Brandborg said, "We need to set an
acreage number here. Ed Wayburn of the Sierra Club said it should be
one hundred and fifty million acres." And they all got talking about how
many acres. Then Mo said, "Dave, how many do you think there should
be?" I said, "There's thirty-six and a half million acres of crown jewels
lands, like up in the Wrangells and Gates of the Arctic." So Brandborg
said, "Well, how about ninety million, Mo?" And then everybody went

back and forth like an auction until Mo said, "Eighty million! Settled."

So that's where the eighty million acres came from! That's the gospel truth about how that happened. It was just a back-and-forth from a hundred and fifty million to my smaller view of what were crown jewels, and then a settlement in the middle.

**Mark:** When I got home to Anchorage in October 1971, we got our local group together and we sent the word out statewide that now there would be a definite consideration of our plan. We had started with five people and now we had about two hundred volunteers working statewide. And so all kinds of information was pouring in. We expanded all our boundaries to be perfect, along rivers and along the tops of ridges. We figured, if this is a dream, go for it! But we could only come up with sixty million acres.

**David:** You couldn't find eighty million acres to save your lives!

**Mark:** We couldn't find eighty million. We worked and worked. We finally threw in wild and scenic rivers, frantically, to try to get up to that eighty million. Eventually we made it, but there were things in there that we thought were on shaky ground.

**David:** Stuff like the Kanuti Flats. Some of these wildlife refuges are pretty damn marginal.

**Mark:** We had marked them as significant for wildlife habitat but we didn't know how significant, even though we had professional State of Alaska Fish and Game and U.S. Fish and Wildlife biologists in our group. Fish and Wildlife itself would not cooperate with us because if land didn't have a waterfowl on it, the top men didn't want to hear about it. So all the lower-level biologists sneaked in my back door and piled up all this information. For Alaska state Fish and Game, helping was even more dangerous. Their employees didn't even dare show their faces around us. They simply slipped information under my front door.

There were trappers who were perfectly willing to help us. Guides that helped us. Geologists, hydrologists, miners, fishermen, draftsmen, construction workers, lawyers, doctors, anthropologists, Natives, cartographers, recreationists, and every kind of pilot that landed in remote places. Even at that, some fine things out in the Aleutians slipped through the cracks.

**David:** Most of those were selected by the Natives, so they wouldn't have gotten in anyhow.

**Mark:** An among-ourselves agreement was that we the Alaskan conservationists would not fight for any lands that the Natives chose. We felt it was their due. They were not being given anything. They were receiving compensation for what had been taken from them. And it broke our hearts to think that they might select the guts or the heart of any of these areas, but nevertheless we felt it mandatory as Alaskans not to dispute the Natives. And boy, we fought with national conservation organizations over and over about that. "No, they've chosen that area," we'd say, "you D.C. people can't fight for it. If it falls out of their selection because they overselect, then we'll fight for it."

**David:** The secretary withdrew for the Natives three times what their selection would be just in case there were prior existing rights that the Congress had allowed for mining claims, acreage that had gone to patent or tentative approval of lands for State of Alaska land selection.

In effect the Natives had a withdrawal for roughly one hundred twenty million acres versus their true selection of about forty-four million acres. Then there was another eighty-three for parks and refuges, et cetera. So the state felt quite squeezed by all this.

The point is that the maps and studies that Mark and the whole group of us had put together were carried to Washington by a fellow named Walt Parker and became the essence of Secretary Morton's withdrawals for both Native and conservation land determinations. They were the *only* maps available.

**Mark:** The secretary withdrew according to *our* boundaries! Isn't that marvelous when you think about a dream? Fish and Wildlife didn't want any part of it and the new refuges were jammed down their throat. They didn't want to worry about bear, sheep, caribou, moose, or deer in Alaska.

Now, the first withdrawal was merely a draft. Then the Interior Department had to go to work to propose their own final withdrawals, and they all started out with our map.

**David:** A fellow named Ted Bingham was the staffer in the Bureau of Land Management that put the final maps together. And, of course, there were a heck of a lot of conflicts between Native interests, the conservation interests, state interests, but the time frame was so limited and the information so scanty that he *had* to use the Wilderness Council's maps.

**Mark:** And we sent them volumes of reports describing each area's resources. Each report's author signed it unless it was too dangerous for that person to sign and then I did it.

I was a neophyte who learned very rapidly. I became an encyclopedia. If you asked me, I could just reel it off! Anybody who didn't know that thought I was an expert. Little did they know I just had the data retrieval button turned on and was spitting back out all the things I'd read and been told by all our volunteers.

Those were very exciting days. We did something quite marvelous. And it isn't just that one person did it. Many, many people worked on those maps and studies and somehow we moved a mountain. It was well worth the time I spent as my contribution. I think that everybody needs to leave something to make the world better.

# Gayla Hites

*North Winds of Romance*
*Skagway*
*b. 1954*

*"There was some excitement that I can't explain," says Gayla Hites of her first trip to Alaska in March 1983. Many generations of newcomers had felt the lure of islands, waterways, and wildlife, but forestry graduate Gayla (named after her father Gayle) was also in love with an Alaskan, Steven Hites, conductor on the White Pass & Yukon Route.*

*The 1900 railway has in recent years operated as a summer excursion line for the cruise-ship cheechakos who fill historic Skagway's streets. During the winter of 1982–83 Steven Hites doffed his old-time conductor's uniform to become a deskbound railway employee in the line's Seattle office. It was there one November day that he met a pretty woman who "just sparkled when she smiled." Steve and Gayla now operate a Skagway tour-bus service complete with antique White buses and 1920s costumes. Steve laughs when he recalls that he had to court his Seattleite for "quite some time—three months—because he was from Alaska, at the ends of the earth!"*

STEVEN HAD come down from Skagway to resume his duties as the passenger manager in the Seattle office of the White Pass & Yukon Route in autumn 1982. And a business acquaintance of mine named Dena was a reservation agent in that office. She invited me out to lunch one day at the J & M Cafe in Pioneer Square. Well, when I got there, Dena was still on the phone. So I sat by her desk waiting for her to finish up. And Steven walked by. We were introduced by Dena between hold buttons on the telephone. A very short meeting, but when I got home that night there was a message on my telephone answering machine asking me if I'd like to go out to lunch the next day. It was Steven! And he had a wonderful voice.

Even though our meeting had been brief, I thought, sure, so we went out to lunch, then out to dinner a couple of times.

We met the first week of November in '82 and we had a couple of luncheon dates and a couple of dinner dates. Then he was back and forth to Alaska and to Colorado for his Christmas holidays. And the next time we really saw each other was about the third week of January. And we were both dating other people at that time. So the relationship was platonic until the third week of February. I just decided one day— he had left my home, and I couldn't stand it. I couldn't stand the fact that he had gone back to Seattle—a two-and-a-half-hour drive from my home. I was going crazy because we hadn't set a specific time and date when we would see each other again. It just hit me like a ton of bricks that I was in love with this guy!

We got on the state ferry about two weeks after that and came north to Alaska. Which was my first trip here. Steven had to come back to Skagway in early March. I think we got on the ferry March 4.

It was a wonderful trip. I had never been farther north than Vancouver, British Columbia. We had a cabin, very romantic! It was sunny and cold and the mountains were covered with snow. The scenery was brilliant. Steven asked me to marry him half a day before we got to Ketchikan. And before we got to Skagway, I said, "Yes!"

But at Skagway I knew immediately that I had made a horrible mistake.

I had never seen a picture of Skagway. The only picture Steven had had with him in the wintertime in Seattle—of course, we had had all sorts of other things to think about and do—was an aerial-photograph postcard. So when I got to Skagway, it was a shock. I felt like it was forty below with a forty-knot wind coming right down the main street of town. The *Skaqua,* the north wind, was blowing.

Dirt streets. Unrestored buildings.

Then I went to the grocery store. No milk! No bread! No nail polish remover! And the grocery barge wasn't due in for two more days. Because I had just had a manicure in Seattle my nails were chipped and I desperately needed nail polish remover. I spent the next whole day chipping off all of my nail polish because I couldn't get nail polish remover. And I didn't have any girlfriends to borrow any from.

However, true love has prevailed. We're very happy, most of the time.

March 12 we were formally engaged to be married. And then we were married the following March 17, 1984, at the Olympic Four

Seasons Hotel in Seattle. It was a very nice wedding. Steven has a small family and they flew in from Colorado to the wedding.

Most of my five-generation family is in Seattle. Including my great-grandmother, who is ninety-five. She was able to attend the wedding and tell me again about how my great-grandfather Robert Stevens came to Skagway in the Klondike gold rush. I hadn't known that until I had gone home and told my family that I had become engaged to this man from Skagway. They had seen it coming, and when I got together at a family gathering with the older relatives, they told me the stories about how Great-grandpa Stevens had come to Skagway on his way to the Klondike gold fields when he was just off the wheat farm outside of Cle Elum, Washington.

My grandmother is the only child of Great-grandpa Stevens. I knew him, but he passed away when I was nine, so I don't remember his ever having told me about the gold rush. But the story started coming out when I suddenly had this connection to Skagway.

I will tell you about my great-grandfather. He was twenty-one when he came. His cousin was twenty. And my great-grandfather, like many, lost his money in a gambling tent on the White Pass trail, and someone gave him money for crackers and cheese and passage home. Which was what Soapy Smith did—because his men would take advantage of these young people, and Soapy Smith, to appear the philanthropist, would buy people passage home so they wouldn't become destitute and start causing trouble for him after they realized that they had been duped. Soapy Smith was the Al Capone of Skagway. He ran the town. He owned the newspaper and what little law enforcement there was here at the time. Most people thought he was a legitimate business owner because he did operate an oyster-bar restaurant and saloon.

And so Great-grandpa went home to Washington. The family sold another team of horses off the farm and he came North again and he eventually did work in the Klondike gold fields and later went into the grocery business in Tacoma, Washington.

Unlike him, I am committed to staying in Alaska. I love interpreting Great-grandpa's White Pass history for the visitors.

Unlike Great-grandpa, I did not come for the gold. It was Steven's voice on the phone that night that first attracted me. And his ability to communicate. We talked a lot. And our courtship was long-distance in the beginning. We started talking on the telephone on almost a daily basis. It just seemed as though we were able to communicate from the very beginning.

We spend a lot of time with our mates in the North. Really listening to the other person is vital to our relationships because we have few diversions compared to Outside. The cold, dark winters break up many marriages.

Some couples mistakenly come to Alaska to save their marriages, but if they aren't talking already, they aren't going to start doing it up here!

# Steven Hites

## On the Patron Saint of Alaskan Tourism
## Skagway
## b. 1954

*In the previous chapter Gayla explained how she accompanied Steven Hites to Skagway, Alaska. There she soon caught the spirit of Steve's mentor, showman Martin Itjen. As soon as she heard about Itjen's unique jitney, she insisted that they revive it.*

*And so the Skagway Street Car was reborn in 1985.*

MARTIN ITJEN. Today he and his wife, Lucy, are buried up in the Gold Rush Cemetery at the foot of the largest gold nugget in the world. It's a boulder spray-painted gold. It says, "Property of the Skagway Street Car Company." And, of course, it is chained securely to a tree so no one can steal it!

Our streetcar company is the same street car company that Martin Itjen created in 1923.

Martin Itjen was such a showman and such an excellent storyteller! He saw that there was an interest in Skagway's story when, wowie-zowie, a hundred tourists might land from a steamship. (Nowadays Skagway can be thronged with as many as five thousand tourists when three or four cruise ships are in the harbor at once.) Well, of that hundred probably seventy-five got away right away and rode the train up over White Pass. But there were still about twenty-five of them that would want to see the town. So Martin with his streetcar was always waiting down on the dock.

Street Car No. 1 was a 1907 Verrick with a Packard radiator and a home-built wooden frame painted up bright yellow and red with black striping that said Skagway Street Car. It was Martin's coal delivery truck. He was also the Ford dealer, so he had lots of Ford parts to keep it running and retrofitted. He was a mechanical genius with levers and wires. He even had a big mechanical bear rigged up on one side of it with fur and bendixes and springs and pulleys. He'd pull this lever and the bear would point the direction he was going to turn the bus. He'd turn the streetcar to the right and the bear would point that way and it would growl—rrrrrrr—and its eyes would light up bright red!

Each one of Martin's streetcars had a whistle and trolley bell on it. And Martin would dress up with a gold-nugget watch chain made out of dried prunes, which he would paint gold. He was an authentic character! He had looked for gold in Atlin and the Klondike and had found some but never enough to make him wealthy. But as a result of his personality and wit, he had ended up back in Skagway doing this multitude of odd jobs.

I guess I identify with Martin because I, too, had to chase after the gold. In my case I was trying to get one of these cushy railroad jobs right where I could be tied in here as a conductor and have a wife and six and a half kids and a great life. That eluded me in the same way that gold eluded Martin Itjen.

So I ended up wearing a lot of hats. Local balladeer. Local theater company. Working odd jobs hither and yon. Part-timing for the railroad. Doing whatever. And at the same time just listening to all the stories.

Like about the time in 1923 the president of the United States came to Skagway. The chamber of commerce had convinced him to be in town for three hours after the ship pulled into the dock. Well, Martin Itjen washed out his coal truck and painted it up and wrote Skagway Street Car across the side and put seats in the back of it. And drove it down on the dock. There were not many motorcars here in those days, and because Martin's had room for everybody in the presidential party, his "streetcar" became the presidential limousine.

Martin gave the president the first streetcar tour of Skagway. At the end of the tour everyone stopped at the Pullen House Hotel for a presidential reception, including Buck, little Virginia Burfield's dog that had gotten loose from the yard and followed her downtown. President Warren G. Harding said, "Boy, do you know how to shake hands?" Virginia Burfield said, "Yes, he does." That was a trick that she had taught Buck. "Shake, Buck," said the president. And Buck the dog shook hands with President Harding right there on the front porch of the Pullen House with everybody in Skagway watching. Wild!

But Martin had a good line. He could tell a good story. He was a promoter. He even dated Mae West! In 1935 Skagway was dying on the vine. No tourists were coming in the middle of the Depression. So Martin wrote to Mae West, "You always say, 'Come up and see me some time.' How about I come down to see you?" Mae West responded, "You're a Gold Rush stampeder? This looks good. Come on down, Martin, and I'll make a show for you."

So Martin put the streetcar onto a ship and unloaded it in Seattle, and he drove the streetcar, handing out brochures in every little town, promoting Skagway all the way down right into Hollywood, California, to the movie studio gate. And Martin Itjen went out to dinner with Mae West.

All the society pages in California did stories, "Klondike stampeder dates movie queen." They ran pictures of big Mae West and little Martin Itjen standing side by side.

He dated Mae West and he did two weeks at the Orpheum Theater in San Francisco. He was the toast of the West Coast telling stories about the Klondike. Because of his promotions, the next year Skagway tourism blossomed. That's why I like to call him the patron saint of Alaskan tourism.

# Pete Isleib

*Alaska Birding Pioneer*
*Juneau*
*b. 1938*

*Because he so often fished commerically near Bligh Reef, Pete Isleib flew out the morning after the Exxon Valdez oil spill to survey the damage to his livelihood. His interest was not just monetary. As one of North America's most zealous birders, he had spent most of his adult life monitoring Alaska's avian populations.*

*Pete Isleib has the honor of having Alaska's most extensive life list, meaning that he has seen more species of birds in the state than anyone else. But even that does not begin to describe his passion for Alaska's first flyers.*

**B**IRDING IS quite a personal thing. A lot of it today is really kind of like a bird golf. In other words, you're counting numbers—how many birds you see in a day, or in a geographical area, or in your life. There is a certain amount of competition involved, but that's not negative. It more or less feeds one's own ego and sense of accomplishment. And this is all part and parcel with an appreciation for birds and wanting to see habitat maintained and promoting conservation. I do a lot of traveling around Alaska seeing strange and new birds. Right now I have seen three hundred seventy-four species of birds in Alaska. There's only been four hundred thirty that have ever been recorded in Alaska. I've seen the greatest majority. I'm way ahead of what anyone else has seen because I have gone to great lengths to observe them. In many cases I was the initial finder of that bird—whether I photographed it or collected it or brought other people to see it.

I compete with a few other individuals, but it is a camaraderie-type competitiveness. I would be most happy to share the experience with somebody else, even my most serious competitor. It's a lot of fun to go find something new and different. Like when I went to Gambell on St. Lawrence Island, where you can see the mountains in Siberia, I didn't see anything specifically unusual, but I accomplished quite a bit. I got a lot of good data on what birds pass through that area in the fall migration. And there are a lot of people in the States that want to know that information. They might want to go there and look as well. And I'll probably end up writing an article about it.

Birding is the self-gratification side of a larger interest, whether it be in conservation or wildlife management or portions of some biological or scientific study. Bird watchers include an awful lot of people that are not scientifically trained, that have no biological background, contributing in a small part to what we know about bird life in North America if they properly record their data. Like today, I have been compiling data from a lot of amateurs, sightings that they'd made around the state, and synthesizing it into a report for a national publication about this year's Alaskan bird population trends, unusual occurrences, reproductive successes.

I was imprinted by birds way back in my preteens. I've been a bird watcher, more recently the term has been birder, for most of my life, starting off in Connecticut back in the early fifties.

The birder image is the little old lady in tennis shoes, either sex. But mostly in Alaska we are definitely not little old ladies in tennis shoes. For most of us up here there is a considerable amount of scientific research involved in birding. I've just returned from one survey on St. Lawrence Island, and I'm going out to Middleton Island in another ten days for the University of Alaska Museum. There's a great deal of data that we're turning up that has not previously been known. It's a frontier. A lot more of us publish or compile reports than would be common in the Lower 48, where they are inundated with bird watchers. In most of Alaska, there's a long distance between people, let alone between bird watchers!

Alaska is a wilderness in how little we know about its birds. Few areas have been covered adequately enough to understand fully avian abundance and distribution. We're here on the edge of the continent, almost a subcontinent, and we've got a lot of remote areas which are only rarely visited by government biologists. Because we are a crossroads between Asia and North America, between the Pacific and Arctic oceans, we get a great number of birds on the fringes of their ranges. It's a dynamic area where a lot of changes are occurring. For example, a Caspian tern colony has just recently been found on the Copper River Delta.

The terns weren't there until just a few years ago, but now there's a large colony. Yet I know many active Alaskan bird watchers who haven't seen that bird in this state because it's just in one location and you have to go to considerable expense to see it. That's an example of the fact that we're living in a sort of crossroads.

For many birds, there are no real boundaries except temperatures, and we get many birds that stray north from their normal ranges in the Pacific Ocean or Asia. For example, this spring on Attu Island I discovered a Chinese little bittern and this bird had been known no farther north than Japan. It was far out of range and had to cross some fifteen hundred miles of ocean to have gotten there. That was an exciting find!

There were other birds this year of the same ilk: windblown strays out of storms. You realize how close you are to Asia and Siberia when you see a lot of such unusual birds.

This year I've also seen a narcissus flycatcher from Asia. It had never been seen in North America before. I also saw a little curlew on St. Lawrence Island, new to Alaska and the Asian counterpart of the Eskimo curlew, which is nearly extinct in North America.

The person who influenced me most is presently a physician in Boston. His name is Al Wills. In Connecticut back in the very early 1950s, I'd already earned a Boy Scout bird-study merit badge when I heard that there was a counselor at our scout camp who knew everything there was to know about birds. I heard that if he questioned me, he'd take my merit badge away from me if I didn't know all I should know about birds!

Well, I knew more about birds than anyone I'd heard of at that time, so I said, "I'm going to go to that camp and find out who this guy is."

He turned out to be Al Wills, a counselor a few years older than I was. We became fast friends. He recognized that I was very interested in birds, and I realized that he had an awful lot more experience with birds than I did.

The following year I was one of the camp counselors with him. My first trips with Al inspired me to think that there was more to birding than I had thought, that there was a lot more to learn than I had suspected, because initially I had had nothing more than Audubon's *Birds of America* (which is a large portfolio) to identify birds with. At the time I didn't even know of such things as field guides!

Al and I built up a lasting friendship. His sons have worked for me as fishermen here in Alaska.

Ludlow Griscom and Roger Tory Peterson, who were eminent

ornithologists when I was in my teens in the early 1950s, took me on numerous bird-watching trips. Their consideration for a teenager who was interested in birds added the acceptance I needed. Roger is still a close friend.

Roger said that there was a future in birding. He carried my boyhood interests along into young adulthood and expanded them. I even worked for the National Audubon Society for a while in the late 1950s in Florida.

When I left my job working for the Audubon Society in the summer of '58, President Eisenhower was signing the Alaska statehood bill. I wanted to go to Alaska right away, but since I was twenty-one years old, I thought it best that I do my military service first. It turned out that I was able to get up here with the air force. Immediately upon arriving I helped to start the Alaska Ornithological Society in 1960. I was stationed in Anchorage for several years and then moved to Cordova when I left the service.

I got into fishing because there was no money in birds here at that time unless you were working for a government agency or a university and had an academic background. My birding experiences were strictly as a field ornithologist.

I started fishing in Cordova in 1963, and I've had vessels fishing there ever since. I lived in Cordova from '63 to '83, and I still have a home there and still have vessels fishing there. Early in the fishing season I'm involved in a herring fishery there that takes place near Bligh Reef at the mouth of Valdez Arm. That fishery was canceled for the 1989 season because of the oil spill. I have since been paid by Exxon for what my gains would have been for that season's fishing, but I have little hope of long-term remuneration from Exxon for future years if the fish don't come back.

I came to Juneau in 1983, where my daughter could take Japanese in high school and become an exchange student to Japan and where my son could go into different sports that weren't offered in Cordova. Now that they're both off to college, I'm not sure what I'm going to do, but I know that I'm not going to live in Palm Springs or Seattle because I believe in contributing to Alaska. That's why I'm involved in many volunteer activities, such as being a commissioner of the Pacific States Marine Fisheries Commission or being on the Governor's High Seas Task Force or working as an adviser to the State Department on North Pacific fisheries.

In some years I have spent as much as ten thousand dollars funding myself to participate in various volunteer activities for the fishing industry with the state or federal government. I'm not unique in that. Mr. Gordon Jensen of Petersburg, for instance, and others might spend up to a hundred days a year for very little per diem to help set fisheries policies.

Because my fishery was closed by the *Exxon Valdez* spill, I had time to go to Washington, D.C., as an adviser to the State Department for the International North Pacific Fisheries Commission, to work with the Japanese and Canadians on the high-seas gill-net issue. Since I was already there, I was able to testify at the first congressional oil spill hearing.

Back in the early seventies I had been very active in the Cordova District Fishermen United, fighting the oil pipeline. I was also on a committee of fishermen that held a major symposium on oil and water back in '77. We fishermen were downplayed very strongly. The oil interests tried to lump us with the Wilderness Society and other groups and said that we were just a bunch of naysayers. Even with our own governor at that time, Bill Egan, although we loved him quite dearly, we were in direct opposition to him on this. He would be swearing at us and we'd be swearing back at him. He was going to put an oil embargo on our ports so we couldn't get any fuel to run our fishing boats. I mean it was really pretty nasty. But we insisted that alternative inland routes to the Midwest should be seriously considered rather than taking the pipeline to the coast, necessitating a marine leg.

And so on that March day in 1989 I could see all our old fears about the coastal route coming to pass.

I felt that things had come full circle when I, representing Cordova fishermen, was once again testifying before Congress on this issue.

Since the oil spill on March 24, probably well over a million birds have died from its results. I think that it will be decades before the last vestiges of the *Exxon Valdez* oil are gone, and there will be millions of birds that will die or not even exist because of reproduction problems, habitat and food losses.

Although the *Exxon Valdez* oil spill affected many aspects of the environment, the effect that seemed to bother people the most was the loss of birds. This indicates to me the importance of birds in people's lives. Millions of people around the world depend on birds for food or for recreation—whether observing them or hunting them or for income as a tourist attraction. But whatever the reason, I believe many people share with me a deep attraction to birds.

To me they represent a free spirit: The air seems to hold freedom, and birds epitomize that. They are showy, colorful, and seemingly fragile but are actually very hardy and can withstand great variations in weather. The sound of the geese flying south in the fall makes us feel sad, while the sight of the first robin in the spring raises our spirits. I am only one of the millions whose lives wouldn't be the same without birds.

# Austin Hammond, Charlie and T. J. Jimmie

*A Tlingit Family*
*Haines*
*b. 1910, 1932, 1952*

*These three generations of Tlingit men are symbolic of the changing attitudes to-*
*ward tradition among Natives in Southeast Alaska. A highly respected Raven*
*elder, Austin Hammond grew up in 1920s bush camps, where he helped his crip-*
*pled grandfather with hunting and fishing and served a ready audience during*
*long nights of storytelling. Austin had to grapple, often unsuccessfully, with alco-*
*holism and with rapid cultural change from subsistence to a market economy and*
*from an oral tradition to assimilation. His stepson, Charlie Jimmie, "grew up*
*dancing," says his mother, Lillian Jimmie; Charlie is the heart and soul of Carl*
*Heinmiller's Chilkat Dancers and is the president of the traditional Geisan*
*Dancers, both in Haines, Alaska. Tommy "T. J." Jimmie, forty, Austin's grandson*
*and Charlie's nephew, is outspoken about steering away from the tourist-oriented*
*stage shows of the Chilkat Dancers toward greater authenticity and spiritual*
*meaning.*

*The Chilkat River Indians were noted until early in this century for their*
*fierce independence and resistance to white domination. Traditional guardians of*
*the trade routes to the interior, they were never conquered and never signed a peace*
*treaty. Recently Austin made his stepson head spokesman for the Coho and Frog*
*clans, an indication that Charlie is the heir apparent as Raven moiety leader. "I*
*respect my father very much. That's why I have to be careful on how I act," says*
*Charlie. "Becoming a chief doesn't happen every day to a person. I come from a*
*very high rank. All my grandfathers were chiefs on my mother's side."*

*For his part, eighty-two-year-old Austin Hammond says, "We never used to have chiefs. Only a big man,* onyadā, *who was a respected man who took care of everybody on our Raven side. Our whole people watched to see who was qualified to be a chief. Who knew how to live correctly with other people and who knew all the stories."*

Grandson T. J. Jimmie is watching and thinking.

A T FIRST there was no land at all, but the Raven was out in the ocean with a canoe. . . .

**Austin Hammond:** My grandfather told me, "Let all the people hear the story." That's why I keep telling it. The part I just told you, that's only the beginning! Then we come to the fire, the water, the tides, the salmon, and all the parts that must be told. The story takes a year to finish, and when I finish telling it, then I go back and begin again.

People keep asking me, "What is your history?" My history is on my blanket. That's how we know it. Our people never used to write or to know about how God created us. You people, you got the Bible and you read it. But us, we didn't have it. We passed on our own knowledge. This is not *my* story I'm telling you. It is the story my grandfather told me. And I don't add any into it.

I have a lot of things in my mind to tell. Our people believe that we've got to respect anything that's growing. Just like the way we respect each other. Respect all what's growing—different kinds of medicine growing, grass growing. Mountain goats, moose, deer, everything will be satisfied from eating what's growing from the ground.

The tree is the head of this world and the world is alive from that tree. This is what we are trying to tell the men that are cutting all the trees—that the rain comes down from water which has gone up out of the trees.

My grandfather told me that the tree is important to everything. The tree gave us shelter. The deer goes under the tree, taking care of the tree, the tree taking care of him when the snow is coming down. Mountain goat, moose, everything. Right now you can see all the birds that roost in that tree.

We can predict the weather from the tree's changing color, from light to dark or to light green. And if the tree makes fire [autumn colors], there will be good weather and sunshine again.

The world is breathing, like we are. That's why we've got to respect everything. The tree is breathing through the earth. He breathes and all the animals are protected under him. If we cut the whole forest, what is going to happen? The earth is going to dry out. When the earth dries, we all are going to be starving. Everything is going to die. There will be nothing in this world.

We have to take care of the land. God created us Tlingits, white people, Filipinos. We've got to take care of the whole world, even the ground itself and its great worms and insects of all different kinds. We can't respect only ourselves. We must respect everybody and everything in the world.

My grandfather used to say, "The Raven will give you knowledge when you need to know it." By the Raven he meant God.

When the first minister came here, an interpreter told us the story of God in the Bible. We had no Bible, but we had the stories of Raven. The Bible says that he will send us a comforter. Our comforter is our grandfather and his grandfather, all that way back. So that's the reason why they used to tell us, "Listen to the elders." This is what I'm trying to tell the children, listen to the minister, to the Bible; that's your grandfather.

It's hard to say about the next generation, but I know my grandfather is pulling for everybody.

My grandfather Jim was blind, so I had to take care of him. I stayed in camp with him ever since I was nine years old cutting wood, hunting seal. My grandma, she wasn't too old yet and we trapped, fished, and put up all kinds of meats for winter in five gallon cans and oil. I stayed in camp all the time till I was fifteen. That's how I learned my grandfather's stories.

**Charlie Jimmie:** I have always loved to dance. When I was four and a half years old, I danced at our Raven House in Haines after I first got here from Yakutat. They put me up on a round oak table and when I danced and sang, people donated money to pay for the dance.

When I was about eleven or twelve, I spent a winter at Wrangell Institute. I was stilll in fourth grade, I was behind in school. The Presbyterian preacher, Walter Soboloff, his name is Dr. Soboloff now, that was his mother that was teaching the girls sewing and Indian culture at the Wrangell Institute. She said, "We have to have a play. Can you do any dancing?" I said that I had danced ever since I was small. "Okay, we'll need you to be the medicine man." I said that I had only seen a real one in Juneau once as a little boy. Well, I was kind of scared, but I danced the part of the medicine man in that play and I have been dancing it ever since.

When I went back to Juneau, I traveled around with my mother and stepfather and grandfather. We used to go to these potlatches at Hoonah which used to last two and three days, some of them. I danced there to say thanks to the people that gave us food and money and gifts. We danced sometimes two or three hours to show our thanks.

When Carl Heinmiller came along, he influenced me more because at that time our culture was just about dead. We Tlingit people had been trying to keep up with our Caucasian brothers, competing for the jobs. That is why we had lost our culture but now we're gaining it back.

I've been dancing with Carl Heinmiller and the Chilkat Dancers for thirty years because Carl helps the young people learn a little bit about their own culture through dancing and singing. And he's helping the young people get spending money.

When the Chilkat Dancers was formed in 1957, it was a Boy Scout troop. They were invited to go back East to a jamboree at Valley Forge and they wondered what they could do for a performance. And since they were proud of being from the Chilkat Valley, they said, "Let's form a dance group and call it the Chilkat Dancers!" And that is the way the Chilkat Dancers was born.

Okay, the troop was half Tlingit and half white, but they were all Boy Scouts. People in our audiences have asked me many times, "How come some of those dancers have blue eyes? Are they . . .?" "No," I say, "they are our slaves!"

We grab the good whites, and a lot of times we'll give 'em names of our people who have passed away. It's like reincarnation. That is why my mother adopted Matilda Lewis and gave her my oldest aunt's name. So my mother reincarnated her sister who had passed away.

He is special that came in a long time ago and was adopted.

There was a colored man that used to stay over by Glacier Point. He used to raise strawberries a long time ago when the army was here. And he was so good a friend of the Tlingits. He gave 'em everything. So they adopted him in turn because he loved the Tlingit people.

It's done in the potlatch so everyone can see all these important namings, adoptions, gift givings, and the paying of debts. A long time ago the missionaries thought we were squandering too much money, but potlatches were where our affairs were settled. For instance, I have some dance gear made out of many pieces of gopher hides and pearl buttons on red cloth. My daughter (who is an Eagle) wanted to fix that up for me as my daughter for free. But it took her a long time, and I wanted to recognize her with money for that at our next potlatch.

Austin Hammond raised me as my stepfather after 1945 until I became a man. When I started halibut fishing with him, I had to be the first on deck and the last to leave the ship after I had checked everything for the next day. It was a tough upbringing.

Austin has been two or three different persons over his lifetime. As a young fellow, of course, everyone played basketball. Austin was called Frisco Star when he played at Fort Seward in Haines. For five feet eleven he used to be a pretty good rebound man. He made some key plays when they won the gold cup in 1942 and 1943. That was a big honor.

As he got older my stepfather drank quite a bit up till middle age or so, when he became chief when his brother, Alfred Andrews, died. There were witnesses to what his brother said in passing on the chieftainship. The succession goes according to our different ranks.

As he was dying, Alfred Andrews gave Austin a copper money piece engraved with the words "Chief of the Chilkat Indians." "It is yours to wear and to keep," said Alfred Andrews.

But my father said, "No, I am not worthy of it. I drink too much."

His older brother said, "You won't continue having a good time all your life. You will settle down eventually."

So my father said, "Well, I'll keep it until I feel worthy of hanging it up on the wall."

My father proved himself as he grew older because he and my mother reopened the Salvation Army and the ANB, according to the wishes of his uncles. Okay, now we even have a hundred-thousand-dollar ANB Hall here. If it hadn't been for his hard work . . .

And now he's got a culture camp that he started up there at Chilkoot, where my roots are. And I'm very happy about that 'cause a lot of young Tlingit kids learn about our culture there. Most of the mothers nowadays don't know anything about our culture, and I think that camp is a wonderful boost.

I think it's worthwhile for our kids to know about this way their grandparents lived. I have grandchildren now. Our history and language should be taught in school so that kids will be proud of being Tlingit. Maybe that pride will help us to forget our wants for alcohol. For instance, I'm a recovering alcoholic, and when I'm really bad off with liquor and feeling guilty, quite a few times someone has come and said, "Can I get you water?" I never forget that kindness. And I will remember that person at the potlatch because any little thing that you can do to help an alcoholic goes a long ways.

My stepdad and I, we have our differences sometimes, but we're out fishing together now and usually he's trying to cram a lot of things into my mind. It's the first time I've gone back with Dad fishing. I've been carving totem poles and going south to work on seine boats and just keeping away from my dad because I've got kid brothers who've got no job. My boys have no place to work, so they always work with their grandfather and I didn't want to push them aside. But since he asked me,

I said, "Well, Dad, if you're in a pinch, I'll go fishing—but I'll be dancing, too, because that's my job."

I've been fishing with him all summer. He's something else. I love Dad and I love to go out with him. Ever since I was small we hunted together, fished together, and trapped together. I even played basketball with my old man! We did everything together.

**Tommy "T. J." Jimmie:** We have an expression we use when we are holding our grandfathers up the highest that we can. *Hadakanuqu.* I accept the responsibility that Austin has given me by sharing these stories with me. He says that everyone should share these stories because that is the only way that our traditions will survive. The more people that listen, the more that will pass it on.

I grew up around Austin. I used to fish on his boat all the time with him and his uncles, Johnny Marks and Willie Marks. They took me around to villages all over Southeast Alaska. Every place that we stopped, Austin introduced me to all the different elders there. And they would sit down and talk history.

There's a lot of wisdom among our people. If they had wanted to, they could have developed a written language a long time ago, but they recognized the importance of being able to stand up and speak publicly from their hearts rather than from things that were written. If the things that you are saying touch other people's hearts, they feel that they can trust you. I think that's a real important part of our tradition.

The stories of Raven are referred to as *yethqutlaq* and are the oldest memories of our people. My grandfather Austin used to tell me them over and over again, always in the same way. But I would always hear something different because I was growing older and more able to appreciate the oral tradition. Before me, my uncle Charlie was exposed to a lot of venerated old-time singers and dancers, especially the Marks Trail Dancers in Juneau. But he is still learning. All of us are still learning.

# Bruce Johnstone

*A Patient Man*

*Ketchikan*

*b. 1909*

*Bruce Johnstone spent most of his life collecting grubstakes to prospect for the gold that was always around the next bend in the creek. To finance this life-style Bruce and his brother Jack hand logged steep slopes in what is now Misty Fiords National Monument. They cut huge hemlocks, cedars, and spruces by hand and towed them to their bush camp by rowboat, then rafted them together for shipment by a primitive tugboat to the Ketchikan sawmill. Bruce, a patient man of the old ways, says that Southeast has run out of the large stands of prime timber that big operators need to be profitable but that gyppos—small-scale loggers—could still make a go of it. A thousand hand loggers could produce the volume the mills need while minimizing environmental harm and retaining jobs for the community. The only problem with the idea, he says, is that hand logging requires too much physical labor and patience for today's impatient people. He likes to tell the story of some sourdoughs who had joined the Klondike rush of 1898 by fixing up an abandoned steamboat on the Tacoma tideflats and taking a load of passengers and freight to Skagway. Then they hauled the boat piece by piece over the pass, reassembled it, and cruised triumphantly to Dawson. Bruce says that he cannot imagine modern people showing that type of endurance. "If they can't do it in a day now," he says, "they won't do it at all."*

**M**Y FATHER was a loner from Kentucky. When things got a little too crowded, he moved. And that's how we came here.

We were living at Deserted Bay on Princess Louisa Inlet, where I was born, about a hundred miles north of Vancouver, and it started to get too crowded, so he flipped a coin to see what it would be, New

Zealand or Alaska. It came up Alaska. We came first to Rudyerd Bay in the Misty Fiords, where there was steep ground, and we went to hand logging.

Hand logging, you do everything. It's not like in a lumber camp, where there are specialized jobs. Mostly though, when I first started, I towed the logs with a rowboat, and that's why I'm so stooped, from sitting hour after hour, ten hours a day, rowing and towing logs by hand. I used to pull two or three logs for five or six miles. Hand loggers figured pulling logs was the easiest job, but I think it was the hardest work in the outfit.

Those boats were made for rowing. The boats nowadays are almost impossible to row because they are made for power.

If two people were rowing, the man in the bow pulled and the man in the stern pushed and steered. But if you were alone, you pulled.

Everybody rowed! Like going to Prince of Wales Island, if you go around the south end, it's twelve miles across. By rowboat, if you could hold two miles an hour, that was a pretty good speed in the old heavy boats.

The winds come up in this country so fast that it's a wonder that half the people didn't die. But they have way more accidents now with the speedboats than we used to have with the rowboats because people had more patience. If they can't do something in a day now, they won't do it at all.

Hand logging was work for a patient man. And it required very steep ground so that the trees would slide. So first we'd row out and cruise a steep slope to find where we wanted to work. In this part of the country, either limestone or lava has the best timber. So we'd look for those formations and for good drainage. The back side of Revilla [Revillagigedo] Island had the best, steepest ground and best timber. It was all Forest Service land; in the twenties and early thirties Jack and I paid a dollar and a half a thousand to the Forest Service for the privilege of cutting this timber. And we'd go to the Forest Service and pay 'em the stumpage on whatever we thought we could cut in the time we had that summer. Then we went out to our falling site on the *Me Pal,* a thirty-foot boat with a five-horsepower engine. We lived on a boat or camped ashore and only got into Ketchikan two or three times a year.

It was hard work to get to the trees we wanted to cut because the ground was so steep and because we might be a thousand feet up from the shore. Sometimes on steep ground we were at least a hundred feet up in the air. We started on the back of the tree and began to chop in holes for the springboards until we had worked our boards around to the steep side. The board had a hook on the end to tie into the hole in the tree. If you were good, you could jump and kick a springboard into position. I wasn't very good at that, but my brother-in-law, Handlogger Jackson, was very agile.

Nowadays we'd use a power saw, but in those days it was all by hand. The real old-timers didn't use a saw, only an axe, but my brother Jack and I used a 7½ Simmons saw. But we'd always chop the undercut in. Handlogger always worked by himself. He rigged up rubber springs to pull the saw back. He said he liked to work with a partner that he could swear at.

We used double-bitted axes because when we felled a tree, it had to be exactly right. With a double-bitted axe we could use one side one day and the other side the next so that the handles wouldn't warp. We needed to have a perfectly straight handle to sight along from the under-cut to where the tree would fall.

If you are not sure which way the tree is leaning, you can plumb it with the handle of a double-bitted axe. Stand back about forty feet, hold the axe handle lightly with two fingers and let it swing itself straight and use that as a plumb.

If the tree got hung up on a stump or a root, we had what we called logging jacks that would lift or push about five ton. But the jack itself weighed seventy-five pounds. So you didn't want to pack it around in the woods too much!

I didn't start growing until I was about sixteen—I don't think I weighed a hundred pounds then—and packing the seventy-five-pound logging jack through the woods was just too much for me to handle. So my brother Jack done most of that until I started growing up enough to help.

I think hand logging will come back. We are almost out of big stands of timber, but there is enough for hand loggers to keep the mills going here for a thousand years. A lone hand logger would only bring in maybe a hundred thousand board feet, but we'd have a thousand hand loggers out. So we could still bring in the volume of timber that the big mills need.

We could take ten miles of coastline and after we hand loggers had selective cut it, you wouldn't notice that anybody had been through there because we would only take the very best. The easiest and the best! We'd take the old ones and let the young ones grow—instead of taking everything, like the clear-cutters do.

The Forest Service is against it. They want to sell to the big com-panies. They don't want to sell thousands when they could sell millions.

And most people won't want to do the hard work that hand logging requires. A lot of times I had to oil my hands to keep their skin from cracking. People don't like to work that hard anymore. But come visit me and we'll go hand logging!

# Sandy Kogl

Dogsled Patrol, Denali National Park
Denali National Park and Preserve
b. 1943

*A California farm girl, Sandy Holloway grew up wishing for something more ex-
citing. In 1964 she enrolled in a graduate program at the University of Alaska at
Fairbanks, but her real goal was adventure. Within two years she had married a
fellow graduate student, dropped out of her wildlife management program, staked
a homesite claim through the Bureau of Land Management, built a cabin, and
begun a subsistence life-style in the Alaska Range. Fairbanks friends gave her
some "hand-me-down dogs and lots of advice." For nine years she and her husband, Dennis Kogl, lived five miles from the nearest road, trapping, fishing, and
using dogs to freight supplies to and from the railway line. But with the nearest
kids eight miles away, Sandy's children were becoming "socially maladjusted,"
which she says is common among even many adult Alaskans. So the need to get
them into a school system brought the Kogls out of the Bush. Sandy's husband
became a dog-mushing outfitter at Denali National Park and Preserve. When he
and Sandy divorced, she was the park's kennel manager, doing back-country
dogsled patrols. In recent years she has been a supervisory ranger, but her book,*
Sled Dogs of Denali, *explains the park's canine traditions to wide-eyed
cheechakos. Sandy says that she is still surprised when younger rangers see her as
a back-country role model. "I still feel I have a long ways to go," she says.*

FROM 1966 to 1974 my husband and I were living on a couple of
thousand dollars a year cash income, and the rest of our needs were
provided by hunting, fishing, trapping, and by what we could sew, build,
or construct on our own. Luckily our needs were few because our area
up in the Alaska Range was not a rich area for trapping and subsistence.

In fact, one of our Fish and Game cohorts had warned us, "It looks like hungry country to me!" He was right. But it certainly was ample for our needs.

Subsistence is one of those vague terms which is hard to define. My definition of subsistence now is much more severe than it was at that time. We always had the amenities of modern technology—rifles, scopes, binoculars. We never did go to snow machines or mechanized travel other than being five miles from the road and six miles from the railroad, where we had access to supply. In 1966 our area did have year-round rail access. The highway between Fairbanks and Anchorage had not been completed yet, so the railroad was the graduate student's access to the Bush. The railroad was flag stop. You could get off at any point you wanted to and you could board at any point. It ran twice a week in winter.

And there was a cache of supplies available up a drainage. We invested in buying those supplies, and we staked some BLM [Bureau of Land Management] land that was available for homesite development. My daughter was born in 1969 and my son was born in 1970, eighteen months apart.

Gradually we realized that we did not want to spend all of our waking hours in a survival mode. That perhaps mankind had advanced farther than that. We needed time for reflection and recreation. So we tried to have the best of both worlds: a remote wilderness lifestyle and yet still not spend all of our waking moments chopping wood and picking berries. But not having nearby kids—our nearest neighbors were eight miles away—made it pretty obvious that our children needed some more socialization. So we started living along the road system. And about that same time there was an opportunity to work here at the park. So I accepted a permanent job with the Park Service and the kids went to school.

Dogs had been our means of transportation back in the Bush. Our way to travel the miles, to haul the firewood, to bring the moose and caribou meat, to haul the kids back and forth. Then my husband started a business freighting supplies into the park for mountain climbers and hauling passengers and ski groups.

By that time I was comfortable with my own abilities to handle dogs and build sleds and equipment to support dog teams. That led to my job at the park's kennel and doing back-country dogsled patrols. My role was also to train rangers to patrol the back-country by dog team. A lot of that was simply teaching basic survival skills to rangers who were new to the North. I had to teach them how to deal with the cold and how to deal with dogs.

From '75 through '85, I patrolled about twelve to fifteen hundred miles a winter by dogsled. We have a six-million-acre park, so realistically we're not going to be covering all corners at any one time or even at any one season. But there are corridors commonly used by visitors coming with their own dog teams or skiing. The old McKinley National Park is a wilderness area where mechanized travel is not permitted off the road at any time of year and not at all during the winter. No snow machines are allowed in the old park.

We used dog teams to make contact with those visitors, to access some of the remote patrol cabins we have, to haul garbage out of back-country areas. Some of the climbing and survey expeditions have abandoned gear. Cabins have burned down and tin roofs and bedsprings have been left. So we haul that stuff out. Wintertime is better for that rather than backpacking it in summer.

Some of it is just a matter of being out. You don't have a thorough appreciation for an area until you're out in it throughout the year. And certainly the winter is one of our dominant times of year.

We do some informal censusing of caribou or moose or sheep traveling through. Packs of wolves. And our just being out serves as a deterrent against some of the illegal poaching. (Most of that is by airplane, however.) Poachers shoot animals from the air, land on skis, and fly out the carcasses or hides. But certainly we don't delude ourselves that we are chasing away the bad guys with our one little dog team, going along at five or six miles an hour, covering twenty or thirty miles in a day. But we do put down a fresh set of tracks, and I know for certain that I have turned around some airplanes that were intent on illegal activities.

And some of it is just a matter of maintaining a tradition. Hey, rangers have been doing this since the beginning of the park. It's always interesting when we have going-away parties for departing staff that are moving on to other parks. Their nostalgia is usually related to their experiences out in the winter with the dog teams. Those memories are pretty important to people.

Actual wildlife encounters are fairly uncommon in winter. In winter a lot of the animals have dispersed to other areas. We encounter a moose or two, an occasional caribou or fox or wolf. More often we'll see tracks in the snow where animals have gone.

It sounds romantic and often it is. Sometimes it's absolutely fantastic. When everything goes right, it's extraordinary. If you have good trails. Say, the temperature is zero degrees Fahrenheit. That's a great temperature to be traveling in the winter. Clear, crisp skies. Frosty. Not bundled up in heavy clothing because you're physically active, running around hitching up the dogs. The dogs are excited to go. You put them in harness. You've already packed your sled. You've got your extra mittens and hat and parka on top of the load. You're all hitched up ready to go. You untie your sled and take off and it's just absolutely exhilarating. It's just fantastic. Especially for me: Having been here over a number of years, I built some of the sleds. I've raised and trained most all of the dogs. So there's a lot of personal satisfaction to have put all this together and seen it through to completion.

You are traveling along at maybe eight miles an hour when trails are good and everything is just great. Sometimes you get off and run to keep the blood flowing and circulating. When the dogs start to tire or you need a break, you stop and put the snow hook in and sit down on your sled and drink a cup of hot tea and reflect on your surroundings. It's fantastic.

On the other hand, there are times that are not so great: when the trail conditions are not good; when your load is too heavy, the weather is too warm, the trail is too soft, the snow too cold and balling up between the dogs' feet, making hard little marblelike balls between their toes and they start limping and you have to physically pull those snowballs out with your bare, frozen fingers. That's not much fun. It is hard, unpleasant work.

If we are off from the main routes and tent camping, it's a laborious, time-consuming task to set up a good winter camp and take care of dogs and people and get your clothing dried out and stay warm. I must admit that I like doing it better at zero degrees than I do at forty below zero. I'm getting soft!

Sometimes I wonder, "Hey, am I going to make a mistake that will cause me to lose some fingers through frostbite or lose my life?" So that burden and stress goes along with it, too.

Not all patrols are successful. I guess that is something I've learned over the years. I have developed a pretty good sense of not fighting it for too long. I've got sense enough to turn around and come back because I know that conditions will improve given enough time. I used to be stubborn. Especially as a female in what was traditionally a male role.

I've been here at a wonderful time to have some really wonderful women role models in the state. Coming from California, I didn't feel that there were adventurous women doing exciting things. But here in Alaska, the things I've done are unremarkable compared to the feats of many women, such as Celia Hunter and Ginny Wood, who were the founders of Camp Denali. Nancy Simmerman from Girdwood. Liz

Berry from Fairbanks. Linda Forsberg of Denali Dog Tours. Certainly Mary Shields. And, of course, Susan Butcher. The list is endless. There are extraordinary women in Alaska.

# Cecilia "Kin-Too" Kunz

Juneau's Indian Village
Juneau
b. 1910

Cecilia Yarkon grew up with ties to both Sitka (where her father was chief of the Wolf clan) and Juneau (where her father's father, Yees-gaa-malth, was chief of the Lee-Na-Dee, the Auke people at Auke Bay near Juneau).

Cecilia is the last person who remembers when Juneau's Native village was a populous home of the Lee-Na-Dee people. She was born in a birth hut close to her present home on Village Street.

The Indians used to live between where the Gastineau Hotel and the City Cafe are now. But during the early mining period of the 1880s the town of Juneau relocated the Natives to ten acres at the present village site (including all the way over to the tank farm). Cecilia's father used to keep his war canoe where the big petroleum tanks are now.

Gradually Native land was simply expropriated until all that was left was a three-acre enclave on tailings-filled land at Willoughby Avenue. Most of the houses have been torn down, but the more serious destruction has been to the culture itself.

The old and new dress photo of Cecilia Kunz's father dedicating his Wolf House at Sitka reminds us of the pride that these traditionalists felt in their ancient ways even as they were adapting to Western life. In 1904 the Kagwantan people assembled from Yakutat, Hoonah, Angoon, and Klukwan for the last official potlatch in Southeast Alaska. Today the pole is on loan at the Sitka National Historical Park.

IN 1958 we got all the people together and told them what was going to happen to our village when Alaska became a state. "Let's petition the Congress," said my husband, Edward Kunz, "so we can have a title to our land." Back then all we had was just a quit claim deed. Oh, I can get a quit claim deed for the Douglas Bridge if I want. That's how good a quit claim deed is!

We asked Congress so the people in the village in Juneau would get deeds to their land. My husband wrote to all those lawmakers, Gruening, Bartlett, and Rivers, and they pushed it through. And when we got it, they gave us a choice of what kind of deed we wanted. Restricted or unrestricted. Now I have a restricted deed and nobody can touch my land. Now everybody, including the ANB, has title to their land.

Before the miners came to Juneau, this was all Indian land. But we were squeezed by the miners in early Juneau into a strip along the beach. Then later, when the Alaska-Juneau Mine started up, they told the Indian people to move the village to ten acres. Ten acres! And now we end up with only three! Where the tanks are, my dad used to leave his big war canoe there. Somehow the tanks started to appear over there.

When I was little, this whole place where the village is now was beach. The tide used to come up almost under this house. Just a big beach until Alaska-Juneau filled up this place with their tailings.

When they were putting that Willoughby Avenue in, they stopped right here at this corner. My dad, Jake Yarkon, he said, "You're not going to go any farther. You stop right there." For two weeks it didn't go while the authorities talked with our Mr. Seward Kunz and Jake Williams from the village, who could talk English. What shall we do, we wondered? Shall we allow the city to put that avenue through? At that time, we used to burn coal in wood stoves. And we used to go uptown in our canoes to get sacks of coal. And that's what Seward Kunz told the people. "If we allow the city to put in the avenue, maybe their horses will bring us sacks of coal." Horses used to pull big wagons in Juneau. And our people liked that idea. "Yeah, that's gonna be good. Okay, let's allow the city to go through." And that's when Willoughby Avenue went through around 1916.

But we gave so much to the city, and the city hasn't done anything for us. When they put that avenue there, you think they'd call that avenue Seward Kunz Avenue? No, they called it Willoughby Avenue. Willoughby wasn't even a Native! There's some bad stories about that man, but I don't want to repeat them. Seward Kunz was the first lay worker among the Indian people. He got his education at Sheldon Jackson School in Sitka. He was one of the Alaska Native Brotherhood founders. Seward Kunz was my husband's uncle. He was a genuine Juneau. The name of the Juneau people is Lee-Na-Dee, and Seward

Kunz was the first lay worker from Alaska's Tlingit people. He worked for the missionaries who were preaching at the Presbyterian church. He was very old at the time I came along and was known as the William Jennings Bryan of the Tlingit Indians.

I met his nephew right here.

Kunz was the name of the Kuk-Hit-Ton chief. A subdivision of Kagwantan. The name Kunz was not German or anything. We pronounce it "q'unz." Just like Yarkon, they spell that all kinds of which way, too.

My husband's name was Edward Kunz, Sr. We went to the same school and church, the Orthodox church, the first religion in Alaska.

There's not too many people in the church here in Juneau anymore. When the priest goes away and stays away, they start joining other churches.

In my days we used to use both the Slavonic language and the Tlingit language in church. But now everything is done in English. It doesn't seem right to me. Sometimes while the rest are singing the Lord's Prayer, "Our Father, Who art in heaven" in English, I just sing silently to myself, "*O china ischsay nepissay*" in the Slavonic language. I can sing a lot of the Orthodox hymns in both Tlingit and the Slavonic language.

There were lots of church people in those days. This time, there's hardly any because we didn't even have a priest for ten years after Father Andrew Kashavaroff died. Ten years! But we continued to have services at the church. My husband used to read the Bible. The priest from Sitka would come over and open the royal doors because nobody but a priest can touch them.

When the Russian Orthodox celebrated Christmas, we used to go around caroling and carrying a big star from house to house. Everywhere people served us refreshments and gave us lots of money, which we turned over to the church.

We celebrated Christmas according to the old calendar, one or two weeks later. We knew where all the Orthodox church members lived and we went to those houses. People used to sit up all night waiting for us! It was always very cold, caroling all night, but we enjoyed ourselves so much that we didn't even mind. And after we were through, somebody would be waiting for us to serve us breakfast at their house.

Oh yes, we knew everybody. There were a lot of people, but most of the houses are torn down now. I'm just about the only one here now from way back. The rest are all other people.

I liked the village better back then. I knew friendly people. We cried together. We ate together. We laughed together. In those days when somebody passed away, you were right there to bring the body to the ANB Hall. And people would sit there with it. Nowadays it's not like that. Working people are always in a hurry to get away. I wouldn't mind to go back to the old way.

I was born right here and I was raised here but my ancestors are from Yakutat. Yakutat people were called Luk-Nas-Edee, and among the Ravens they were well-to-do because we were the tribe that brought the copper, they call it *ti-nah,* from Latuyu Bay all the way down the coast to Ketchikan. And people bartered copper for one slave, two slaves according to the size of the copper because copper was valued for knives. Our people were considered well-to-do because we had so many slaves.

That's why it used to be the prayer of an Indian woman to marry into the Luk-Nas-Edee tribe. And the men, too, they'd say, "I wish I could marry a Luk-Nas-Edee female."

When my sister got married, the Eagle tribe came to Juneau to talk to my dad, asking him for the hand of his daughter. Her name was Elsie. In the Indian way they were speaking for the bridegroom. There were Eagle representatives from Hoonah, from Sitka, from Taku, from Kluk-wan. Four branches.

And when Elsie died, I had those four tribes come here to act as a pallbearer, just like at her wedding. People represented Hoonah, Taku, Sitka, and Klukwan. Her husband was from Taku. That's why a Taku man had to be a pallbearer.

When I was first married, in 1929, I married a Sitka man, Dan Paul Kunz, a Kagwantan, the opposite tribe from me. When my sister got married, it was in an Indian way. Not me, though. Dan's family wanted my wedding like that, too, but my mother said no, "let her get married the white man's way because her father is already dead and cannot speak for her."

So we got married in the Russian church.

I had gone to Sheldon Jackson School in 1919 for one year. I only knew a few words of English before I went to Sheldon. Even now I can't carry on a conversation in English very well. My husband and I used to speak Tlingit at home.

Just very few of us can speak our Tlingit language now. Recently I started going to the senior citizens' lunch here in Juneau and I meet some of my old schoolmates and we talk about our school days at the government school here in Juneau when the government was keeping Indians away from the white school. It took the Alaska Native Brother-hood to break that.

The Alaska Native Brotherhood did a lot of things for our people. They fought racial discrimination. Signs, for instance in a beauty shop, "No Indians Allowed." And the Alaska Native Brotherhood fought that and brought it to the legislature here in Juneau. And I used to follow the people that talked there. That time in 1946 the antidiscrimination bill came on the floor, the senate chamber was so full the doors were open! People were standing on chairs so they could see and hear what was going on. Some of the lawmakers said mean things and some of us cried. They called the Indians mean names. One lawmaker said, "I'm not going to sit near a stinking Eskimo!" But the Alaska Native Brotherhood stood their ground and said that this was our land. One white lawmaker, he was so mad about that that he got up and kicked his chair back and he started to stampede out. Everybody booed him. But we made it. We won. It went through and the governor signed it—no discrimination in Alaska from then on!

# Leo Land

*Adopted by the Ravens*
*Haines*
*b. 1917*

*Leo Land is known throughout Southeast Alaska as the scourge of the letters-to-the-editor columns, quick to right any slight to military veterans. So at first glance this pen-wielding gadfly is an unlikely cross-cultural ambassador. But that is what he has been for the five decades since he married Edna James, a Tlingit Indian from Haines, Alaska.*

*As recently as the turn of the century Haines was a bastion of the Tlingit's Russian/Native culture but by 1940 the tribe suffered from discrimination, poverty, and addiction. Infantryman Leo Land faced anti-Native prejudice head on in 1940 when he married blinded-by-cataracts Edna James. Even Edna's mother, famed Chilkat robe weaver Jennie Thlunaut, was initially against the match because she worried about the hardships of mixed marriages in prejudice-prone Alaska.*

*However, this cook and ex-soldier was adopted by the Raven clan, counterpart to the Eagle clan, of which his wife was a member. Outsider Leo refused to dance in his own naming ceremony, but he won the hearts of many Ravens, thus his Tlingit name, Ah-Ka-Eesh, meaning "Kind Father" or "Best Father."*

**W**HAT DID Edna see in me? Well, I don't know! She *couldn't* see. She was so blinded by cataracts that she had had to quit school in the third grade.

What did she see in me? Maybe she liked my voice? I had met her shortly after I transferred up here from Spokane in the army in August 1939. There were four of us soldiers on an Alaskan steamer when we landed at Haines August 19. That fall I took a trip to Skagway on the

old *Fornace,* an army tug, and I met Edna on that boat. She was shy but
our eyes just locked, sparks flew, and that was it.

So on January 11, 1940, I went from Chilkoot Barracks down to
the Raven House in the Indian village to get permission to marry her.
Her mother, Jennie Thlunaut, disapproved of Natives marrying the
white people because she thought it caused too many problems. Which
was true. You couldn't go to shows, some restaurants. Even in the little
theater they had here, Natives had to go upstairs. And you had to sit on
one side or the other. You couldn't mix.

Oh, sure! Even in Juneau some restaurants were "No Natives Allowed." That's right!

In Haines the army had regulations which made the Native village
off-limits for soldiers. You could meet Natives uptown but you had to
stay out of the village. If you got caught, why, they'd throw you in jail
and bust ya.

When I got married, if they called me a squawman, that was a nice
word compared to their other words.

I was a quiet person. One day at the post as everyone came in for
early-morning coffee in the kitchen before breakfast, something came
up and I said something to a buck sergeant, which wasn't a slur against
him, but he said to me, "At least I didn't marry a shit eater."

Right there I turned white. It was lucky I didn't take the knife and
kill him. I was crying when I went in to see the first sergeant about it. I
said, "If he does it again, the least I'll do is punch him. I'll kill him!"

So the first sergeant told the buck sergeant, "Never say that word
again to Land or you'll be in deep trouble."

I didn't stay in the peacetime army long after that. But after I got
discharged in February 1940, I didn't have no job. My mother-in-law
and father-in-law accepted me and treated me just like their own son,
staying at their house in the village.

The Pioneer Bar kinda hesitated hiring me because I was married
to a Native even if they did allow Natives to drink at that bar. But I did
work there for thirteen months as a cook until Uncle Sam asked us re-
servists to volunteer for active duty. I talked it over with my wife and
went back in over here at Chilkoot Barracks.

I used to cook for the officers' parties once in a while. . . . One day
when we were out on the parade ground drilling, the lieutenant took
me out of formation and he talked to me for that whole thirty minutes.
"Please, you can move your wife and kid. You'll have your own quarters
if you cook for the bachelor officers." But I said, "No, I want to do
straight duty."

So then they took all the privates of both companies and sent us to

Sitka as longshoremen for the navy base there. We worked eighteen, twenty, twenty-two hours a day unloading ammunition and supplies, day after day. It was killing me and I ran away from Sitka and came back to Haines to be with my wife. I spent eighteen days in the guardhouse, mowing the lawn, and was court-martialed and fined five dollars and sent back to Sitka.

My first sergeant's name was Peasner. He would get drunk and go sleep in his tent for a day or two at a time and get away with it 'cause he was a first sergeant. But anybody else who was an hour late or something, he'd punish 'em with extra duty. That went on all the time and I wanted to punch him.

So I transferred to General Buckner's Alaska Scouts at Fort Richardson near Anchorage. Just before we were sent to the Aleutian Islands I went AWOL again to stay with my wife and baby. The Fourth Infantry left me alone until the day we were leaving and then they court-martialed me again from sergeant to private. Then in the Aleutians I served with my company at Adak [Station] and transferred to the Alaska Scouts.

In the meantime I had got my wife Edna moved up to Anchorage, where she worked at an Anchorage laundry. In fall 1943 I managed to transfer to the Anchorage 232d MPs at Fort Richardson so I could stay home with my wife and kids. But here she was bleeding from complications with her pregnancy, and all she needed to do was to go next door to phone an ambulance and they would take her out to the army hospital. But she didn't do that. She waited for dear old Leo, her hubby!

So here I come. I grabbed her at noon and I grabbed the landlady's car and drove through the MP gates and took her to the admitting desk. There was a civilian lady at the phone. She said, "The captain is eating. Take your wife in the little room there and wait." So we went in and Edna was sitting on a chair and she was Indian but she was pale and the blood started dripping on the floor.

That did it! I walked back in to that lady's desk and I hit the desk with my fist and that phone jumped a foot and I said, "You call that captain right now or I'm going to punch you in the face."

She did and boy was the captain mad 'cause Edna pretty near died getting out to the hospital.

At the hospital there was a master sergeant who happened to have her type of blood and it saved her life.

But I noticed immediately a change of attitude in her after that. From then on she was no longer that little meek lady that I had married. No. No more, "Yes, dear; no, dear." No more of that!

So I wanted to shake that man's hand for saving her life; then I wanted to punch him in the face for giving her that new feeling that she could outrank me by having a master sergeant's blood!

When I married Edna in 1940, the Tlingit culture was all brand-new to me. The same year I got married, the Ravens were having a convention and all the Indians of Southeast were invited. That was when they gave me the name Ah-Ka-Eesh because I had helped cure one of Edna's nieces who had white stuff running out of her eyes. A friend of mine was a medical corporal at Chilkoot Barracks and I asked him for some medicine 'cause I could see she was going to go blind. He gave me something which cleared her eyes up. We stole it! I put it in her eyes in the Raven House. (She's a grandmother now and can see fair, though she is still legally blind.)

They always have ceremonies when someone is adopted into the Raven Clan. They wanted me to put on robes and dance. But I bowed out and ducked. I'm no dancer. I'm too shy! I still won't do it!

But they named me Ah-Ka-Eesh, which means "Kind Father."

I had to make some adjustments when I started living at the Indian village. I had to learn to eat seal. Hunt seals. Call 'em. Make a noise and keep hidden while the seals come because they're curious.

I lived in the village after my discharge from the army in 1948. I liked living in the village because I liked the freedom and the honesty of the Indians, especially back in those years. Even now they respect each other unless they're under drugs or alcohol.

My grandkids . . . It's a tough deal for 'em because like any mixed race they're in between and get hell from both races.

My sons used to make eulachon oil, but I could never stand it. I hate castor oil or anything like that. I can eat seal if they don't use too much of it in their cooking. Some white people just go crazy over it. Herring eggs; I don't relish 'em! But all the family and the grandkids, they love 'em. Every one of 'em.

I don't know why.

# Jack McCahan

*Hanging Iron on the Dalton*
*North Pole*
*b. 1944*

*In a state so relatively devoid of roads it is remarkable the role roads have played in people's image of themselves as Alaskans. For instance, not long ago only hardy souls arrived from Outside via the Alcan—or Alaskan—Highway. There are still many people who define themselves by whether they live within the road system or beyond it in the Bush.*

*Jack McCahan drives an eighteen-wheeler across the wilderness on the Dalton Highway, the haul road to Prudhoe Bay. In the Brooks Range and on the North Slope he and the other drivers are jake braking and CBing their way into trucking history. But Jack is a modest, soft-spoken former Oregonian, once a logging truck driver and still so woodsy that he refers to his wife as "the old snag." His Alaska is a hunting and fishing paradise, and he is there for the long haul. Alaska trucking is a "real challenge," he says, but he would rather truck in Alaska than in any other state.*

EVERYBODY GOES off the road eventually, but I have only done it once in eight years. That's not too bad!

Winter of '87 I was going north down the Beaver Slide at about the one-hundred-twelve-mile marker on the Dalton Highway. Old Ray Wagner was a quarter mile ahead of me, already halfway down the Beaver Slide when I broke over the top. I never like to follow anybody real close down that hill in case something goes bad for them or me. Because the Beaver Slide is a long, long hill, about two, two and a half miles long from top to bottom.

Anyway, I always drop down in a fairly decent gear so I don't get running too fast. But this time when I started down off there onto the Beaver Slide, boy, it was slick! My tires, instead of rolling, they broke loose and started skidding. In other words I was going down the hill too slow; so to keep from sliding, I had to go with a higher gear—and *instantly,* if not quicker. I had to pick them gears up two or three at a time and get those tires rolling or else I was going to crash!

I ended up in the high hole coming down that hill and I was catching old Ray Wagner real fast. And another trucker was coming uphill toward us! My CB wasn't working and I couldn't holler at Ray to tell him to get going. By this time I was doing about seventy-five and I was real nervous. So I had only three choices. I had to either take her out over the bank into the snow or tail end Ray, which I wouldn't have done, or pull out around him and take that other guy head on—which I definitely wouldn't have done.

I held in there. It scared me to death, too. I held in there, and I just barely had enough room after that southbounder went by Ray Wagner, I just had time enough to whip out around his trailer end and let her go.

After that run down the Beaver Slide my knees were pretty shaky!

Before we get to them hills in the wintertime, we'd better be on the CB asking how slick they are. Like if I'm going north and I see headlights coming from the other direction, I say, "Hey, southbounder, what's it look like up there on Chandalar or Atigun, or Gobler's?" I have never known a driver yet to say, "It's good, go for it" and get up there and have it be real bad. We try to look out for one another. I have never heard of anyone setting a guy up to get into a bad spot. If you wreck a truck or dump a load of fuel . . . I don't care who it is, whether you like a guy or not, if you're up there in that cold weather and an old boy is broke down, you stop and help. You definitely don't leave another trucker sitting on that road freezing to death. Even back in '81, when the trucking outfits were going nonunion, the big boys in the Teamsters told their guys, "When you get out of town up on that north run, you're all brothers. If them strikebreakers need help, you help them."

Any kind of hill at all, if it's just a touch slick, it'll get you to spinning. If you're going up there at night and some ole boy has spun out an hour or so ahead of you and slicked up the road, and you go whizzing up there thinking it's cold enough for good traction and you get into his spinning marks, you're going to spin out and possibly go backward yourself. And sliding backwards feels terrible. You just think, "Oh gosh, what am I going to do?" And you start trying to get her in reverse and keep her straight to keep your wheels from spinning and locking up. You just do the best you can to get her stopped so you can get out and put on a set or two of chains.

After a year or two running up there, you get real used to hanging iron, I'll guarantee ya. You chain up quite frequent when it's slick or you'll go off the road.

When the road's right in winter, good traction and good weather, the Dalton is really good truckin'. I like it! I really do. There's lots of times in winter when the weather's good and there's no fresh snow, just cold, and you might go several trips and never have to put on a set of chains. You just run up and back.

Lots of times it can be good all the way until about sixty-two miles out of Prudhoe Bay. That's where Pump Station Two is on the pipeline. From there on in to Prudhoe Bay it's all flat, and lots of times that wind will blow for two or three days and make big drifts across the road. If you don't just absolutely have to go through one of them blows, you're better off to set back a few miles out of it. Because when you get into one of them whiteouts, I guarantee you won't hardly be able to see the end of your hood. 'Cause it blows terrible bad. I don't know anything on the haul road which will make a guy's nerves worse!

There's no big canyons or nothing up there on the Slope, just a four- or six-foot drop-off. But it's bad because if you get in them blows and get stuck in a drift, your truck will suck a lot of snow up in the air breathers and when they get plugged up, they quit running. That means you're going to get really cold. And if it's thirty below and you have about a fifty-mile-an-hour wind, you better have some real good survival gear or you're going to die. I guarantee it.

# Con Miller

*When Santa Comes into the Country*
*North Pole*
*b. 1913*

*Con Miller is so identified with Santa Claus in his hometown of North Pole that he even named his daughter Merry Christmas! The Millers are also identified with politics. One son worked his way up through the state house of representatives to become lieutenant governor. Cancer cut short that career in 1989, but another son is now accumulating house seniority. "We're quite a political family," says Con.*

I WAS NAMED after my grandfather, Conrad Mueller. My father, Bob, changed our name from Mueller to Miller when he came up to Alaska to hunt gold. He hadn't found any and had returned Outside, but I had been excited by his stories.

I was born in Colorado and I got all my schooling in Wyoming. My wife and I had just gone from town to town getting small jobs. There was no future in that, and in 1950 we made up our minds to go north. I and my wife and two sons and a dog, we started out to Alaska in an old 1936 Chevrolet with bad tires.

We had a hard time at the border because they asked us to show so much money but we only had about a hundred dollars. But it was all in one-dollar bills, and when the Canadian customs man asked how much I had, I said I had several hundred. He said, "Can I see it?" And I flipped through all those bills. "Oh," he said, "you've got plenty of money."

Fifty miles inside the border we saw a truck drive up, and the fella who ran the place just dropped everything and said I could go ahead and finish filling up. He yelled, "The mailman's here!"

After the mailman had handed out mail and packages and had driven away, I asked what was so interesting about the mailman. "Well, we only see him once a week. He takes our money to the bank and he does this and he does that."

After the border I remember that we had enough money to stop for one pretty good meal as we fought our way up the Alaska Highway. I could make about fifty miles without a blowout. Then I'd have to stop and fix it and go another twenty-five or fifty miles. It was that way all the way through to Anchorage.

I didn't like the looks of Anchorage and neither did my wife. I said, "Let's go up to Fairbanks."

We stopped at a trading camp on the way to Fairbanks and hocked my gun for some gas.

When we were close to Fairbanks, I got to thinking about how excited those people had been about the arrival of that mailman with his deliveries. So when we got to Fairbanks, we got two old Quonset huts and put them together and made a store. And soon I went out on a circling route to peddle cheap stuff to the Natives in the villages.

Each Native had a government check, so they had money. Many spent it on booze, but a lot of 'em didn't. My business just grew and grew and grew and I upgraded my merchandise. And the more I upgraded, the better everything sold.

Anyway, it come Christmastime 1950. I had made a contact with a store that handled damaged materials. And in a box from them I found a beautiful Santa Claus suit. I put it on. (That was damn cold in the wintertime!) And my wife made up a lot of little packages and I bought three bottles of whiskey for some of the old-timers that I knew.

Well anyway, I went out on Christmas in my 1936 Chevrolet and I stopped at every house and every village on the way. And that was the first time they had ever seen a walking, talking Santa Claus!

When I first came into a village, they were afraid. But they knew the old Chevrolet from my trips before, so they guessed that I must have something to do with that suit. That went over so big with all the people that I was able to establish a good route.

I only went three years because we moved our store out from Fairbanks to North Pole in 1952. This area out here was growing. There were five or six homesteader cabins and a couple of houses. They called it North Pole because one of the old homesteaders, when he went into town, they kidded him for being from the North Pole because this spot had the record of the coldest temperature in Alaska. So I was going to call this the North Pole Trading Post.

One day when I was digging out the basement, a carload of Natives from down south came in and spotted me. And, of course, by now they knew I was the guy with the Santa Claus suit. A kid rolled the window down and said, "What are you doing, Santa Claus, building a new house?"

I thought that was so cute that I named my new trading post the Santa Claus House. An old-timer who was a painter came up over the road and offered to paint the place Santa Claus colors. He even put lights that went off and on. And that's what started the Santa Claus House and post office at 511 Santa Claus Lane. I was postmaster.

There have been so many experiences as Santa Claus over the years. The first year I wore the suit—which I still wear every Christmas—a fella passed me real fast on the highway. Later he stopped and I honked and waved at him as I went by. He saw me, threw his hands up, and he went into the bank.

The following year was something that really makes me feel good. A couple with their daughter, they had come up to Alaska like we had come up. They had come up to look around to see what the opportunities were. It was at Christmastime 1953, and they were having lunch in one of the camps along the road when I came in with my Santa Claus suit and ringing a beautiful set of bells. That little girl almost went wild!

Later they lived over here and they told me why she had been so excited. All the way north the little girl had been saying that she didn't mind going to Alaska but that "Santa Claus won't know where I'm at."

This woman said, "When you walked in that door, I almost fell off my chair."

The girl jumped up and down, "He's here, he's here!"

That made her Christmas!

# Debbie S. Miller

*Arctic Classroom*
*Fairbanks*
*b. 1951*

*In 1975 at age twenty-three Debbie Miller found herself attempting to teach tra-
ditional junior high subjects to Athabaskan kids in Arctic Village, one hundred
miles north of the Arctic Circle on the south slope of the Brooks Range. An ideal-
istic cheechako from the Bay Area, Debbie soon discarded her past teaching experience to learn from the parents of her Gwich'in-speaking students. While she was
teaching sixth, seventh, and eighth graders, her husband, Dennis, was creating a
high school in the living room of the Millers' shack. With the help of a bilingual
assistant he made it possible for Arctic Village's teens to attend high school locally.
He had no chalkboard but he scrounged butcher paper, felt-tip pens, and books.
His small kitchen table had to seat five kids while the others sat on the couch. "It
was pretty folksy," remembers Debbie.*

*After two years the Millers left teaching to live in an isolated wilderness
setting. They built a cabin thirty miles into the Bush from Arctic Village, and
Dennis became a pilot, surveying caribou, wolves, and moose. Debbie spent more
and more time in the Arctic National Wildlife Refuge. Over the past fifteen years
she has explored more than one thousand miles of the Arctic Refuge on foot and
by kayak. Her arctic experiences became the basis for her 1990 book,* Midnight
Wilderness.

*Debbie Miller's story is part of the changing of the guard among Alaska's
conservationists. Her heroine is Margaret Murie, one of Alaska's best-loved writers,
who moved to Fairbanks for the 1911 gold rush and became the first woman to
graduate from the University of Alaska. After marrying pioneer wildlife biologist
Olaus Murie in 1924, Mardy spent many years living in the Arctic wilderness.*

*Mardy's influence on Debbie is partly her deep concern for wilderness but also her compassion and exuberance for life. Mardy is now in her late eighties yet still cross-country skis, hikes, and works with students at the Teton Science School. Debbie, now a mother of two, shares Mardy's enthusiam for life. It stood her in good stead in 1975 in the hunter-gatherer culture of northeast Alaska's Brooks Range.*

THE WILDERNESS is why we live in Alaska. It either gets in your blood or it doesn't and you leave. Our first wilderness experience was through the eyes of the parents at Arctic Village.

Coming from the Bay Area, I had never seen caribou-head soup before. Nor did I expect to see eight-year-olds out getting their ground squirrels from their own trap lines. But because children are brought up to appreciate all the wild game that surrounds them, they prefer dried fish, dried meat for snacks.

School begins at the end of August in the village, and that traditionally is when the caribou come back. We came into the community just when some caribou had been harvested. We had bought about a year's supply of food and shipped it up, but it had not arrived yet. The people were very warm and generous and gave us portions of the caribou. Some of the elders sewed us caribou mittens and caribou legskin boots.

The freshly killed caribou was a surprise. In California we had eaten lots of vegetables and salads, not meat, and then here we were in Arctic Village, where the meat-eating culture was a tremendous change in diet for us. We ate mainly caribou (and occasionally moose) for about six or seven years. We grew to love eating wild game.

Villagers utilize every part of the caribou. From the bones they can make various tools. The hides they use for clothing and bedding. What impressed me most was not only that they went out and hunted for this wild game but also that nothing was wasted.

Looking back on my almost twenty years in Alaska, I realize now that I was the one who learned the most in my Arctic classroom. I still have a close connection with my old students (now young adults) and co-workers from Arctic Village. Today I am fighting to keep the Arctic Refuge wild, just as Arctic Village people and their Athabaskan neighbors are protecting their way of life by fighting development pressures. We are still working together.

*The following passage is from Debbie Miller's* Midnight Wilderness:

Along Datchanlee, which means "timberline" in Gwich'in, I can picture the canvas wall tents of many Arctic Village families, dotting the ridge near the edge of timber, with hunters nearby in search of the returning caribou. I can smell smoke from the campfire, the steaming black tea brewed in an old blackened coffee can, a caribou head roasting beneath a tripod of spruce branches, and the pungent scent of a ground squirrel's fur coat singed off by the fire.

I can picture young children with their fathers and mothers walking near camp, checking their ground squirrel traplines, and hunting for ducks at nearby ponds and lakes; old women, their weathered skin coffee-dark at summer's end, sitting in tents on caribou hides cushioned by underlying spruce boughs, sewing intricate beadwork designs on handtanned whitened caribou hides, making caribou-skin boots and mittens for their grandchildren, and telling stories in Gwich'in that have been passed down from generation to generation.

I remember the stories of several elders who vividly recalled accounts of starvation during their lifetimes. There have been years when the caribou, the life and blood of these people for thousands of years, were not to be found. Elders remember the extremely cold winters where ptarmigan and fall-caught ground squirrels were the only sources of food for survival. It was not unusual to hear stories of some family members dying of starvation. There was a time, not so far in the past, when caribou hooves were used to make soup when there was nothing, or little, to eat. One day I saw an elder hanging hooves on a spruce tree near her camp, and I asked her what she planned to do with them. She told me that she still saved the hooves for survival, for "hard times."

It's not surprising that today's Arctic Village residents, along with Athabaskan residents in several other villages in Alaska and Canada, are vehemently opposed to the oil companies' industrializing the calving grounds of the Porcupine caribou herd, a herd that has sustained their people and ancestors for at least ten to fifteen thousand years. The idea of tampering with a zone where tens of thousands of caribou bear their young is unthinkable to those who have depended on the herd; and there is scientific evidence that a major oilfield development, with the activities of up to six thousand people and the proposed web of roads, pipelines, and facilities, would indeed disturb the caribou. As predicted in the Department of Interior's 1002 report to Congress, the caribou would suffer the effects of habitat modification, reduced access to insect-relief habitat, and displacement from preferred calving areas. It is expected that such loss of habitat and related disturbances will change the distribution of the Porcupine caribou herd, and, the report notes, there is risk that a population decline could occur.

In the words of one resident, as spoken at a 1988 [U.S. Fish and Wildlife Service] hearing in Arctic Village: "I don't depend on that damn oil. . . . I'd rather have my land right in my hand. I'd rather have piece of meat right on my table. That's what I've been raised up on. Not only me, but all these one hundred people right in Arctic Village . . . How are we going to live without caribou?"

Another resident, Timothy Sam, spoke of conserving resources for the future: "Let's save it. You got kids . . . You got to think about them. If we use up everything: our resources, the oil, and so on . . . what will our kids use in the future? Let's not deal with now. Let's deal with tomorrow or the next day. We don't have to go up there and drill it. We got no business. We got kids . . ."

**The Reverend Peter Askoar**
*Russian Mission*

**George Attla**
*North Pole*

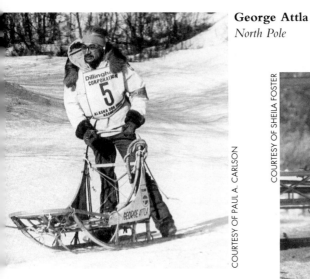

**Porky Bickar**
*Sitka*

**Buster Benson**
*Haines*

**Al Brookman, Sr.**
*Sitka*

**Sharon and
Chris Butcher with
daughter Meryl**
*Talkeetna*

**Roxy Wright Champaine**
*Salcha*

**Henry Chapman
(second from right)**
*Anvik*

**The Anvik Mission**

**Jeff
"Coggie"
Coghill**
*Nenana*

**Helmi Conatser**
*Eagle Island*

**Doug Geeting**
*Talkeetna*

**Vernon Evan**
*Marshall*

**Timothy and Anna Gologergen with granddaughter Gillie and daughter June**
*St. Lawrence Island*

**Peter Hackett**
*Anchorage*

Mary Hansen & Her Siberian Team    Big Delta, Alaska

**Mary Lenzi Hansen**
**(from an old postcard)**
*Big Delta*

**Wally Hickel**
*Anchorage*

**Olaf Hansen**
*Wrangell*

**Mark and David Hickok**
*Anchorage*

**Gayla Hites**
*Skagway*

**Steven Hites**
*Skagway*

**Pete Isleib**
*Juneau*

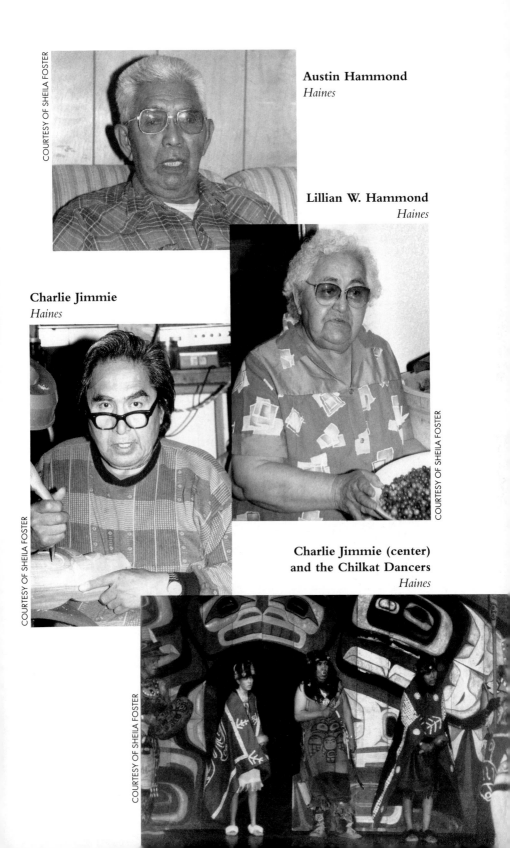

**Austin Hammond**
*Haines*

**Lillian W. Hammond**
*Haines*

**Charlie Jimmie**
*Haines*

**Charlie Jimmie (center)
and the Chilkat Dancers**
*Haines*

**Bruce Johnstone**
*Ketchikan*

**Cecilia "Kin-Too" Kunz**
*Juneau*

**Wolf House dedication**
*Sitka*

**Jack McCahan**
*North Pole*

**Debbie S. Miller**
*Fairbanks*

**Rie Muñoz**
*Juneau*

**Walter Northway**
*Northway*

**Anne Hobbs Purdy**
*Chicken*

**Senator Bill Ray**
*Juneau*

**Vi and Joe Redington, Sr.**
*Wasilla*

**Monty Richardson (left)
with the author**
*Seward*

**Josephine Roberts**
*Tanana*

**Ollie "Pigooruk"
St. Germaine**
*Point Hope*

**Norma Jean Saunders**
*Anchorage*

**Mary Shields**
*Fairbanks*

**Willie Smalley, Jr.**
*Marshall*

**Larry and Shelia Smith**
*Sitka*

**Molly Smith**
*Douglas*

**Bill Spear**
*Juneau*

**Connie Taylor (center)**
*Cordova*

**Drenda Tigner**
*Fairbanks*

**Jack and Edie Trambitas**
*Juneau*

**J. D. True**
*Skagway*

**Tishu Ulen**
*Wiseman*

**Joe Vogler**
*Woodchopper*

**Lee Wallace**
*Saxman*

**Marleita Davis Wallace**
*Wrangell*

**Orville Wheat**
*Juneau*

# Rie Muñoz

*Smiles on Their Faces*
*Juneau*
*b. 1921*

*One of Rie Muñoz's favorite artists is Marc Chagall. His angels floating over Russian shtetls are not Rie's levitating Eskimos, but they share an airy effervescence that brings a smile to our lips.*

*Reared in Holland, Rie Muñoz is a self-taught watercolorist and probably Alaska's most prominent contemporary artist. Each year she does about eighty paintings, of which a dozen become prints. She is well known in the Seattle art scene (still the sign of success for an Alaskan artist), but no Outsider would mistake her colorful fishermen, Natives, kicker boats, drying fish, and staked-out dogs for anything but Alaskan motifs.*

I CAME TO Alaska in 1950. At that time I was working at the Broadway Department Store in Los Angeles decorating windows. And I had a vacation coming up. I had X dollars and I was trying to figure out where the heck could I go on this money. So what I did was make a radius from Los Angeles to the distance I thought I could go and I made a circle and the most interesting spot it hit was Juneau. So I went on a passenger boat from Vancouver and got here. The boat was going on to Skagway, then back to Juneau and Vancouver again.

It was one of the old Canadian steamships, the *Louise*.

When the *Louise* landed here on the first of June, the sun was shining and it was just magnificent. Gorgeous mountains (which you can't see now). So I thought, "I'm going to get off here and see if I can get a job and a place to stay while the boat goes up to Skagway and back. And if I can, I'll just take off my suitcase and stay. If I can't, I'll go back to the Broadway Department Store."

Anyhow, I got a five-dollars-a-week room and a job at the newspaper doing political cartoons. And that taught me the discipline to quit fooling around and to finish something. I read the *Empire* at night and then did a cartoon for the next day's paper pertaining to the local news of the day. This was a lot of fun and very good practice.

Gosh, when I came here, this place really inspired me to paint! There were no galleries in town at all, just an annual art show, but I did some pictures for it and they all sold. So that was very encouraging.

Then I started painting more and more until a bookstore finally asked me if I would put my paintings and stencil prints in their window, and they sold quite well.

Soon I married a geologist, Juan Muñoz, and we often went prospecting in our boat throughout Southeast Alaska, especially to Prince of Wales Island, and stopped in at Native villages to buy supplies. I liked to sketch those villages and the bush cabins where we stopped to visit.

Then in 1951, to make a grubstake, we decided we'd take teaching jobs. We went to the BIA [Bureau of Indian Affairs] and asked for a remote village because if you go to a remote village, you can't spend any money. My former husband, Juan Muñoz, did have a degree in geology. I didn't have any degree, but they were hard up in those days and so they took us for King Island, which is a tiny island in the Bering Sea. And I did a heck of a lot of sketches there and at Nome during those nine months.

Soon I met an artist named Diana Tillion, who had come here because her husband was in the legislature, and we went to places like Haines together to sketch old canneries. Then she and I and Juneau artist Dale De Armond went often to St. Lawrence Island to paint and to Nome and Kotzebue. Those places were very different then. One of the reasons I enjoyed sketching them so much was because I realized that their lifestyle was not going to last. I wanted to capture my feeling of the lifestyle there even if my paintings weren't photographically accurate.

People in those places loved to fish and hunt and gather berries. That was their whole lifestyle. Almost everywhere I went there were a few people that were really helpful. Like when I went to Gambell on St. Lawrence Island, I stayed at the university house, which belonged to the University of Alaska. And the caretaker of that was a man called Walter Slwoko and he was a little bit of a grump but his wife was incredibly helpful. You know, when you go to some of those villages, people are wondering what the heck are you doing there. Mrs. Slwoko was, as one woman to another, very helpful. She built us string games and gave us clues about what to do and where to go. Her village was very small, only about five hundred people. So we walked all over and sketched all the time and could pretty well see what was going on ourselves. Furthermore, what Mrs. Slwoko thought was interesting, like a gorgeous sunset, might not interest me at all. It was the everyday life in the village which interested me.

I have a hard time saying that I have a favorite village person because I really don't know them well at all. There is one person in Noatak who sticks out in my mind just now because she was quite an old woman, but her house was full of little kids. Here she was cleaning a nice big salmon on the table with about seven or eight little kids walking around. I said, "Are these your grandchildren?" And she said that they were children from parents who had gotten into drugs or alcohol and could not take care of them. I thought that was a sad and remarkable thing to see.

Once I overheard someone asking somebody, "Do you know Rie Muñoz's art?" "No, I don't." "Well, wait till you see it. Everybody in her pictures, they always have a big smile on their faces." And I said, "You're wrong. I've only done one picture with a smile." But they get that feeling because they put a smile on *their* face. It's kind of neat.

The one picture that does have a smile on someone's face, it's called *Loose Dogs in Gambell*. Once when I was there, a dog had broken loose. They're tied up all the time on a chain, and so when they break loose, they go ape and run all over the countryside. And very often they visit other dogs, who get so excited that they break loose, too. So this time there was a lot of yelling and screaming in the town and everyone was yelling, "The dogs are coming. Don't run! Don't run!" All the six women I was with, they huddled together, myself included, because no way was I going to run. There was a little kid there, and as these dogs whizzed by he laughed. He thought it was great fun!

So that's my only smiling picture. This little kid has a smile on his face.

I usually spend a week to ten days in a village and I just walk around. I just came back from Kotzebue five days ago and Atlin just before that.

When I go to a village to sketch, I take color notes, shorthand for what color everything is. And then I come home to paint it and I use any old color I want.

I never loosened up until I started painting with watercolors. One reason was that canvas and paints are pretty expensive, and so I wanted to do it perfectly right. But that was a big handicap. With watercolor, I can slap it on and if it's no good, I just throw it out. And I throw out a lot!

Later, when I am in my Juneau studio ready to paint, I do a bunch of two-by-three-inch attempts until I get what I want. Then I ink it in and project it onto a piece of watercolor paper on the wall so I can lightly trace the major points.

I sketch in bright colors because I feel very good when I'm sketching. I'm a bright-color person. Other artists feel great about the mountains and yet do them in gray colors. I feel really good about my subjects, and so I want to celebrate that by doing them in bright colors.

# Sadie Brower Neakok

*Iñupiaq Judge*
*Barrow*
*b. 1916*

*Misperceptions between Native and Anglo individuals have long been an under-current of northern life, often with tragic results. Sadie Brower Neakok is an in-spiring teacher, welfare worker, and judge who has not only bridged the gap be-tween the Eskimo and white cultures but also made it easier for others to move between these two poles of Alaskan life.*

*Charles Brower was the first white settler in Barrow, America's northern-most town. He operated a whaling station there in the late nineteenth century and a fur-trading post thereafter. He married an Eskimo woman named Asiang-gataq and had ten children, including Sadie Brower. Educated Outside, Sadie re-turned to Barrow, married an Iñupiaq whaler named Nate Neakok, and raised thirteen children of her own plus many foster children. Sadie was appointed to be a bush magistrate in 1960, and her work eventually established the precedent of using Native languages in court when the defendant did not know English. The following reflections are taken from Margaret B. Blackman's* Sadie Brower Neakok: An Iñupiaq Woman.

THERE WERE blunders, too, in my work, where I got so scared, going forward on my own without any orders. Like we were instructed to never use our native language in court, but here was this man who couldn't speak a word of English. The state trooper brought this charge before me, and I arraigned the man. What had happened was that he was charged with petit larceny, taking something away from the base area that was surplus, that to his mind was good stuff that he was going to put to use with his family who needed it. But he didn't tell the superiors that he was going to take some of the stock, and when the state trooper apprehended him, he knew he had made a mistake, and he refunded everything that he had taken.

But here this case came up, and the trooper never told me anything about him refunding the stock, and he pled guilty. I was speaking my native tongue all the time. I advised him of his rights, and he said he didn't want to use his rights, he wanted to waive them and admit to the charge that was before him. We did it in such a manner it was on record—tape—and I had to interpret the whole thing so the court system would know what the case was all about. But I didn't know that base up there was federal property, and the trooper made a state charge instead of a federal charge out of it. So four days later the federal authorities arrest this man and take him to Anchorage before a federal court. I got this phone call over at the Wien Airlines terminal from the chief justice of the Alaska Court System about that case.

I was asked to come to Anchorage and demonstrate how I arraigned this man. "Did I, in fact, have so-and-so in my court on a charge?" "Yes. The state trooper brought the charge, and I heard it, and this case was disposed of." "Well, we want you to come down and demonstrate before the federal courts how you did it." I had to go down there. And I had never been in a big courthouse, let alone in a robe. And they railroaded me into this big courthouse and put a robe on me, and as the prisoner was being brought in, we all had to stand for the gavel. This we did in my court when I came in, but not that formally. My heart was in my throat. I explained that I did it all in my native tongue because there was no alternative. There was no way that I could make this man understand what his rights were until I used his own native language.

So they bring in the prisoner, and who should it be but that same man I had arraigned who didn't know one word of English. As they brought him in he was looking down, and he looked up and he recognized me and you should have seen the beam on his face: "Hi, Sadie!" Right there in the courthouse. No formality of any kind, not knowing why he was being brought there, but recognizing me. He didn't even know I was there, but when he looked up and recognized me, the smile on his face, and then for him to say, "Hi, Sadie!"

And then I demonstrated. Well, after I demonstrated to them, I told him in Eskimo, "We have to go all through the same thing we went through in Barrow." And he did beautifully. He pled guilty. And then I asked the state trooper what was the charge there, was this true? Because when someone gives himself up to me on a plea of guilty or admission of guilt or *nolo contendere,* then you ask the defendant if he has anything to say where we might show cause for leniency. He came up with the statement that he did let the trooper know that he [had] returned all the items he was charged with, and [that] they were back at the base. And then I asked the trooper, "Is this true?" He said, "Yes, it is true." "Well, why didn't you mention it?" And then they knew what kind of a person I was. I wanted the full information on any case that came up before me. I told them I was stumped: I couldn't read his rights in English; he couldn't make head nor tails out of it; and he didn't know anything about the law, nor did he know that he stole. He was just taking something that was going to be thrown away—he just took advantage of it—and so, all those things, they [had] never [come] out.

The court system had planted some people in the back, listeners who were from my town, to record and to translate back in English what I had said in court about the man's rights. When it was all over, I was told, "The chief justice would like to see you in his chambers." My heart is still in my throat, and I thought, "This is where I get thrown out." I was so scared. But when I got to his door, there he was in a white shirt just relaxing, smoking his pipe in his chamber. And he said, "Hi, Sadie." The voice that he greeted me with had no hurt in it whatsoever, and he said, "That was the most wonderful demonstration you performed. From now on, it will be a rule of the court to use the language of the people." So from there on [c. 1964], they started using the native language.

Having been born and grown up here, there was a time when there wasn't drinking. It started coming up after the base was settled. Our menfolks and our young people started consuming alcohol, and I could see where the fights were coming from—assault and battery, assault with dangerous weapon, or whatever. The laws say that you cannot use alcohol as an excuse and bring it into court—"Because I was drunk, I don't remember doing it." Well, you can't use leniency, because he was drunk and did this. In evaluating cases, most of the time, if that type of complaint came in and it was signed by some member of [the] family caught in the same situation [also drunk], automatically when they sobered up, they were no longer fighting, they were friends again. If they had broken anything, if they had wrecked something, I would take the criminal charge away, and let them pay restitution, and just let them go— with warnings that they could go to jail for a certain amount of months or days the next time. And it worked. So, much of my feeling went into my work, and I talked to my people. And knowing them was even harder, because I couldn't believe some of the charges against my own people, when the law says drunkenness is no excuse to do an act. That was even harder for my people to believe, when they sobered up, that they did something like that. Shameful.

My main concern in that job was to make my people learn about the law, and to learn about what rights they had. Some would be mad at me, because they were held in jail and didn't know what their rights were. At arraignments they would ask, "What is that?" And it used to take me fifteen or twenty minutes longer to try and explain and make my people understand what their rights were—rights to a lawyer, rights to remain silent, and oh, they had many rights that I had to read to them. And when that initial period was over, then it was much easier for me to hold court. And when the city adopted all the misdemeanor laws as city ordinances, on Monday mornings my courthouse was like a schoolhouse. I had so many the police had picked up over the weekend, when liquor first came into Barrow in the early sixties, and I had to find out a system to take care of each and every one of those as fast as I could. So I used to let them line up in front of me, and I divided them into who could understand English and who could not understand English. I was asked to use my native tongue to make them understand what their rights were. So, I could read their rights to the ones who were able to speak English and understand it, and have them line up. And then the ones who were not able to understand fully what the English language was all about, then I would do it in my native tongue. And then their charges are right in front of me; so like a school roll call, I would call each name and ask them, one by one. And when a person admitted to the charge before me, there were set fines. If it was an ordinance-violation [that] the city had given me on a first offender, it was a suspended sentence. If the same offense was committed for a second time that month, then a ten dollar fine. The third one, the fine tripled, until you had five or six charges against you. Then it became a state matter, instead of a city ordinance.

I was in the habit of searching for solutions to better our situations, because by Monday I would have thirty or forty cases in the morning— the same alcohol-related charges. The police that we had there would just throw them in jail. Or, if they were transporting liquor while under the influence, that was another charge—one of the ordinances, too. You could just walk out your door here with a can of beer and get arrested. Your property didn't mean that you were in your own private prop-erty—didn't mean a thing to the police, because we didn't own our property then. We were squatters on the land until BIA decided they would give us the lots and area where our houses were, and they were sectioned off. But before that it was such that you were a violator under the city ordinances, and I was collecting all these fines and making some six or seven thousand dollars a month at the time for the city through their ordinances, because the fines stayed in the community. In those days the menfolks and most everyone in this community were earning big wages, and those fines didn't mean a thing. It wasn't a punishment to them. They would go back, walk out of the courthouse and do the same thing, and they would be right back in my courthouse. They just handed the fine over, and the city was getting richer fast from those ordinance violations.

So, when that didn't seem like a punishment to the people, then I went to the council and asked if there were some way we could put these people on a work release program, clean up program, or help out somebody in need with building their home, or whatever. And oh, you should have seen the effects of that one. People who came from well-respected families said, "Oh, I'm not going to be seen out there doing silly work—clean up, or. . . ." "Either that, or you sit in jail." It was a choice. And that jail we had wasn't a very pleasant place to be. The solution wasn't very popular, and people hated me for that, because people who classed themselves well-to-do did not like to be seen out there in the street, cleaning up because they had been picked up. That was the most effective sentencing in those times, to put somebody on a work-release program. People didn't like it, and they started thinking about themselves.

In the matter of sentencing, I waited until I looked into the family situation. Sometimes this is [unorthodox], but it was my practice. I knew the people, but I had to get more information—why this was happening, if it was a repeated offense. If I had to sentence a person on their plea of guilty, or if they were found guilty, I had to look into the background of the family, or ask questions of the defendant after the case was all formed, that might allow me to show leniency or give me an idea what type of sentencing would be proper. Then I would have to explain why I am giving it. It helped to look into the family matters at times.

In areas like Fairbanks and Anchorage my system would never work, because I wouldn't know the people. But I made it a point, if I didn't know the person standing before me, to ask them questions—where he is from, and how long he has been here, and how long he expects to stay, and what type of work he is doing—those types of questions. I wanted to know the whole story so I could evaluate the case properly before me and get to the core of it, what caused it. And after a plea of guilty or a no-contest plea, then I could ask that person to give me his views, what he felt, talk to me freely so it wouldn't happen again.

They did talk freely; they never kept back. And later on, some of the whites who were looking down on me got to know me better. They didn't shun me anymore. That was quite hard to come to, and they found me a different person. Sometimes they would knock on my door and come in and apologize for their attitude.

# Walter Northway

## My First White Man
## Northway
## b. 1876

*Walter Northway, of the Northeast Interior village of Northway, has lived from the end of the Stone Age to the space age. He has gone from a hunting and gathering culture to one in which men walk on the moon. The following reminiscences are from the 1987 book* Walter Northway *based upon a 1982 interview in Upper Tanana Athabaskan by Shirley Jimerson.*

I WAS BORN June 10, 1876, near Moose Creek, where we call it *K'ehthiign*. I was the third child out of eight. I had three sisters, Elsie, Laura, and Maggie. I had four brothers, Bill, Lee, Danny, and Stephen. My grandmother was *Ts'ist'e'*, meaning "Old Medicine Woman." My father was *T'aaiy Ta'*, meaning "Strongman." Later he was called Northway. My mother was *Ts'attleegn*, a nickname meaning "funny blanket," because when she was born they wrapped her in a ragged blanket. Her real name was *Ts'atch'iil*. Later she was known as Anna.

Captain Northway came by steamboat up to Nabesna. He was going to the Chisana gold rush. He met my father, *T'aaiy Ta'*. He gave him the name Northway. This was around 1908.

The steamboat used to stop at the mouth of Moose Creek. I can remember seeing a lot of boats with a lot of men going up to the Chisana gold rush. We used to sell them moccasins and meat. Then we would buy tea, rice, tobacco, flour, and other things from them.

I was fourteen when I saw my first white man. My dad and I were hunting ducks by the mouth of the Chisana River. We came to that point by moose-skin canoe from *K'ehthiign*. We were hunting with bow and arrows. My dad and I were on the bank roasting ducks and making tea. I told my dad that I wanted to go for a walk. While walking down by the river, I heard voices, weird voices that didn't sound like us.

I ran back to my dad and told him I heard voices and they didn't sound like us. He told me to watch for them.

They came straight to us. Their clothes were ragged, shoes torn. They were starving. They came to where we were roasting ducks.

When they saw the ducks roasting, they asked for them. My dad clapped his hands over his ears, letting them know that he did not understand them. Then they pointed to the ducks and made motions that they were hungry.

Dad split the ducks in half for them and gave them tea. When Dad gave them the ducks, they were very hot. The men dipped the ducks in a puddle of water nearby to cool them off so they could eat them fast.

After they were done, I took one of the men across the river in my canoe and came back for my dad and the other white man. Then Dad and the white man walked over to *K'ehthiign*. I traveled back by boat.

Kids all surrounded the men when they got to our camp. They stayed with us until they regained their strength. They worked and helped us. Then they asked my dad if anybody could lead them to the Chisana gold rush. Joe Demit's dad, *K'ost'un'*, and Chief Sam guided them. After these two, white men came like ants.

# Dorie O'Toole

*In Hot Water*
*Tenakee Springs*
*b. 1915*

*At Tenakee Springs on Chichagof Island a fissure of one-hundred-six-degree bathwater became the basis for Ed Snyder's general store in 1899. By 1990 the community numbered over one hundred souls, mostly spread out along the town's only street, a shoreline trail named Tenakee Avenue.*

*By all accounts this predominantly white town has been a close-knit community. Dorie O'Toole, longtime storekeeper, says, "For the most part if something happens to somebody, everyone gets together and helps. Tenakee is like a big family." When local residents decided to invite the state ferry to stop at Tenakee Springs twenty-five years ago, however, outside influences began to change what had always been a down-home hunting and fishing life-style. Improved access brought a surge in housing values as rough cabins became expensive second homes for Juneau folk. And when television arrived, folks stayed home to watch it instead of going down to the dock to see the ferry, bathe at the pool, or kibitz at the store. With telephones, suddenly people could phone each other rather than walk down the path to chitchat.*

*Dorie O'Toole "helped with the bookkeeping and waited on trade" at the general store. She says that coming as a cheechako from Seattle, she did not know what to expect. The books she had read made Alaska sound like "a land of ice and snow, and no fresh meat, and everybody traveling by dogsled."*

DERMOTT AND I flew out from Juneau in a little plane and landed on the water here. That was quite an experience for me. And there were more Natives here at that time than there are now. Some of 'em would sit on the floor in the store and nurse their babies. The children spoke very broken English because they spoke their own language at home. They would come in the store and say, "I want one candy bar." And I'd ask, "Well, do you want any more?" "No. One candy bar." And I'd get 'em their change. "I'll have one more candy bar." They could only figure out their cash for one.

At first I had a hard time understanding the Natives. One came in to ask for a herring net. I thought he wanted a hair net! And, of course, when they came in and asked for twenty-two shorts, you didn't know whether to go to the underwear section or the ammunition.

Then there was one Finnish fellow that wanted *fiddley rings*. I had him repeat it, *"Fiddley rings?"* I said, "Can you see 'em anyplace?" Finally, he said he'd wait till my husband came back. What he wanted were violin strings. Fiddling strings.

Once a cook from one of the seine boats was in, buying supplies, and he was standing near the shaving mirrors. And he said, "Give me one of these mirrors. I'm tired of the guys swipin' my pancake turner."

The baths were very democratic. We women went in in the nude after leaving our clothes up in the dressing room. We exchanged recipes and news about our children while we were sitting around in the pool. And the men, my husband always told me about all the deer that were shot and all the fish that were caught down in the bathhouse.

The water bubbles out of a natural crevice at about one hundred six degrees. Now the pool room is about eight by ten, concrete, but when I first came here in 1938 it was a log structure and much steamier because the ceiling was lower. That was better because people benefited from both the hot water and the steam.

After bathing, we used to lay on the benches and cover up with our blankets. Women's hours were from nine in the morning till noon, and then men's hours from noon till five o'clock, and women's hours from five to nine, and then the men had the bath all night from nine until nine in the morning.

Because the hours changed from women's to men's at nine P.M., men used to wait at our store. We were open from nine in the morning till nine at night except our day off, Tuesdays, and Sundays when we opened at noon. Our store was the only place in town that had a light. We had a Delco generator system in the store and one streetlight out in front. So men stood around our stove waiting for the hours to change. I think they came mostly for the sociability. The store was the only place that was open. There was no social hall and no clinics or health nurses. There was really nothing else here. Everybody just came to the store.

I always enjoyed meeting people. The hours were long, nine to nine, but that was our way of life. My husband and I, we were together twenty-four hours a day, working together, living together, practically for the whole fifty years that we were married. We managed. We both liked to read whenever we had time. 'Course in those days, there was no TV. But we kept busy. We operated a radio-telephone, our only communication, at eight in the morning and eight at night. And a lot of times Dermott was called out, for emergencies.

If anything went wrong, why they came to my husband. Whether it was for first aid or a fight breaking out or whatever. He was the mediator, the first-aid man, and the one who sometimes had to pull bodies out of the bathhouse after heart attacks. Yes, that's happened. They'd stay in too long. It's recommended that you don't stay in for longer than five minutes. And the first time, you shouldn't even stay in that long. And you shouldn't go down by yourself, either. You should have somebody with you.

But the steam is very beneficial. Yes, very much so! A lot of people have come here on crutches with arthritis or other ailments and leave their crutches when they left. A lot of the miners and construction workers from the Interior would spend the winter here, taking the baths.

My husband had lived here since he was five years old. His mother and father met here in Tenakee. He was born in San Francisco. So he came back and started working at the store during vacations. And kind of grew up with it. So it was always intended that he would take over when Mr. Snyder retired. I came in 1938, and Dermott and I worked with Mr. Snyder until he died in 1942. Then we worked with Dermott's aunt, Mrs. Snyder, until we took over the store in 1945.

I seemed to fit in all right, and I decided that it was my way of life. I had met Dermott in Seattle when he was going to business college. I was an accountant and we were staying at the same boardinghouse. Dermott had to come back up to Tenakee in January 1938, but I didn't make it up until May. We were married in Juneau May 3, and then we came out to Tenakee. I have been here ever since, fifty-three years.

At first I had big plans. I had always wanted a kitchen that was red and white, but when I got here there was only a little three-room cabin. Somebody had painted the chairs, but they'd been cheap and had only painted the fronts and not the backs. All the paint had run down. So I thought, well, this is just like camping out.

When I first came, we had no refrigeration and all the staples were bulk. Bulk rice. Bulk sugar. Bulk beans and cookies in the racks, and they were all bulk, prunes, apricots, all the dried fruits were bulk. We had a sack of one of everything. And people bought different than they do now. Maybe they would buy one-hundred-pound sacks of potatoes, and a dozen lemons. In larger quantities. A slab of bacon.

We had a weekly mailboat on which we could get supplies from Juneau. And then there was a freight boat that came from Seattle once a month. And we had boat coal instead of oil or wood; we'd sack up the coal for people to burn.

We had a fourth-class post office in the store office. I was postmaster for thirty-some years. We moved the post office into a building by itself when we sold out in 1979.

My husband, Dermott, was very versatile, very helpful. He never got flustered, no matter what the challenge. Once a boat caught fire at the dock and they brought the man up with just skin hanging from him. I mean, there've been a lot of . . . But Dermott always did whatever he could. Sometimes there'd be shoot-ups. Seemed like he always managed to calm people down and act as a mediator.

Tenakee Springs has changed, though. I mean with the advent of phone service and TV and ferries. It seems like we're not so isolated as we were. We used to have more fun get-togethers, pinochle parties, and dances. There was nothing here that was manufactured.

We had to make our own fun.

# Arndt "Lonesome Pete" Pederson

*Jack-of-All-Trades*
*Meyers Chuck*
*1892–1983*

*Traditionally rural Alaskans have had to be jacks-of-all-trades in order to survive. Norwegian immigrant Arndt Pederson of Meyers Chuck was a man who had a money-making skill for every season. By turns he was a trapper, boatbuilder, prospector, and fisherman. Fishing especially was "a wonderful life."*

*Arndt Pederson was born in Frederickstad, Norway, in 1892 and arrived in the North in the late 1920s. His Alaskan nickname was Lonesome Pete not because he was actually lonesome or antisocial but because there were so many other Petes when he came into the country that they had to name him something different. The following chapter was edited from a 1978 interview, courtesy of the Kettleson Memorial Library, Sitka, Alaska.*

I'LL TELL you how I got my nickname. After I built my boat, I came to the fish buyer to sell my fish and he said, "What's your name?"

I said, "Pete is the only name I go by."

Well, Hawaiian Joe was standing there. He had come to see me once in a while when I was living alone on Zarembo Island. So he told the fish buyer about how I had taken almost two years to build my boat.

The fish buyer, he said, "Pete, there are five Petes here in the harbor." [Whiskey Pete, Kodiak Pete, Rescue Pete, Mulligan Pete, and Halibut Pete.]

So Hawaiian Joe, he said, "Call him Lonesome Pete because when he built that boat, he was all alone on that Zarembo Island."

So that's how I got the name.

When I came to America, I done so many things! Working as a draftsman in a machine shop, working as a contractor. I went from one thing to another, mostly to see how the American people lived. I even worked in Newport News for a while when they built that flagship *Pennsylvania*. Yes, I had a job there and had twenty men with me. And then I went diamond drilling for a few years to see the country.

I started fishing in Alaska when I came up here from Pennsylvania on a vacation. From where I was camping on the beach, I saw there was a lot of fish. So I went out fishing in a rowboat. I soon made up my mind that I was going to stay because I saw how people were living here and I thought it was a wonderful country, a wonderful people. There was an awful lot of Norwegians!

I liked the climate, the scenery, and everything else. And it was so easy to find something to do because I could start working at repairing engines, building boats, prospecting, fishing, and trapping. Because it was a territory, we didn't need any licenses.

When I first came up here, there were so many salmon in the streams that you could walk on them. There was so much fish here that there was no closed season. We fished the whole year around. The prices were low, of course. White salmon even went down to ten cents a pound.

I tried every kind of fishing—my boat was strong enough to handle any of it—but I fished mostly trolling. I saw how the others did and there wasn't much to it. We had hand gurdies and we used cotton line and trolling poles. I kept experimenting, getting a little deeper with my line until it hit the rocks and broke. But that is where you've got to fish most of the time, right around the rocks, in and out, here and there.

I fished by myself because I experimented so much with different gear. I made my own spoons and so many different things. Wooden plugs. In my shop I put a hole through one of them wooden plugs and put blood and herring scales in there and that fished good for a while.

I'd see a school of fish—I could tell by the seagulls and eagles—and maybe I put on a brown spoon and I went slower, then speeded up a bit just to tease the fish!

I'd open up a salmon to see what it was feeding on. Then I got an idea what to use. Lots of people don't do that, so consequently they don't get the fish. You've got to attend to business. I fished in a derby here one year with a couple of fellas. I said to them, "You're not fishing."

They said, "Oh yes, we're fishing."

I said, "Pull up your line."

And they pulled up their line and there was grass on it and all kinds of dirt. I said, "The fish is not a vegetarian. He don't eat grass!"

So there you are. There is all kinds! Some people come up here to fish and they just can't make it. They mortgaged the farm and bought a nice big boat and they come up here. Some of them camped right alongside me when I was building my boat on Zarembo Island, and they had their family with 'em. And they couldn't catch any fish at all because it wasn't in them.

In the early days Norwegians were a majority when it came to halibut fishing because they had the gear and the boats. Now the majority fishing are Americans, born and raised here.

I liked the fishing and I done good. I had a couple of days, a hundred dollars when I got into heavy fishing. Yes, and I was not high boat by a long shot! No, no, no! Because when I got a little ahead and had enough for the winter, then I took only the cream of the fishing. I had built my cabin and I said, "I'm going to fish for another hour or two and then I'm going to buy a circle saw or buy a flexible shaft for my outfit or a short-wave radio" when that came along.

I didn't put in the hours others did because I saw how they killed themselves. It's pretty hard when you haven't got any money and you never had any money, then you get into fifty or sixty dollars a day. Young husky fellas from Norway came over here, and when they saw the money that was in it, they got up at two or three o'clock in the morning, in rough weather, without having anything to eat, took a cup of coffee, and went back in the cockpit. They kept on fishing, fishing, took a day to unload if the sun was shining. At the port of Alexander on the south end of Baranof Island, there'd be maybe forty boats waiting their turn to unload their fish. And then they'd start right up and go out again. With a little ice in the boat, they stayed out for a week and loaded up.

A lot of these Norwegians, they had stomach trouble. One was a big giant of a man and his lungs were gone. A lot of them inhaled all that carbon monoxide from the idling engines in the harbor. They're not around anymore. And quite a few of them died because they had put in days and days without sleep.

Well, it's a fine game, though!

Now trollers have power gurdies and stainless-steel-wire gear. We used to pull by hand. We had three leads on there. Ten fathoms down there was a ten-pound lead. Then probably down to twenty fathoms there was another ten pound and another ten pound again. Three leads. Maybe you'd have thirty pounds on a cotton line and then you pulled it up by hand all day long. That was hard work, believe you me!

Some of the boats here were not fit to go out in because if they got into a storm, those men would stay out in the Pacific forever.

But you've got to be a realist and a fatalist. You can't say, "Well, she's gonna blow now; I'd better get out of here" because that's when the fish are biting good.

We didn't have any Pioneers' Home when I built my cabin and when people got sick . . . Some of them retired from prospecting up around Nome, Kotzebue, and those places, and they quit and come down here and they lived in tents on the beach, hand trolling from rowboats. Some of them did pretty good in their rowboats because there was good fishing but when they got old and sick, many a one I took in to the hospital. And some of them died right there in the rowboat. In the tent.

We had no radios or anything in them days, and oh gosh, the Pacific Ocean, there is nothing pacific about it. All these straits and currents and tides. Oh yes, I have seen some awful storms! Out at Hazy Island, for instance. But my boat was a North Sea style with sails on it if the engine quit. I built it so strong that I could go in any kind of weather—which I had to do sometimes.

There are many signs you can watch for out on the ocean. For instance, sometimes, depending where you are, you can see great big rollers coming in. Then you know there is a storm behind that. But sometimes it takes an hour or two maybe before the real blow hits you. So when the rollers started comin', then I went home. And men on the other boats hollered to me, "What in the world are you going home for, Pete? Stay and you'll get a lot of fish here."

"Yeah," I said, "I'm hungry. I've got to go home and eat."

And they'd have an awful time!

Many of us up here have taken the fellas in who lose their nerve altogether when they get in a storm and maybe the engine quits and there they sit. You can't be that way. You've got to be happy-go-lucky and able to take care of yourself. If you can't do it anymore, well, you can say good-bye because there is nobody there to help you.

I saw one man who was afraid to even come up on the bow and throw me the line so I could tow him in. He sat in the cockpit.

Yessir, so I couldn't help! It was real rough! Blowing, too. So I hollered to him, "You've got to get up there and throw me the line so I can tow you in." No, he just sat there in the cockpit. He couldn't move.

So I said, "I'll go in and get a man to go with me. Then I'll jump over on your boat and tie it up."

And, you know, I did. I took about half an hour and I took a man off of the beach and we took a rowboat and went out there. His boat was going up on a rockpile. And you know what? When it hit, then he jumped off his boat and he run between the breakers.

So I rowed in there—you've got to watch for the third swell and then there's no danger—and there he was. Soaking wet and laying up in the woods.

"Well," I says, "my goodness, you've got to come. You can't lay here. It's getting dark pretty soon." So I had to put him in the rowboat. When I took him into town, he says, "Good-bye, Pete. I'm going to go down where I belong."

No, out in the ocean, you've got to know what you're doing, all right. And even then if you haven't got the right equipment . . . Some halibut boats, here comes a breaker and they don't watch it and they are lost.

But it's a wonderful life, though. It really is!

# Anne Hobbs Purdy

*Tisha Reveals Her Secret Blueberry Patch*
*Chicken*
*1901–1987*

*Anne Hobbs Purdy influenced a legion of fans who never had the good fortune to study in her bush classroom. The title of her 1976 book,* Tisha, *refers to the way kids pronounced the word teacher in 1927, when she arrived by pack train in Chicken, Alaska.* Tisha *is a beguiling book, but one that pulls no punches about the rigors of bush living and about many pioneers' anti-Native prejudices.*

*In 1977 writer Sharon Haney visited the old teacher on the fiftieth anniversary of her arrival in the Fortymile country (near the Yukon border). Long fascinated by the Fortymile gold discoveries at Franklin Gulch in 1886, Haney lived near Delta Junction for two years in a Mongolian yurt while panning the still-mined Fortymile for historical nuggets. When she met Anne Purdy, a friendship bloomed quickly. A single woman, Sharon was fascinated by the life-styles of single women in earlier times—how they obtained food, cash, house repairs. The following story, originally published in the* Fairbanks News-Miner, *is Sharon's tribute to Anne, who died in 1987.*

HARDY AND tenacious as an Arctic poppy, Anne Hobbs Purdy bloomed in the Fortymile country after her arrival in Eagle, Alaska, on September 4, 1927. The events of her many years cast a character unique to this land, but it was her initial teaching assignment in the mining town of Chicken that established her as one of the area's most controversial residents and which subsequently made her known worldwide as the subject of the book *Tisha*, edited by Robert Specht.

Meeting Anne Purdy for the first time, one was easily charmed by the spice and vinegar of a sourdough who claimed the right of an old woman to say exactly what she thinks at any time and in any place. During the course of my first meeting with Anne in 1977 and before reading the book, I accepted an invitation to visit her home on "Poverty Hill" in Chicken.

I set out on the road to Chicken forearmed with friends' stories about a young libertarian who had had the courage to treat Natives and outcasts as equally educable citizens in days when it was unfashionable to do so.

Barking dogs greeted me as curious eyes peered out of the paned windows of the weathered, two-story frame house. The door opened with a squeak and a scrape and Anne beckoned me enter. The blue-flowered blouse she wore accented her bright blue eyes; her slacks and tennis shoes were also blue. Silver-gray hair was pinned back behind one ear. She offered her hand.

"Hello, I'm Anne Purdy," she said, motioning to a cushion-covered cot against one wall. "Won't you have a seat?"

It was very warm in the house. The Olympic woodstove that was the main feature of the front room was heating a tea kettle. The large room was sparsely decorated, the furniture was functional, and an orderliness predominated. A long cloth-covered dining table filled one side of the room. On the wall at the end of the table was a large blackboard over which hung the brown-toned portrait of an ageless and beautiful Native woman, long hair flowing.

"Lynn, bring our guest book," Anne called to another room. She explained, "We always have our visitors sign in so we can keep an accurate count of how many come by." Then she asked, with an eye-to-eye look that searched deep, "What brings you to this part of the country?"

In describing my plans, I recalled for her the circumstances of our first meeting, when I had come across Anne's daughter, Lynn, and Anne in a wide-brimmed sunbonnet, filling more than thirty one-gallon water jugs. Break-up and mining had made their local watering holes temporarily unusable, so they were hauling water from a friend's house in Tok, sixty miles away on a dirt road. It amused Anne that she had forgotten.

Lynn appeared with the guest book, and I remarked over the book being already half-filled with names.

"We've always had lots of visitors," Anne said with a smile. "The people in Chicken have always sent strangers up here—long hair types and people who scare 'em—because they know I'll talk to them. The book brought a lot of visitors wanting me to autograph their copies, but even the summer before the book came out we had five hundred visitors. So far this summer we've seen about two hundred."

She tapped on the table. "It's the letters! Last year, I got fifteen hundred letters from as far away as South Africa, Australia, and every state in the U.S. Sometimes they are so sad. I answer a few with a card or a kind word if it's needed. It's the book makes people feel they can write to me."

Lynn brought several copies of the book, and we spoke at length about it. In 1977, there were two hundred thousand paperback copies in French and English in addition to the hardcover editions circling the globe.

Anne's eyes glowed whenever she discussed her story's success. *Tisha* was serialized in an English woman's magazine, on British television, and on Canadian radio. Additionally, *Reader's Digest* in 1976 selected it for condensation in its annual "best stories" book. *Tisha* was also being considered as a movie property by Cine West, a Utah-based movie production company that has already shot footage in Utah and Alaska.

Before selling the rights to her book, Anne said she and Lynn earned their livelihood by holding yard sales, selling berries, and taking orders for Lynn's knitting and for autographed copies of *Tisha*. Anne receives no Social Security income and said she was disqualified from her teaching pension because "they say I taught too long in Oregon." The women asked young miners and other friends for help with the heavy work, but as far as the rest of backwoods living goes, the two obviously made it on an abundant supply of bush savvy.

Anne agreed to talk "officially" for this interview while we picked berries, after first insisting that I swear an oath of absolute secrecy concerning the whereabouts of her favorite blueberry patch.

We arrived at the site, and before I even had my buckets in hand, Anne was down the hill and out of view. Guessing at her direction, Lynn and I stumbled into fruit-laden bushes. It was quite a time before a faint "Halloo, halloo," chirped out from the edge of the burned spruce to the east of the clearing.

"Come over here! The berries are thick!" she exclaimed.

I followed her voice, my hound dog at heel, leaving Lynn to finish stripping the bushes in her methodical manner. We got to where the voice had been and the bright blue, floppy sunbonnet Anne wore popped up. Dressed head to toe in blue, she belonged in the midst of all those berries.

"We get ten dollars a pound for these in Eagle," she boasted, "and what we don't sell, we put up into jam and give away."

She called to Lynn again, but Lynn insisted on picking where she sat. So the dog and I followed Anne.

"You know," she spouted suddenly, "a lot of people thought I was a heathen because there is no mention of God or church in the book. I've gotten letters from every denomination except the Catholics—I guess they figure 'what's the use?'—offering to save me and promising that I'll be reunited with Fred when I die if I'll just join their church. Well, I read I Corinthians 13 and the Beatitudes every day of my life and that's enough for me.

"Some years ago, the people of Chicken sent two itinerant preachers up to our house to inquire about the religious needs of the community. After long arguments about the necessity of organized religion, I told 'em, 'Well, you can build your churches if you like, but nobody in Chicken will come.' And to this day, Chicken remains unsaved!"

She chuckled heartily before continuing, "You know, there's no game here anymore because the government waited until it was all gone before they closed the area to hunting. We had lots of game here before they put that highway (the dirt-and-gravel Taylor Highway) through. When I first got here, you'd be out in the woods like this and hundreds of ptarmigan would fly up from a ways off and you could hear their wings thumping the air like drumming. I never hear that sound anymore. It's been ten years since I saw a caribou. Still, I think that if someone wants to come out and try to make a living from what's here, they ought to be able to try. That's a basic human right! I get so angry when the BLM comes in and tells someone who's been *living* here for years, maybe as long as me, to leave!"

We picked in silence. It became apparent that the real secret of the day was Anne's ability to wander over the entire patch, gesticulating to punctuate her stories, and still gather as many berries as Lynn and I, who picked continuously.

The following day I arrived at the Purdys' at an hour when many are still in bed. Anne and Lynn were just pouring the paraffin over dozens of jars of hot blueberry jam. The aromas of jam and baking bread filled the house. Colorful bouquets of flowers adorned the table, and a flowered china tea service steamed a welcome.

Previously, though Anne had been vocal and blunt about her philosophies, she had been reserved in discussing her family. That morning things were different.

"I used to feel badly that I hadn't given birth to any of my children, but I don't any longer," she told me. "I adopted three children before Fred and I married, and we adopted seven after, all Natives or part Native, and some with health problems. I am part Kentucky Indian myself.

"Let's see, in the order they were adopted into the family, we raised Chuck, who is now deceased, and Ethel. Then came George and Jack, Eddy and Doris, who is also deceased, Marie, Lynn, Hank, and Barbara, the youngest."

Tisha fell in love with Fred Purdy her first year in the state, yet did not marry him until ten years later. I had to ask why.

"Fred and I just preferred to stay away from each other because of the pressures of his family and the people here," she recounted softly. "He was half-Eskimo, a 'siwash' to most of these people. Then, when I was teaching in Eagle the winter of 1937-1938, I went out to the Fairbanks Ice Carnival. Fred and I met accidentally, and after some heart-to-heart discussion, we decided that we were mature enough to decide whether or not we should marry. I gave up my teaching job and moved into our log house as a happy bride, but his family was not glad that we finally married.

"But I can say this truthfully. Although Fred and I had very different upbringings due to race, which made us think differently, we got along beautifully. Fred was self-educated after he quit the third grade. I taught him mathematics and geography at first, until I ran out of brains. Our children always asked Fred their questions, not me.

"Fred was a trapper, even though he thought trapping a 'heathenish' business. It was only a means for him to make money in the Bush. He was a gentle person who liked to laugh, and he knew Alaska as few people ever do."

After a solemn moment of reflection, she smiled broadly. "In '39 or '40, we brought the very first car into Chicken. It cost us four hundred dollars to have 'Old Betsy' shipped in piece by piece by plane. She was a 1927 Chevrolet. We drove that car without roads, without lights, without brakes, and the radiator leaked so we filled it with dog food. We drove that car *everywhere,* even on the tussock flats!

"Once when we had the car all filled up with people, bouncing over a flat, I turned around and counted the people in the back seat. 'Fred,' I said, 'you better go back right now, we've lost Billy.' He'd bounced out on one of the larger hummocks, but he was just fine. And in the winter, Fred would mount skis on the front and rig up sails and we'd sail down the Fortymile River on snow picnics."

She was silent for a time, then added, "Fred never minded all the visitors. I didn't always want all the people who came, but early on Fred and I decided we would always treat people as we would want to be treated ourselves. Fred was full of jokes for the company, full of laughter. A man like that comes only once in your life."

Asked about the people who have had the greatest impact on her life, Anne stated, "There have been several people who influenced me greatly. I think it is most important to understand that you will meet the people you are to meet who will influence you. It is a pattern. People go out of your life when sometimes you don't want them to, but it's all part of the pattern of your life. Some people stay. By and by, all the pieces fit together and it becomes a tight-woven tapestry."

Anne has remained a resident of the Fortymile country despite many hard times. Her lessons on cheerful stoicism, positive thinking, and good works have for fifty years inspired students and others to call her by the honorable title, "Tisha." What has been the most important lesson this teacher has learned in her years in Alaska?

"With all the race prejudice I've been surrounded with," she began, then paused. She collected her thoughts and began again. "Undergoing all these difficult things has enabled me to look at people with tolerance and compassion. When I first arrived, I wasn't aware that there were people in this world who could be so mean. But I believe there is a law in life which forever causes a balancing of the scales. I have always had great compassion for the underdog. But when the underdog was me, for people to hate and do evil unto me, to learn how to deal with them with tolerance and compassion, that is the most important lesson.

"I cannot hate people. I am only made sorry by intelligence wasted or spent on living for nothing. Living through all these years with hate, thwarted at every turn, taught me the best lessons about living. They were lessons that I otherwise would not have learned.

"Well, this life I chose. It may have been difficult. It may have been foolish. But I chose it! At any rate, it doesn't matter now that all these things have happened. What does is that Fred and I always felt the same."

# Senator Bill Ray

*Keeping the State Capitol in Juneau*
*Juneau*
*b. 1922*

*The level of misinformation Outside about Alaska is always astounding, but people can probably be forgiven for not realizing that Juneau (pop. 26,000) and not Anchorage (pop. 230,000) is the state capital. Former bartender Bill Ray represented Juneau in the state legislature for twenty-two years, and he understands the difference very well. Largely because of him, Juneau held on to its statehouse against the designs of populous Anchorage in the 1960s and 1970s.*

*In the state house and senate Bill modeled himself on some of Alaska's colorful solons, such as Harold Strandberg, Jay Hammond, Terry Miller, Ted Stevens, Nick Begitch, Ralph Rivers, and Bill Egan. His chief mentor was Senator Johnny Butrovich of Fairbanks, whose calm, straightforward manner he admired.*

*Senator Bill Ray, the savior of Juneau, describes his constituents' feelings toward him: "They said, 'He's an SOB, but he's our SOB.'"*

JUNEAU WAS a mine town and they were running three eight-hour shifts a day. It was just as active at four o'clock on a Thursday morning as on a Saturday night. There was people coming and going at all times of day and night because of the shifts.

The people off the cruise ships today are only in Juneau because the ships happen to stop here. In the old days you came because you wanted Juneau as your destination.

When I first came here, I was broke! And in order to work in the wintertime I had to go get some warm clothes. Some of the guys told me to "go to one of the clothing stores and tell old Shelley Graves that you want some clothes." So I did and I told him what I wanted and he asked when I was going to go to work and I told him. He said, "When are you going to pay?" I said, "As soon as I get the money, probably the first of the week if I can get on. I'll be in here and pay." "All right, take what you want."

That's the way they were.

And the smallest piece of money was a quarter. The only time you saw pennies was up at the post office. And everything was silver dollars. We never used paper money. Only silver.

It was considerably different than it is now.

The only way you'd leave was by the boat. And when the boats came in there'd be maybe two hundred people waiting. They'd usually blow the fire horn one time as the boat was coming up the channel, and everybody would migrate down toward the dock to see who was coming in. And you'd see who was leaving. It was kind of like a happening every time.

And then we had what they called the blue ticket. If you were not wanted in the community, if you were of bad character or a bum, the police would give you a blue ticket—in other words, a ticket to the next town. And [you were] told not to come back.

And if you skipped out on a bill, the merchants would look at the passenger list or somebody would tell them that they saw so and so leaving on the boat. If you owed money, they'd tell the marshal and he'd wire ahead and pick you up at the next port and take you off and bring you back to pay your bills.

Most of the time you knew everybody. You never locked your doors because nobody would take anything. It's a lot different now.

When I first came to Juneau, the only method of getting here was by steamship.

I came from Wallace, Idaho. I'd just graduated from high school in 1938, and it was depressed up in the Coeur d'Alenes at the Sunshine Mine and the Hecla and Bunker Hill and Sullivan and all those big gold and lead and silver producers. My sister had just gotten married early that year, so that just left my father and myself and my mother. There was no future in Idaho. And a friend of my dad's came down from Anchorage and told him how great the country was and how things were much better than in Idaho. So my folks started talking about Alaska, and we just sold everything we had—which wasn't much—and went to Seattle. When we found out how much it cost to come to Alaska, all we had was just for my dad and I to get to Juneau. Tickets on the steamship *Baranof.* We had to leave my mom in Seattle because we didn't have enough money to bring her.

So we came up steerage. That's where you carry your own blankets and you sleep in the hold of the ship. That was quite an experience because those sleeping quarters were noisy, stuffy, and really bare bones. We had steel bunks, two and three high. And what passed for a lounge was the dining place, which was right in the stern over the engine screws. When we weren't eating, then we were playing cards, spinning yarns, and telling lies.

They used to have four steamship companies coming in here: the Alaska Steamship Company; Northland Transportation; Canadian Princess Line; and Alaska Transportation. And Alaska Transportation was more or less a freight outfit.

When we got to Juneau, it was in the wintertime, about December, *cold.*

I started in longshoring down at the longshore hall as an extra. My dad was a professional gambler and he started playing cards. The next thing we had enough money to bring my mom up. And life went forward.

My father died about three years ago. He was ninety-six. Died very peacefully in bed with his shoes off in the hospital. Just wore out. Long ago he'd retired from playing cards. He had been playing cards in the old country and that's how he had come across to the New World, through gambling. He was just a kid and he went to work in the coal mines in Minnesota up in the Iron Range. His name was Elijah Rajacich, Eli Ray for short.

Dad ran poker games. Like he would run a bar. In those days they had open gambling in Juneau. Blackjack games and poker games. The "pan" game, that's more a disease than a game! It's played with eight decks of cards, and they take the eights, nines, and tens out of it, and they play it similar to rummy only you collect chips for runs of threes, fives, sevens, and so on.

He was my stepfather. My mother had divorced my real father when I was six months old, and I had never known anything about him. This was my stepfather my mother had married when I was eleven years old. He was the only father I ever knew. He was of Yugoslav descent, talked broken, but looked like an ambassador. Very nice dresser and always was a very nice man but physically one of the toughest men I've ever seen in my life, pound for pound. I mean I've seen him whip guys four times his size without even exerting himself.

He was tough but he was a gentleman and he was very well liked. I guess I have always hoped to be that way, too. Tough enough to take care of myself without being obnoxious to other people.

I'll tell ya a story! I was through with school and was sixteen years old when I first came to Juneau. And they had a police chief by the name of Dan Ralston, and my dad went to Dan and asked for permission for me to go in and play cards in the Imperial Bar. To play pan and rummy. Dad didn't want me running around with a bad gang, so he felt that it would be better for me to go into an open place where everybody could see me instead of running around. It kept me off the streets, you might say.

I was only sixteen years old but as big as I am now and probably looked damn near as old! So old Dan said, "As long as the kid don't take no drinks, he can play cards. But the first trouble he gets into he's got to stay out."

So I had permission to play cards. I used to play in all the places. Poker, blackjack, pan. Did they take advantage of me? I don't think so. No. My dad was a professional gambler and I had grown up with cards in my hands. I could never beat Dad though!

In 1940 I left Juneau and went to Sitka and went to work on Japonski Island when they were building the Naval Air Station. In Sitka you did anything that you were big enough to do, but if you weren't big enough to do it, somebody would cut you down fast. Sitka was tough. That was a fishing town. Just a *tough* town!

It's not that way anymore. No. All of Alaska is tempered out. I'd say the very, very last frontier outpost is Fairbanks; they've still got some orangutans up there.

But Sitka was wild. In fact, one time over in Sitka when I was nineteen years old, there were two fishermen named Big Walt and Little Walt. Big Walt was about six foot three and about three hundred pounds and Little Walt was about six foot three and a hundred and sixty pounds. And they were partners in a fishing boat. One Christmas Eve everybody was celebrating and I come walking into the Silver Foam, which was a bar where my dad was running all the gambling. I saw this Big Walt pull back his fist to hit my dad, so I run over there and jumped up and hit him and the fight was on. Everybody started in to fighting and they knocked over the stove and the bar and it was a terrible thing. Finally they got this Big Walt outside. My dad had just cut him to ribbons. Just beat the so-and-so out of him. So they locked the door and my dad was still stomping around in there. His friend was a guy by the name of Bulgarian Jimmy, a hard-rock miner who weighed about two hundred pounds. My dad weighed maybe a hundred and eighty and was about five foot eight. So old Bulgarian Jimmy jumped on my dad's back and put a full nelson on him to control him. My dad continued just walking around just like there was nobody there. He grabbed on to the door handle and he pulled that right out of the wood.

Finally the police got us quieted down and put us in jail on Christmas Eve. So guess who comes down to get us? My mother! And things weren't very good after that.

My mother was a super lady. I mean she was really a lady and she could cut you up just by looking at ya and you'd feel about this big. And not only me—I was her son—but a lot of people had the same feelings.

She was great. Everybody called her Ma Ray. She was only five foot four maybe. She had a very nice personality and had very sensible attitudes.

After she got a look at us at the police station, things weren't very jolly for a while. You can imagine on Christmas Eve! But she got over it.

In later years, after I had been in the service, my folks had a small bar here in town called the Midget Bar down where Admiral Way is now. I went to work for them.

Later they built a bar downtown and we named it the Pamaray Club. Pa, Ma, Ray. That's what they called it because everybody called him Pa Ray and everybody called my mother Ma Ray.

The Midget Bar was small and it wasn't what they wanted. So when they opened up the Pamaray Club right after the war, 1946, 1947, they really made a nice place out of it. They made a glass bar with lights on the inside. It was really a showplace in town, up about where George's Gift Shop is now. I'd say it was the nicest bar in Southeast Alaska at that time, including the Baranof or anything else.

There's different styles of bars. The Pamaray Club was a middle-class family bar, not like some of the bars down on South Franklin, which were Native hangouts with drunks and that type of trade.

A lot of ladies came to the Pamaray Club. We used to have two floor shows a night. Music—a three-piece orchestra, four-piece sometimes! We had two bars, one in the front and one in the back. We had promotion nights: Montana Night, Wyoming Night, and all that kind of stuff. Amateur Night. Dancing. Tables. It would be jam-packed.

My dad tried to figure out attractions to keep the place going. I used to get a trade magazine for show people, so I wrote away for comics. So I would be the emcee, putting on two shows a night. That was fun. One liners right after the other, talking about Alaska.

On Montana Night we used to hang a guy. We had a sign on him, "Horse Thief" or "Cattle Rustler." It was a fake dummy that we'd hang up in the middle of the dance floor. We had drawings and giveaways. It was a regular going concern. And all the bartenders wore bar jackets, ties, and white shirts. Two or three waiters going back and forth.

We were operating!

Bars are confession places. They're places where people go to do things they couldn't do at home. I don't even remember half the stuff that happened when I was tending bar back forty years ago. I remember a lot of fights and stuff. I had to separate people from fighting. Fishermen and miners and just regular guys. You'll still find fights on South Franklin every Saturday night.

The Bucket of Blood was farther down on South Franklin. We had a two-man police force, Roy Hoffman and Kenny Junge. Roy was about six foot three and about two seventy and Kenny was about six foot five and about three twenty. And they had an old red delivery truck, a panel job, and they'd go down to the Occidental Bar, to the corner door, and they'd open up the truck, then go into the bar. You'd see 'em come out with a guy under each arm and throw 'em in the truck and take 'em down to the village and warn 'em not to come back uptown again.

In those days, when the police walked the beats, there was a lot less trouble. I used to live up above the Pamaray Club. And Saturday nights when I wasn't working, we'd be sitting up there and all of a sudden we'd hear a ruckus out in the street, guys fighting to beat the band. And all of a sudden somebody would say, "Look out. Look out." And the police car would come driving by. The fight would stop and everybody would just stand there until the car got up around the corner and then they'd start in fighting again.

Juneau was lively because there wasn't much to do in the inclement weather. There wasn't much to do on Saturday nights except play cards and drink.

I think the reason that people drink in Alaska is that in the olden days everybody was single. Even though you were married, you came up here by yourself trying to make a living. And when you didn't have a family to go home to every night and you didn't want to go home to an empty room, you'd gravitate to a place where there was a little action. The action was in the bars.

When I first came to Alaska, the proportion of men to women was about seven to one. They had a red-light district down here on South Franklin. It was accepted by the city and the girls were all inspected by the doctors.

But there was actually a more restrained attitude in bars then than now. You didn't see as many women in bars. In the Baranof we used to have afternoon cocktails and the ladies would all show up with their hats on, suits, and dressed out nice.

I always liked class. When I was on the House Finance Committee, my hero was Johnny Butrovich. I just liked his style. I mean he had *class!* When he stood up to talk, everybody listened.

Sometimes a guy stands up to talk and everybody turns off.

I had a lot of guys that I learned from. A guy by the name of Harold Strandberg; I learned from him. Terry Miller: I learned from him how to conduct myself and how to get across my ideas in a manner that was acceptable and interesting. Anybody can stand up and harangue, but in order to sell something a legislator has to be able to cajole, even threaten sometimes. But he has to know who he can do that with. Be friendly. A little arrogance. Humility. He has to be an actor.

My second year in the house we wanted to do some refurbishing of the legislative halls and I went around and got the votes for it. Barry Jackson, this baldheaded guy from Fairbanks, said he'd go along with it. I had to have three votes in finance out of the five members. So the two Republicans, Strandberg and Haugen, voted no. So there was Kerttula and me and Barry Jackson. But when we voted, Barry Jackson, he votes no. I took a recess and I asked Kerttula, "What do you do when a guy lies to you and doesn't keep his word?" He said, "You take him out and talk to him." Well, in the parlance that I came from, the vernacular of the street, you know what that meant! So I said, "Can I see you, Barry?" and I took him outside and I bounced him up and down the hall. I banged his head all the way up and down until he got it through his noggin. Then we went back in and he changed his vote and that's how we got it.

But it's a learning process.

I don't say that I was popular. I was popular in Juneau, where a lot of 'em said, "He's a real son of a bitch but he's our son of a bitch, so leave him alone." I went uncontested two or three times. I was bringing it home!

I had offers of a house and job in Anchorage just to get me away from here so that they could move the capitol. But the people in Juneau were awfully good to me. Awfully good. And I was very, very proud to represent them to the best of my ability. I think that the thing that I liked most was when some little guy called up and said, "Hey, do you know what they're doing to me? Blah, blah . . ." I said, "Oh, yeah?" Well, I investigated to see if that was happening, then I told whoever was doing it, "I'm just giving you a warning now and if you don't stop that, I'll take it to the governor or to the legislature. But you quit that!" And that gave me the biggest pleasure of all to help the little guy fight City Hall.

I never considered myself any better than anybody else even though I was a senator. I just thought that that was what people wanted me to do.

In fact, I almost quit after my first term when I had been getting invitations to dinners and lunches and cocktail parties. Hey, I'd show up at all of 'em. I'd be every place. People would be talking and I'd listen and pretty soon I started to have real self-doubts. Man, these guys are talkin' different than I believe; this isn't what I think. I must be out of it. I must not know what's going on. And I thought, by golly, if I'm that far off, I'd better get out of the legislature.

So I sat down and I thought about it again and then I took a tabulation. I said, wait a minute. Seventy-five percent of those people there are always the same people. And they're trying to pass their opinions on to me. And the real people, you never see them at the cocktail parties, but those are the guys that I represent.

So I stopped going and I got a terrible reputation for not going to cocktail parties. It was a feather in people's hat if they could get me to a dinner or something. I was very highly selective.

Where I used to feel the public pulse was down in the supermarkets. Foodland or SuperBear or any of them. The ladies'll tell ya. The men, you don't pay too much attention to. But if the ladies say, "Hello Senator, hello Bill, I have a question for you," you know with the first smile that you're doing a good job.

You've got to remember that I had one of the hardest jobs of all because I had to keep the capital in Juneau. That was my big responsibility and I was successful in doing that. But it ruined all my chances of statewide or national office. People in Anchorage used to think I had horns and a tail and a pitchfork. Honestly, you couldn't believe how Anchorage had editorials once or twice a week about that SOB down in Juneau. Sweet Old Bill, I guess that's what it meant.

But if the government left Juneau, there wouldn't be anything here except a wide spot in the channel.

# Vi and Joe Redington, Sr.

*Trailblazers*
*Wasilla*
*b. 1924, 1917*

*Vi and Joe Redington, Sr., created one of America's favorite races and are the living embodiment of sourdough Alaska. Vi Redington is the unflappable partner who helped Joe accomplish his dream of moving north, mushing dogs, and claiming a chunk of the last frontier. "When we homesteaded on the Iditarod Trail in 1948," says Joe, "we learned a lot about mushing dogs from an old-timer that had been the trail's last mail carrier." Nowadays Vi and Joe are passing on their knowledge and leasing some of their four hundred dogs to would-be Iditarod mushers. And Joe is still competing in the 1,100-mile race. He even led the pack across half of Alaska in 1989, a feat that had much of the state's population cheering with glee.*

*The Redingtons have worked hard, mortgaging their own property to make the Iditarod a success. They have an obvious empathy for both dogs and people and insist that their dog drivers use the outdated but romantic command "mush!"*

JOE: WE came to Alaska to mush dogs after reading Jack London's books. We didn't know what kind of dogs we would need because very little information about Alaska was available back in Pennsylvania. We didn't know what the hell to expect, so we brought Dalmatians and English sheepdogs.

When we stopped at the border for gas, they was pumping some gas out of a barrel into the Jeeps and we seen these two puppies running around. Vi asked about the puppies and they said "You can have one of 'em if you want." We named it Dodger, and the following year it had nine male puppies and two females. So Dodger was where our kennel started from.

**Vi:** When I saw those little huskies at the border, the first ones I had ever seen, I thought they were so cute! But I think the lady was glad to get rid of Dodger!

**Joe:** That was 1948. It took a little while to get up to what we got now. But we kind of lucked out because when we came in here, I immediately went to work for the Air Force 10th Rescue. They had discontinued the 10th Rescue's dogs, and we bought some of those dogs at Fort Richardson and started working for the army on contracts. Instead of them having the dogs, why, they hired a civilian. We took airplanes off of mountains and we worked right on up with the dogs in all kinds of rescue. One of the first jobs we had was when we took a team of dogs into Elmendorf, flew 'em into Willow, put 'em on the train, and went as far as Kashwitna Bridge, got off of the train, and went in and made a rescue seventeen miles west of Kashwitna. While we were there we took out a F-80 that had gone down in one of the big swamps. We hauled logs in with the dogs and jacked that jet up out of the water and came back the following winter and flew it out on skis.

I went on all kinds of rescue work, and I worked on the White Alice sites and the DEW Line.

**Vi:** When we got into Palmer, they said that Knik had just opened up for homesteading.

**Joe:** When we stopped in Wasilla, there were only three or four buildings in town, and May Carter was the postmaster and everything else, too. There was one garage-gas station, one bar, the roadhouse, and a store, and that's all there was. And May Carter at the post office said, "We don't know whether you can get to Knik or not. There hasn't been no car over the road yet." And that was June the second.

When we started out in our Jeep, they were starting to work on the road some. That was June, which should be one of the driest months, but it was just a dirt road with dips that held water. In fact, that next spring, after using the dogs all winter to go to Wasilla and back, we had to start walking because of the mud. In the spring we hunted ducks all the way into Wasilla and back. We'd go along and shoot ducks in these mudholes in the road, and by the time we got back home we had a good bunch of ducks and some groceries.

That was early homesteading. We probably came as close as anybody to living off the land for several years. At our hunting lodge at Flathorn Lake we put up a ton of potatoes in a big root cellar. Vi grew all kinds of vegetables, and we put up five hundred king salmon just for ourselves and our dogs. Hung 'em up and dried 'em. We shot beluga whales for dog food. And seals. We put up five hundred seals just for the dogs. We had an island where we got our eggs at. We'd go down to Egg Island before the sea gulls started laying their eggs—which are twice as big as a hen egg, twice as rich. We'd start checking the island every day, and when we found that they had started to lay, we'd gather every egg. Then the next day, if we found two eggs in a nest, we figured that we'd probably missed that one. So we got fresh eggs all the time. And as long as we kept gathering eggs they kept right on layin', just like chickens would.

We put up these eggs and had 'em pretty near all winter. We dipped 'em in hot water to seal 'em up. As long as you seal 'em up and turn them every month the yolk won't stick to the shell and spoil.

I was a veteran, so I didn't have to clear my homestead to prove up and get ownership. We had our homestead here at Knik, next to my father's, and we had our big-game hunting lodge at Flathorn Lake thirty miles out the Iditarod Trail. We used to go back and forth by dog team all the time on the Iditarod Trail after we got the trail reopened again. When we first came into this country, the Iditarod Trail had not been used in many years, and it was growed up bad.

I guided hunters and I commercial fished and I worked for the army and air force going into all these villages on rescue work and on intelligence missions, such as recovering photo balloons which had been sent from Europe over Russia. Top-secret work that they called reclamation! I got into those villages in the sixties and there were dog teams behind every house 'cause them people had no other means of transportation. They'd get a mail plane once a week during the winter. Nobody had wells, so they pulled their water from the river. There were no trees in that area and the wood all came down the Yukon and then the wind blew it up along the coast. Nobody burned oil, only wood. So everybody had a small dog team to haul wood off of the beach. Very few racing teams because Dr. Roland Lombard and his leader, Nellie, were winning everything and all the Natives were dropping out of speed racing.

But when I went back in the later sixties, there were snow machines out in front and the dogs had almost all gone. The richer villages, like Unalakleet and them, almost every team was gone. Most everybody had a snow machine. Some of the other villages, like Teller, that weren't as prosperous still had dogs. So I thought to save the dogs we had to have a reason besides work for having the dogs in the villages. Let the snow machines do the work and let people use dogs for recreation and pleasure. And that's what the Iditarod was all about.

In 1967 there were three of us that really believed in it. That year we had a twenty-five-thousand-dollar race on a very small part of the Iditarod in honor of the Alaska Centennial Purchase. Dorothy Page was chairman, and when I flew one of my sons into Willow to race in a speed race, she asked me if we could plan a long-distance race on the old Iditarod Trail. I said yes, a short race, over the part we were using every day.

When we moved over there in '53, we didn't have time to build a cabin. We put up a sixteen-by-thirty-two army tent. We put a barrel stove in both ends of it, put a cookstove in the middle, dug a hole in the sand in the middle for a root cellar (that we could put our eggs and things in), and we mushed dogs every day the entire winter. We traveled back and forth from Flathorn, cutting out the Iditarod Trail in places that hadn't been used in thirty or forty years. That winter of 1953 and 1954 was the best year we ever had in Alaska!

Then that Christmas we was going to come in to her mother's in Anchorage after we got back to Knik, following the Iditarod Trail all the way through for the first time. Nobody had been over this part of the trail in fifty years. It had growed up real bad. But there were always blazes and things that we could find if we searched hard enough.

We started out on a real nice day. We each had a team of dogs. And we had Timmy and we had food enough for the dogs for four days. Timmy was three and rode in the sled. We started out and made twelve miles that day, which was good because we were hauling a big load of stuff. And making trail at the same time. This was out of Flathorn up to the Iditarod Trail.

We camped where we found a wooden frame from years earlier. We just stuck a tarp over it.

It snowed three feet that night. Just covered up everything. It snowed enough that we could just barely see the handlebars of the sleds. The snow was so deep that we decided the only way we could go on was to put all the dogs on one team and leave one sled behind. I would snowshoe ahead of the dogs and find the trail. We didn't want to leave the trail because we'd be lost if we did that. But we could only make about a mile a day. And pretty soon our dog food ran out. And we didn't have the airplanes flying in those days like you do now. Vi and I were eating army C rations, but from now on we had to save those for Timmy. Vi and I, for two days there, we didn't have anything to eat. And working hard, too!

Finally I shot a moose, but it was the poorest, skinniest little moose that I ever saw. It must have been having the same problems that we was because I could almost carry the whole moose.

We fed that to the dogs but before I brought it in, I took one of the kidneys on a stick like you would a hot dog. And for some reason it seemed like that kidney was what I wanted. I never ate a kidney before or since. And I brought Vi one and she ate it. We just roasted them on a stick. And I carried part of the moose in and fed it to the dogs raw.

Then we went on another mile and another mile and another day and another day. Finally at the end of ten days we were still twenty miles from Knik.

Vi's mother and father got worried because Christmas came and passed and we wasn't in Anchorage. They had a friend who was in the Civil Air Patrol, and they asked him to look for us. At our tent in Flathorn we had left a note on the wooden door that said, "Left for Anchorage Dec. 22 by Iditarod Trail." So the CAP went up in the air and they found the sled. Back in Anchorage they had a big deal on television that they had found an abandoned sled and couldn't locate us. We heard all that on the radio we had with us.

The next day I went out to make trail for another mile, and here they flew over and seen Vi and Timmy at the halfway-house cabin on the Iditarod Trail. We had put our tarp over the door because somebody had took the door off and burned it. At that time we was getting people up and down the rivers doing things like that. We had cut up a barrel, took the axe and cut the door in it, and made a barrel stove. And took some five-gallon cans and made a stovepipe. So we had a place in there to keep warm, and her and Timmy was there and I went out making trail again.

So I'm out on the trail and they found Timmy and Vi there and they circled and dropped a note, "If you're the Redingtons, walk in a circle." So Vi walked in a circle. They came over low and dropped a little teeny package of navy-type food and then flew away. We heard that night on the radio that they had found Vi and they figured that I was lost or gone or had abandoned them or some damn thing. So everybody in Alaska heard it over the damn radio that they'd dropped food to Vi.

They'd actually only dropped this one little old candy bar and a little box of raisins, and we gave it all to Timmy. Anyway, that was a big deal on television because that was the first year they had TV in Anchorage. And, oh boy, they made a big deal out of it!

The next day the weather was bad. I didn't even dare leave there because I wanted to get ahold of them if I could. So we sat there and waited.

The next day they came back. I had made an arrow on the crick pointing to a lake a half-mile away so I could get 'em to land on their skis. That damn circling don't do you no good! And by the time they landed, I had gotten to that lake. They said, "We thought you was either dead or gone or had abandoned Vi and them." I said, "Hell, no, I'm here. I was just out cutting trail!" They said, "What can we do?" I said, "Go out to where I work at the army base there and tell them that I need some rations and some dog food and they will send some out." So he took a note, but the next thing we knew, here come a damn helicopter. An H–19 landed and said, "We came out to get you." I said, "Hell, we ain't leaving. We've got dogs here and all we need is some dog food." The pilot said, "I've got to take somebody in. These rescues cost a lot of money and I came out here to get ya."

I said, "You ain't gonna get me or Vi. We're staying with the dogs." We asked Timmy if he would go, and he said yes, he'd go in to Vi's mother.

The pilot said, "You think I can take that kid?"

I said, "Hell, yes, he'd go in anything."

**Vi:** At first Timmy cried. I said, "What's the matter, Timmy?" He said, "I want my raisins!"

**Joe:** The pilot thought Timmy was crying because of being taken away but all Timmy was worried about was that little box of raisins!

Then they got the note back to where I worked at Elmendorf doing "reclamation," and here come a C–47 and they started dropping C rations. I mean we had to get in the cabin because it was *dangerous.* That C–47 dropped us about eight fifty-pound bags of dog food and it must have been two hundred great big cases of C rations. We hauled C rations all winter, gave everybody in the country C rations, hung 'em in trees, and every damn thing all winter long.

But anyway after we had fed our dogs, hooked 'em up, and come into Knik, camping one more night out, Anchorage sent word to us that they wanted Vi and I to come down there on television, so we both escaped back to Flathorn Lake and they never got us down there on TV. They had said that we was lost, but we wasn't lost. We were just delayed.

Then the CAP guy wrote up a big story in *Man* magazine telling all about the deal. It kinda embarrassed us because we hadn't been lost. We knew exactly where we were all the time. We were on the Iditarod Trail!

# Monty Richardson

*Earthquake!*
*Seward*
*b. 1918*

*Alaskans reacted to the earthquake devastation of Good Friday 1964 with char-*
*acteristic resourcefulness and gumption. The epicenter of this megatrembler was*
*beneath Miners Lake in northern Prince William Sound. Eleven people died at*
*Seward, a railhead port of twenty-three hundred people, many taverns, and in-*
*numerable fishing stories. Today Monty Richardson is a familiar figure on the re-*
*built waterfront, where he hires out his 1978 Chris Craft, the* Irish Lord, *to*
*sports fishermen. Monty retired in 1976 from a teaching career that began in a*
*Colorado one-room schoolhouse. But his greatest challenge came not in the class-*
*room or at the tiller but on the streets of Seward.*

I'D GONE through drought and dust storms in Oklahoma back in the
drought-ridden thirties, and I had had about all I wanted of that. And
I felt the lure of the last frontier, the uncrowded vistas, and the hunting,
fishing, so I talked the wife into it. I loaded her and two kids in the station wagon and brought all of our earthly belongings over the Alcan. It
was quite rough, you bet! It was all gravel. We busted a windshield and
busted the trailer way out in the wilderness of the Yukon. We had a lot
of adversities here and there but we've never regretted a minute of it.

In my early days in Seward, there was a lot of elbow-bending.
There still is. Seward is a hard-drinking town. In winter it's cold and
dark and not many diversions. Yeah, this is still pretty much of a free and
open town. A lot of dissipation goes on. Always has.

My wife is a good old solid part-Cherokee Indian. I guess you
could call us Okies. Yeah, although in 1956 we had never been to Cali-

fornia. That's what the true making of an Okie was in the Dust Bowl, having been to California. We went to Alaska instead of California, and by 1964 we were both working in the schools here and we called Seward home.

On Good Friday I was up at the house, 519 Third Avenue, in the middle of Seward at five thirty-seven in the afternoon. I'd been ill with the flu. Fortunately there was no school that day because it was Good Friday. I had finally gotten up out of bed to get to the barber shop before six o'clock to get my hair cut. I walked outside and a friend, a local policeman, stopped by to chat a few minutes. When the earthquake hit—we had had earthquakes right along—we both remarked casually about here was another one. But then it increased in intensity, and when I saw his tires bouncing off the ground in that undulating, rolling motion, why I knew something serious was happening.

It was such a long, long four minutes. Nine point two on today's Richter scale! North America's most powerful earthquake ever recorded.

About a minute and a half into the earthquake, why Standard Oil's big gasoline storage tanks blew sky-high. Flames and smoke went hundreds of feet into the air. My friend roared out of my driveway and lurched down the street in his police car to the waterfront.

I remember looking up and seeing the top of Mount Marathon just trembling and trembling like it was going to tumble right down on us. And as the shaking went on and on and on, the thirty-five-foot-high chimney on the grade school across the street from us swayed back and forth and back and forth until in slow motion it came, whumpf, roaring down. Our own chimney bricks almost hit me in the head. Finally the wife and kids stumbled outside and we huddled and huddled while everything fell around us.

Fires raced down Seventh Avenue and caught fire to thirty-one loaded fuel tank cars that had overturned. And they all went off like the most giant firecrackers you can imagine. The wife and I decided we'd better get out of town before we got roasted. I did have presence of mind enough to shut our electricity off and grab some clothing. By the time we got out of town and drove to the head of the bay, the pavement was wet from a high tide, but we figured we were safe. Half an hour after the earthquake, about seventy-five or a hundred other people were milling around there watching the tanks explode and buildings catch fire.

Nobody was thinking straight, of course, but the tide was way, way out. I had never seen so many mud flats! That should have told us that if it went out, it was darned sure going to come back in. And then I saw a big, white frothy mass out in the bay. I thought, "Well, what's all that snow doing out there?" We were looking up the bay toward Fox Islands about twelve miles out at what looked like a bunch of snow on the bay. I couldn't figure out . . . I had never seen anything like that, though I had been on the bay many times. Then soon, even with the crackling of the fires and people chattering excitedly, I began to hear like a freight train in the distance. And then it got louder and louder. Then we could see skip, skip, skip just like a snow avalanche coming down a mountainside. Well, it began to dawn on people what it was! A *tidal wave*. And it was really barreling in. We finally began to yell, "tidal wave," and started running away from the beach to our cars. Several didn't make it. They got killed right there on the spot. One old couple, a man and his wife, I can still see 'em, just frantic. They couldn't get their car started. Flooded it or something. And they were killed.

We were racing as fast as we could up a little old, dim dirt road, right straight away from the bay, or we wouldn't be here to tell the story. All sorts of timbers and boats and debris came crashing down around us and we just barely got away.

We drove about a mile farther to a place called Three Bridges, where the Resurrection River divides into three parts. And that was as far as we could go because the earth had sunk six foot and there were the bridges hanging up in the air.

We and other people turned around and came back, but not too far back because the fires and tidal waves had everybody panic-stricken. My wife remembered that she had the key to the little four-room school where she taught a mile and a half out of town. So we decided to go up there. No way could we get back into town because the tidal wave had thrown monstrous amounts of debris across the road. So we opened up the schoolhouse, not knowing what we would get in the way of wounded people or even dead people. Sure enough, people came straggling in there. Some with bruises and scratches but nobody badly hurt. About a hundred fifty adults and children spent a harrowing night in that schoolhouse.

All the facilities were overburdened almost immediately, so we decided to go up to an old Quonset hut where the government had stored some civil defense supplies years back and see what we could get to help take care of all the people. We took flashlights and jumped over some big earthquake fissures and knocked the door in. Big, old wooden crates were stacked to the ceiling. They had codes on 'em but we didn't know what the codes were, so we heaved and struggled and got a couple into my van and got them back to the schoolhouse, hoping that we had some stuff for food or shelter or warmth. But when we pried open the first crate, it was full of bedpans.

The four toilets were plugged almost immediately, so along about midnight we eased back down to the bay to get some water to flush those toilets out. We started walking and walking out across the mud and sand to fill our garbage cans. We should have known. . . . Earlier in the evening should have told us that if we had to go that far out in the mud with no real water there, then, by golly, the bay, it had run out again, tilted, and was sure going to come back in. But we were a little bit wary by that time. When we heard that roar coming, why we threw our garbage cans down and took to our heels and got out of there. We came within an inch of getting caught in another tidal wave that came roaring in like a freight train. We got out of there with our lives just before it came crashing in.

Twice in about six hours we had almost got caught in tidal waves. Again the monstrous force threw all sorts of debris up in the timber. It threw a freight car clear over across the bluff, a mile away from the beach.

We stayed in the school all night. Nobody slept because the aftershocks came on with terrifying frequency. Every ten or fifteen minutes a booming aftershock hit. We heard about five tidal waves come crashing in. Some people became hysterical, afraid the waves would come up there and get us. The beach was a mile away but we didn't know what to expect and women and children screamed each time another one roared in.

During the night a few people reached us from town over Mount Marathon, winding their way through the timber and the snow. They told us wild stories about how much of the town had burned.

At daylight we were able to ease our way back to town through an eight- or ten-foot-wide strip bulldozed through the debris. We found that the fires had laid a massive layer of soot on the streets and snow. Our foundation was cracked, the chimney had tumbled down. The back porch had pulled away from the main house. It was just a royal mess inside. Broken glass and dishes and pottery, fallen shelves, stuff all smashed up.

Yet we were lucky to be in the center of Seward. Houses down along the waterfront were totally destroyed by the tidal waves and fires. For a small community of seventeen or eighteen hundred people, some eighty-five to ninety homes were completely demolished.

Yet we never thought of leaving, even though we didn't know if we still had teaching jobs or not. I had a wife and three small children to support, and fortunately the schools were only closed ten or twelve days. The Civil Defense and military jumped right in and began repairing the high school to use it to house and feed people. They didn't want anybody lighting fires here in town. There was no water. Most of the chimneys and flues and heating systems had been shattered and they didn't want anybody to light fires. So they went up and down the streets with bullhorns encouraging everybody to take their meals at the army field kitchen at the high school. Some people whose homes had been destroyed were bedded down there on cots for a goodly number of days and nights.

After about two weeks they were able to patch up all three schools enough to where we could get through the rest of the year. So we teachers were only out about fourteen days. The authorities wanted to do something with the great amount of kids that were wandering around getting in the way of cleaning up the debris and getting the facilities of the town working again.

The people of Seward showed real intestinal fortitude. I'd say the majority of them were gutsy people that pitched in and cooperated and helped solve the problems. However, Alaskans come in all stripes. Unfortunately there were a few, as there would be in any community, that instead of helping solve the problems, they added to the problems.

For days and days we were isolated because there is only one road out of here and it was shattered. Of course, the only planes that were flying in here on a damaged airfield were military and Civil Defense. But some people, by golly, with all those aftershocks still coming on and the town just devastated, they took off and they left and they never came back. But the majority of them, even though everything was gone and they had not much more than the clothes on their back, they all pitched in and started building their lives again.

The wife and I wanted to stay because by that time we had been in Alaska seven years. Alaska was good to us. We liked it. We were getting our roots down. When we sized the situation up, we knew that it was going to be a long, tough struggle, but we felt we were equal to it. In many respects the town became better after the earthquake. Gutsy people rebuilt everything bigger and better and more prosperous than it had been before. The federal government gave us a new small boat harbor, the commercial harbor, and other facilities. And the Red Cross, Salvation Army, Civil Defense, and other agencies pitched in and by midsummer we were beginning to struggle to our feet.

Today we earthquake survivors all have our own phantoms to chase. Many of us are fatalistic: "If it's going to happen, it will." If

Seward people were worried about earthquakes, they'd go someplace else. In 1964 the wife and I, we didn't really have anything to go back to Outside. We had cut all ties when we left there in '56. Things had not been too good for us Outside and Alaska had become our home and our future.

# Josephine Roberts

*"When kids go to high school, they're lucky."*
Tanana
b. 1922

*When Josephine Roberts takes a grandchild for a walk along the Yukon River, metal skiffs line the bank and dogs strain at their stakes near fish-drying racks. In some ways the life of the river remains the same as it was during Josephine's youth. A large proportion of Natives still get by through subsistence fishing and hunting. But modern technology has allowed more people to live permanently in the village, and that has been a factor in the improved educational opportunities for kids like this grandchild. Josephine Roberts is wistful about the chances she might have had but thankful for the cultural blessings she has enjoyed. Her story that follows is from* Josephine Roberts: A Biography.

ENYAS PAUL and his wife with their two daughters and son, Old Wholecheese and their kids, Helen and Sam Stannish, and my dad all decided to go up the Novi and hunt muskrat and beaver. We could shoot beaver those days. They didn't want to leave us too long so they decided to take the whole family. We walked all the way from Galena to the head of the Novi.

In the springtime the snow melts in the day and freezes over at night. So we started in the dark about one-thirty or two o'clock walking and kept on going until we fell through the snow about eight o'clock in the morning. Then we make camp, rest and sleep.

The men take a couple loads ahead to where we'll camp with the dogs. We have another sleigh with the little kids in it and our clothes. We can only take a few clothes. Maybe two shirts and like that. When they reach the camp site they pitch up the tents and pass out. That's one thing the mothers were for. They start cooking.

We stayed in Ruby a couple days while Dad took a load ahead. When they got back we started walking again. It was nice walking out to Long Creek and Poorman. From there, there were cabins all along we stopped in. Good to stop in the cabins. All kinds of old movie magazines in them. We used to feel like we wanted to take those magazines with us. But we wouldn't do it because it belonged to somebody. Isn't that something? We sure would like to take them, stick them in our pack-sack, but we wouldn't do it. We know it belonged to somebody.

When we got to the Novi they set up main camp. Tents all around and dogs tied in three rows around the camp. All the dogs that came over with us. They were going to go further up the river and leave us there at the main camp. They make canoes and went still further up. I was kind of young so I don't remember too much. I think I had a gun and I was taking care of my brothers and sisters. All the Mr.'s and Mrs.'s took off and there we were, just us. Dora and Reba were older, Lorraine and I kind of younger, and Susie was younger still. All Eenyas family.

They told us don't sleep too hard. Anytime you hear the dogs barking just watch. That's what we did. We were all right up as soon as we hear the dogs barking. Right up looking through the tent seeing if there was any kind of animal. We were in kind of an open place so we could see way back. We had a good camp in case a bear came around.

They stayed out about ten days at a time. When they came back, they get all their fur taken care of. Stretched and dried. And all the meat taken care of and off they go again. Three times they did that. We started from Galena in April. In first part of June they built the boat and we left that camp. They sawed their own lumber to make a scow. Loaded down with fur. No grub. We ran out except for a little flour and meat. We stopped some places and picked those last year's low bush cranberries. And we'd get those wild rhubarbs. Mom cooked those for our fruit. Dry meat, tallow, and those berries were good. We had ducks and dried moose meat, bear fat. When you're hungry anything is good.

Andrew Wholecheese and I paddled the whole way out. My sister, Mary, couldn't make it. Every time she tried to paddle, she'd miss the water with the oars and fall backwards. She's smart, you know. I told her that too. I said, "I give you credit, you were a smart girl. You just pretended you didn't know how to paddle. You'd just miss the water, fall backwards and cry to get out of it."

She said, "Oh, I was spoiled anyway."

I didn't want to be spoiled.

Three scows. Eenyas Paul and them had their own and Old Whole-cheese and them had their own. We follow each other. Once when we were paddling through the canyon suddenly we heard someone shoot ahead! We stop paddling and look up. "Don't look!" Mom said. Of course we can't look in case it's black bear, but here it was wolf. Eenyas Paul shot it on the bank. We landed right there and they skinned it.

Then they got dry wood and burned the carcass right there. They didn't want it to rot so they burned it. See how they used to take care of their animals. Kind of out of the way place so nobody will walk all over the place either. They've got a superstition about wolf for that.

After that we stayed in Galena till we got all cleaned up. Clean house and wash clothes and ready to go out to fish camp. After fish camp when we had a whole lot of wood to cut, we move to wood camp. Otherwise we stay in town falltime.

We had a one-room schoolhouse in Galena. Mr. Peck and his wife and Miss MacElroy are the two teachers I remember best. Mrs. Meagan is another one, too. They did all they could to teach me. I always regret I never went to high school. All these children who can go to high school are lucky. I had to take care of my mother because she's always having babies and I have to do the work.

We never had much recess and our schedule was right there. We start with the pledge to the flag and singing. Then we do reading and arithmetic and spelling. Teachers used to save old newspapers for the upper grades. We try to read about Hitler and Mussolini and all of them. I didn't know it was that important. I never paid much attention about what a powerful man he was and all that. It seemed far away from me at the time. I didn't know that they were going to raise havoc in the world. After we read the papers we have to make a report about those big people.

My dad thought it was important that we go to school but I don't know about my mother. She never went to school herself. When we were small she always used to tell us she's not raising us to marry white men. I don't know what her hangup on that was. She used to tell us that a number of times. She just didn't like the idea. Maybe she thought we won't be treated right if we marry white men. But all my sisters married white men. I didn't. I don't know if that was from being obedient or not.

Miss MacElroy wanted to take me to Seattle to put me through school. She said I was really smart and I should go to school. All the way through college. I didn't even know what college was. But my mother wouldn't part with me. Who was going to help her?

Then they were going to send me to Eklutna, a BIA boarding school. When it was time for me to go they sent Mary instead, my sister. Mom was going to have a baby and nobody to help her so Mary went. She lasted not even a year. I should have gone. I liked school. Really. So I always think when kids go to high school, they're lucky. I didn't get to go. Didn't give myself a chance.

We always used to talk our language at home but pretty soon we find out we can't talk our language in school. They told us that we're not going to be able to learn anything in school if we talk our own language. I believed that. So we try to talk English in school until Charlie Evans taught a couple winters there. He never said anything about not talking Native because he was part Indian too, and he could speak Athabaskan himself.

I believed what they told us but I'm glad I learned my own language. I'm sorry I never taught my kids how to talk. Now they ask me why. They say I should have taught them because when people come to visit they can't understand us. We're sitting around talking and my kids wish they had learned the language so they could be talking with us. They're all there and here we are talking Native and they don't understand us. I think that's bad and I always promise I'll teach my grandchildren. If I start from when they're babies it'll be easy. That's the way the Eskimo do it. They just talk their language with their kids so even the younger generation talks their language. You always hear them.

I believed what they told me about not speaking Native in school, but I still liked to talk with old people like Mrs. Bogie and Mrs. Abraham because they used to tell good stories. Stories that have been carried from way back. It's gone from me now. I forget them. But around the Koyukuk River they still tell a lot of them. Catherine Attla said they used to tape Chief Henry when he was alive and now they tell them to each other. I'd sure like to listen because I bet they are some of the same ones I used to hear from Mrs. Bogie and them.

Mrs. Bogie was old. I always remember her as old. People used to call her a medicine woman. I was around her a lot. I guess I was her favorite for some reason. I was the oldest of the kids and she had all that wood on account of me. After we got tired of playing on the beach, we used to say we're going to carry some driftwood for those old ladies, Mrs. Bogie and Mrs. Abraham.

We carry all this driftwood so far every day and before you know it, it's there in her yard. Just load her yard with driftwood. If you see a picture of her yard, you'll see all that wood. Certain length is stacked right here, certain length right there. And the stump wood is piled up with a gunnysack or old canvas over it so it'll stay dry. We used to do that a lot for her, especially her, because she used to make these fried bread. That's just like giving us candy. She's smart. She gets most of the wood.

Most important thing I learned from the old people was sewing. They weren't very good cooks. Oh, they could do the main things like how to make rabbit stew in the oven or bake fish, but nothing fancy. Everything was cooked plain. Fried, baked, boiled, or roasted. But they used to tell me a lot of things, especially Mrs. Bogie, like how to take care of myself.

When a girl first becomes a woman, that means when they first get their period, that's when they say you're going to be an adult. For me it was before that because I had to take care of my brothers and sisters. It was up to me to keep them clean, wash clothes, clean house, and besides, go to school.

When I first became a woman, Mrs. Bogie told my mom, "She's got to come down to me so I can give her grease." I always heard about this before and I thought, oh, I'll vomit.

Then I went to her place and she said, "Oh, I'll give you fish oil."

"Okay," I said. So she put it in a cup and she put warm water in there. I tell her, "What's this for?" I know what it's for because I already heard it, you know.

"This is so that you will never be hungry," she said.

"Okay," I said.

"You can go without eating for a long time and you wouldn't be hungry," she told me.

"Okay," I said, but I felt like telling her, well, I hope so. So I drank this thing.

When I was down in Ruby last time, my younger sister ask me, "Do you dye your hair?" She looks older than me and everybody thinks she is older. I tell her, "Mary, every time I see you, you ask me if I dye my hair. If I really dye my hair, I must use good dye."

"Do you remember," she says, "what Mrs. Bogie did to you? What kind of leaves she give to you?"

I said, "Oh, Mary, I forgot all about that." Here in springtime everything is thawing out. All around in the woods there's these round leaves that's just green. It stays all through the winter and in the springtime that's just green. Just like it never died off or anything. Well, Mrs. Bogie had this and she said you put it in your boots and leave it there all the time until you lose it. She made just like insoles out of it. And she had a little pillow for me, too. She said it has the same thing in there. She calls it by the Native name, but I don't remember the name now.

"This is so you'll hold up good under old age. You'll have a good life. You'll have a good, healthy life," she told me.

"Okay," I tell her and I thought again, I hope so.

Medicine woman. I still think about her. I wonder if she knew. I don't think she did. But it happened that way. She told me not to eat salmon berries that summer because when you eat salmon berries you get old fast. So I never ate salmon berries that summer. And another thing she said, the only kind of blueberries you can eat is the kind that are oval shaped. Not round ones. Gee, I thought, that's hard to find because when you pick blueberries you hardly see any like that. But I picked berries that summer and I found a few so I ate it. She said that was so I'd have more boys than girls. And I did. I had seven boys and five girls.

# Ollie "Pigooruk" St. Germaine

*A Smile for Strangers*
*Point Hope*
*b. 1923*

*Ollie St. Germaine's Anchorage dance troupe, the Ahnuvuk Point Hope Dancers, performs regularly for tourists. Composed mostly of family members, the group harks back to a time not long ago when privation, wind, and cold on the northwest coast of Alaska could only be survived by communal effort. Dancing and singing were part of that tradition, as was hospitality.*

**M**Y FATHER named me after his mother. My maiden name was Pigooruk Ahniksoak. Pigooruk means "Little Hill."

There were no white people around when my grandmother Pigooruk was born. Those were hard times with no modern things like rifles. Times were so hard that my dad let his sister take his first daughter when she was born. Then my mother was mad about that, and when she got pregnant again with a daughter, she gave that baby to her stepsister. So when I came along I was a loner. I didn't have nobody to play with because my sisters were with my aunties. I spent a lot of time with my grandmother.

The old folks used to sing to me. "There is Pigooruk walking down to the beach. Her hands are way out and she's dancing while she's walking because her namesake has arthritis so bad. So Pigooruk is dancing for her."

My grandmother had such bad arthritis that she was bedridden when I came along. But she would always sit there and talk to us. She couldn't bend her hands, her arthritis was so bad, so we'd cut meat for her. My cousins and I, we'd fight over sitting beside her because she always made us feel good.

I was about five years old when she died. I remember her and I still crave her traditional foods. So I go to Barrow when they have the Whaling Feast. Everybody gives me some *muktuk* to take back to Anchorage. I have to have it at least twice a week because my stomach gets upset by all the junk food I eat. So if I have one piece of meat dipped in seal oil, then my stomach calms down. Seal meat. Walrus. Whale. Caribou. Fish.

Seal oil has a little more flavor than Wesson oil. I used to try to trick my children sometimes. When I made some boiled beef heart—that's how much I crave meat—often I only had a little bit of seal oil, so I saved that for me and gave my kids Wesson oil. "Mom, this seal oil don't taste very good!" they said. So I had to share my seal oil with them.

My oldest son is a meat eater, that guy. Good hunter, too!

Like I said, I was a loner, the youngest of five girls. My only brother always took me to help him with the boat. I used my stepdad's .30-.30. My brother knew that a caribou calf wouldn't run away, so once when I went hunting with him, finally I hit that calf. Then we dried the meat and took it back to the village.

I was born after we had Coleman stoves and lanterns, but if my brother-in-law killed a seal in wintertime, that blubber, cut into strips, was the only heat we had. My mother and sister had to use it to cook with in a Yukon stove. For light and heat they burned seal oil in a little lamp with a moss wick.

My mother danced and she and my uncles were always willing to show me. My uncle would say, "Come on, *panik* [daughter], let's dance." There were lots of people around and I couldn't say no. That's how I learned all these motion dances. For instance, the Welcome Dance we do for the tourists. My dad's second cousin, I call him my uncle, too, Jimmie Killigvuk used to dance that. A real powerful guy. He was a person that just loved to dance. I think most of the time everybody danced at his house 'cause his mother was still living when I was a little girl. He went to Nome in the early thirties and he brought home a motion dance he got from a friend who called it the Whiskey Dance. Now we dance it here in Anchorage but we've changed the name of it to Pepsi Cola or Coca-Cola Dance because of all the abusing of alcohol and drugs. My grandchildren love to dance it.

After I buried my mom in 1961, I stopped at Kotzebue for a few days to visit my sister. And my uncle Paul came over. Uncle Paul was my mother's first cousin. "Big Snow up in the Mountains" was his motion dance. He said, "*Ooyouho* [Little Niecie], when you need help with the dances, I can drum. I'll be glad to come down and help you." "Good," I said. That following spring he died of a heart attack. In the meantime I was pregnant with my boy, so I named him Koomulook (which means Something Shiny), my uncle's name. Today my son is happy to see his own nephews dancing that same motion dance.

In my mind, old songs like that motion dance pop up and I sing them. That's because when I was a little girl, my mother used to take me to the Eskimo dances in other people's houses. And I'd go to sleep, it just pleased me so much. Now I sing those Eskimo songs to *my* grandchildren and they go right to sleep.

Hospitality used to be very important, sometimes a matter of survival. Like if my grandparents had visitors from Kivalina, Noatak, or from Port Lee and Kotzebue, they welcomed them. Guests stayed for days and days, just like relatives. My grandparents or anyone else just welcomed the visitors and fed them and if their clothing needed fixing, the women fixed it up for them. My mom's great-uncle used to tell me, "If a stranger comes to the village, give him a smile and invite him for a drink of water or hot tea because when you grow up, you never know when you're going to need that smile from the strangers to make you feel good."

# Norma Jean Saunders

*Denali Solo*
*Anchorage*
*b. 1959*

*When Palmer High School sophomore Norma Jean Saunders first became interested in mountain climbing, Denali, the Great One, was always just over the horizon. At 20,320 feet, its south peak, the highest point in North America, attracted as many as nine hundred climbers annually—despite the severe risks posed by the unpredictability of its weather. Norma Jean first tried to reach the summit in 1980 with five other women but was forced down by a gale when she reached the 16,000-foot level. More frustration followed when she worked as an assistant guide for several years but was not promoted to full guide, because, she thinks, she is a woman.*

*Mountaineering is a sport made of firsts. Famed adventurer Naomi Uemura made the first McKinley solo ascent in 1970 and died in 1984 trying to make the first in winter. That honor went to Vern Tejas of Anchorage in 1988. After Norma Jean Saunders's 1990 trip, her ninth on the mountain, she, as far as anyone knows, became the first woman to reach the summit of McKinley un-aided.*

*Norma Jean understands the dangers and has had to retrieve the bodies of partners who have fallen to their deaths. "Reaching summits isn't worth dying over," she says. "I'll never solo McKinley again."*

IT WAS the spring when I was twenty-seven that I was to guide a group of women up the West Buttress of McKinley. I had been keeping fit by running and training with weights and when the trip fell through, I decided to try to solo the mountain. I had heard that no woman had ever soloed Denali. Although an Italian woman claimed that she had, many people said that she had actually roped up with others and had joined other teams for food and shelter.

On the spur of the moment that May in 1986 I decided to try. I maybe wasn't in the best frame of mind, with no definite career and ending an extremely rocky marriage. My husband was a bar-type person, always drinking and partying while I was out skiing and climbing. When he got involved in drugs, I left.

My second day on the mountain my tent was destroyed by wind and I had to sleep in snow shelters. But I was doing pretty good until at high camp at 17,200 feet a woman climber became very ill with pulmonary edema mountain sickness. Her partner, an old friend of mine, asked me to help him get her down to 14,000 feet. Since I was the only other person at 17,200 feet, I felt I should help, even though it meant using up a rare spell of good weather.

I rested a day after helping her down, then returned to 17,200 feet but that night bad weather moved in and when I tried for the summit the next day, I was only able to reach the summit ridge at 19,900 feet. The winds were so strong they kept knocking me over. Not being roped to anyone and with the winds increasing, I decided to return to high camp. After waiting out a nine-day storm, I ran out of food and fuel and slept in snow caves with whomever had a little extra food to share. When the weather broke slightly, I headed down and ended my twenty-three days on the mountain.

Finally later that same year, on my sixth attempt, I reached the summit of McKinley. I was working as an assistant guide for Genet Expeditions (with Vern Tejas as lead guide); we made the summit on a good day and it all seemed a little anticlimactic.

A few months later I went up with a small group of friends, including a guide named Clark Saunders, and again made the summit, after a seventeen-day climb. The significance of that was that Clark and I were dating and the climb got him to thinking about me pretty seriously. He and I decided to fly paragliders in Utah, where his family was living. We settled for the winter at a ski resort to ski and paraglide. Each day after work we skied until late afternoon and then rushed down the canyons to get a long evening flight in.

In the spring of 1987, we bicycled up the West Coast from L.A. to Seattle. We again spent a couple of months on McKinley. This time Clark was assistant guiding with Dave Staeheli for Genet Expeditions. Unbeknownst to me, he was planning to ask me to marry him if his group made the summit. For a while it didn't look good because one of his climbers succumbed to altitude sickness and Clark had to lead him back to safety.

I was coordinating climbers and glacier pilots from base camp's radio hut when I received Clark's CB call from the summit. I thought something had gone wrong because normally you don't radio from the summit unless something unusual has happened on the climb. Clark was so nervous and his microphone was shaking so badly that all he said was, "Will you marry me?" I said yes, as long as he'd ask me again when he was at a lower altitude and had more oxygen in his brain!

That conversation was heard by radio operators all over the state, and many of them jumped in with their congratulations. It was really sweet. Clark and I were married on September 1, 1988. We both felt that we couldn't have found a better friend or partner for life.

That winter we honeymooned by working at a ski resort near Anchorage. In spring 1989 we began our own paragliding school, Raven Adventures, at Palmer, Alaska. By the next winter we were back paragliding in Utah, managing a ski rental and retail shop and teaching telemarking. It was during that winter of 1989–90 that I decided again to complete my unfinished business from 1986 and to solo McKinley. I began to cross-country ski on a sixteen-kilometer run that took me from 7,600 to 9,400 feet. And I learned to skate ski, one of the hardest forms of training I had ever attempted.

When we returned to Alaska in the spring of 1990, we continued to backpack up a 3,000-foot "hill" in order to launch ourselves into the sky. Do that several times a day carrying a fifteen-pound glider and you are getting in shape!

After two months of that, I felt I was ready for some serious planning. After all my earlier expeditions I had a small warehouse of equipment, but I still needed a one-man tent and a crevasse-bridging device. Dave Staeheli (our friend, fellow guide, second man to winter-solo McKinley) loaned me his tent and described to Clark how to rig a ladder for crevasse protection.

I took eighteen days' worth of freeze-dried food for a total summit attempt cost of sixty dollars! I had my gear down to the absolute minimum. My entire load, including the food and fuel, weighed only one hundred twenty-eight pounds. Carrying a fifty-pound pack and towing seventy-four pounds in the sled, I could take the entire load with me (without having to portage any of it) and drop food and fuel off at my various camps.

Clark saw me off May 29 in bright sunshine at the Kahiltna landing strip at the 7,200-foot level. I hoped I could move strongly enough to be home soon, but excitement about the climb overcame any other thoughts.

Good weather and all my training enabled me to move very

quickly along the West Buttress route, completing a carry, moving gear to the next camp, in half the time it had ever taken me before.

I had my first bad weather at 14,00 feet, where a blizzard kept me and several other parties trapped for five days. On the sixth day (my ninth on the mountain), though the weather was still grim, I moved to the high camp at 17,200 feet because that would be a better position to be in if the weather opened up. From 14,000 feet to 17,200 feet I had to break trail carrying a pack so heavy, seventy pounds, I had to hoist it up in two stages. I was gasping with every move. I was really focused and I was really together but I thought I was going to have a heart attack.

Some other climbers had caught up to me by the time I reached the high camp. The wind was whipping snow about so violently that I could not see my hand in front of my face. I dug a tent site out of the blowing snow and settled in to brew up hot drinks, make dinner, and think. Because I had only brought five days' worth of food I began to worry about lasting out another long storm.

The next day dawned with little wind, but clouds were still scudding around the mountain, a sure sign of unstable weather. I kicked back to rest for the day when we heard on the radio about some Japanese high above us who needed assistance. They were frostbitten and lost and one had died. I thought, "Oh God, not again." I was worried I'd get up there and wouldn't be able to complete the climb again because I'd be involved in a rescue.

I helped break trail to meet the Japanese that were stumbling down to the 17,200 camp. Then we made hot drinks for them. I offered to take them down but fortunately some rangers came for them, and eventually the Japanese were helicoptered out from the 14,000-foot level. It angered me that these people had risked their lives and the lives of the people who had had to rescue them. One person was dead and it seemed so unnecessary.

As that entire day went by, I could see the weather was improving by the minute. I kept asking folks at high camp if they were heading up after the rescue. No one knew, and by nine-thirty P.M., when all the Japanese survivors were down, I decided to go up. I could see a front system moving in like a great gray wall. I figured I had about eighteen hours before it would arrive and bring more bad weather.

I headed up in the dark. At Denali Pass I looked back and saw that many climbers from the high camp were finally setting out. So far I was the only person up at 18,200 feet. It felt good to be alone, really alone for the first time on the solo. I did meet the body-recovery party, who were in tears, and I had to step over the one Japanese man who did not make it down alive. His body was recovered two days later.

When I made it to the summit ridge at 19,800 feet, about the height I had reached on my last solo attempt, I speeded up in order not to be caught by the others. I reached the summit at four A.M. as the sun rose above the clouds and the mountain was bathed in a bright pink. The clouds glowed iridescently yellow. To my right the full moon was still casting shadows in the valleys below. Because the sun rose to my left, on my right was a huge shadow, the shadow of McKinley itself, with the moon beside it. The summit view was beyond description and frighteningly beautiful.

I sat down to think about the climb, what had made it successful for me, and what climbing had meant to me all those years. I thought of the dead Japanese, who, like me, had set out to make his dreams come true. Wondering if it was worth the hardships (yes, oh yes, in every way!) and if climbing is fair to the loved ones who must worry at home, I mainly thanked God and my husband and family for their continued care and support. They were what got me up there successfully.

I was able to spend forty-five minutes alone on the summit before the first of the other climbing parties arrived. I headed down slowly so as not to make a fatal mistake descending, as is often the case. (I knew that if I had broken my leg or fallen, then it would have been, "That stupid woman!") I was hugged by each climber who passed.

Glacier pilot Jim Okonek was waiting for me at the base camp with the best surprise of all, my husband, Clark! For me the climb ended where it had begun, hugging Clark on the glacier.

During that solo I learned that I had more strength and power inside me than I had ever known. I am not sorry that I spent all those climbing apprenticeship years to gain experience. By always climbing with people more experienced than themselves lots of mountaineers never learn their own inner limits of what they are willing to do. They never learn their own reactions under maximum stress.

In climbing, as in most other sports, men have led the way but women have learned fast. Even more women would climb if there were less competition between men and women and more learning from each other. I believe, as Wanda Rutkiewicz did, that we should worry less about competing, men against women, and just talk less, climb more, and learn more.

People ask me what helped me most to get to the summit alone. It is as my heroine and mentor Junko Tabei said of climbing, "Technique and ability alone do not get you to the top; it is the willpower that is the most important. This willpower cannot be bought, or taught, or given to you by others. It rises from your heart."

# Gretchen Schmidt

*Accepted in Fairbanks*
*Fairbanks*
*b. 1956*

*During the last hundred years Alaska's many booms have lured the hopeful north with tales of wealth for the taking. In February 1976 a Renton, Washington, nineteen-year-old named Gretchen Schmidt [not her real name] arrived in Fairbanks after reading a newspaper ad that said, "Dancers Wanted, Fairbanks, Alaska." Her goal was to make enough money to buy a sound system so that she could conquer Manhattan as a Cole Porter cabaret singer. Instead her job as a Two Street [Second Avenue] go-go dancer evolved into a striptease act in the final year of the pipeline construction frenzy.*

*Fairbanks pays its respects to some of its past entertainers and ladies of the night in such names as Barbara Street, formerly trails leading to brothels. Yet the greatest recent shrine to the good-times boom town, the First and Second Avenue bar block, is now mostly a parking lot.*

I AM A part of history that got tore down. It's just physically not there anymore. There's not even a plaque that says, "You are now standing in what was a famous block where Indians from all over the state came to vacation."

The bar block was across from the visitors' center, where that big parking lot is now. First Avenue was the Stampede, the Gold Rush, the International Pancake House, and then the French Quarter and the Pastime Bar. So you could party for days and never leave that block. Just go in circles.

And in the old days, before my time, all the bars were connected by doors. Like on the other side of the Flame was the Gold Rush and

**211**

through the Roustabout was the Stampede. In those they used to open the doors. I knew how to get through from the Flame to the next bar without ever going outside. And then there was the alley behind the Flame, which was supposed to be so scary. I walked through that alley all the time, and nothing ever happened to me back there. I didn't know that you were supposed to be scared.

Beyond the Flame Lounge and the Roustabout there were several Indian bars. Across the street was the Mecca, where the Tiki Cove used to be in the downstairs. In one of the Indian bars there was a liquor store.

And so there were all those Indians on Second Avenue messing with the hookers. Some pretty funny stuff would happen, these old guys from the Bush that had never seen that kind of life.

The northern Native people were usually smiling and laughing and were not that rowdy with strangers. They'd just stand out there and tease the girls, and the girls were always pooh-poohing these little old short guys who were following them around. I could stand out in front of the Flame for hours laughing at the things going on, at the local kids throwing stuff at the whores. All these young people had never been exposed to any of this, either.

That block was the Natives' Waikiki. Just think how white people would feel if someone went over to Waikiki and turned it into a parking lot. Bullshit! The city council decided that it was too disgraceful for all the refined visitors to see whores and puking Natives on the streets, and so the city council just got rid of 'em. They did the same thing in Anchorage. They called it "cleaning up" to get rid of these unruly, drunken people. And I said, "Shit, go to Waikiki and watch what Americans do, these refined people. Whites are not any different doing it, they're just not Natives."

We used to smoke pot where the visitor's center is now. Natives and anybody who needed to take a nap used to sleep on that site. I slept there a lot of times myself. Just go down there and sit on the edge of the river and wait for the bars to open back up. Unless you had somebody that had a car and could go out to the Boatel 'cause the bars on the outskirts of town opened at eight [A.M.]. Town bars didn't reopen until noon. And on hot summer days, shit, you don't know what time it is! It don't matter. It's broad daylight.

I came to Fairbanks in February of '76, right before the end of the pipeline period. There was a lot of people coming off the Slope in '76 and showing up in town. So the bars were packed twenty-one hours a day. Most of them only closed for three hours.

I stayed stoned on pot. At first I didn't even drink hard liquor. I drank Bud. But they taught me how to drink Chivas on the rocks and things like that. I like to have fun, so I talked to everybody. I'd sit and listen to their spiels. Everybody was spieling me to find out where I was at. All the whores wanted to know if I was going to work, because if I was they wanted me in their stable so that they wouldn't have to work as hard. And I listened to all these jive guys, "Gee, honey . . ." They tried to talk me out of my paychecks every week by "doubling my money" for me. I didn't do coke at that time—I was an acid freak, reds and pot, to me coke and heroin were the hard drugs—so I had my little limits of what I would do.

I had never been in a strip joint before, so I worked at the Flame Lounge go-go joint down on Second Avenue with all the street trash because of my morality. I wouldn't set foot in the Bare Affair because they *took their clothes off* in there. Actually the Bare Affair was a beautiful club. No whores table-hopped in there. No unescorted women. It was a showhouse, and all the strippers were from Las Vegas and had tons of costumes and their own light and sound people. They were professional strippers.

I always felt that I had to live my life during the pipeline days in a way that didn't make me uncomfortable. Mom and I discussed it before I took the job. And she said, "As long as you can feel okay about what you're doing, then it's fine, but when you start feeling guilty and start compromising yourself, then it's time to quit. 'Cause it's gonna wear on you and you're gonna feel bad." So I never felt bad about it!

But I thought the Flame Lounge go-go joint was gross! It was dirty and full of freaky-looking people. The dancers freaked me out. One of 'em was about fifty years old and she was scary. And then this other one was really big and fat. But she was very nice, and may she rest in peace, she died in a fire; she had five little kids and her husband was a GI. And then there was this little Japanese girl . . .

At the Bare we didn't show any pussy or anything. I mean you couldn't spread your legs or any of that kind of stuff. My job was just to party with people. So I loved it. I was being paid to sit around and bull-shit for eight hours a day. I really believe that in isolated boom towns like this the workers have got to have a break. When the men came to town they were just so weird after being up on the Slope without seeing any women. So I'd say to them, "Hi, how are you? Where did you come from?" and half the time they wouldn't say a word. I'd just sit there and chatter away.

At first I was a terrible dancer. I wouldn't move my hips because I thought that was disgusting. I was a rock-and-roller. I did "the Pony." I played Tina Turner music, none of that funky disco crap.

I changed a lot, though, and I started running around with a couple of the hookers. For some reason they really liked me. I didn't understand it at the time, but it was because I drew the customers to them.

The whores called me "Free Fuck" 'cause I'd have a boyfriend for a week. But he was my boyfriend and there was no money involved, so I felt okay about it. The whores thought I was crazy. I always went for the young, cute ones, and the whores said I should go for the old ones, who were quick.

I could trust the whores. They never hurt me. I used to wander all over the bar block, from bar to bar. Nothing ever happened. I trusted the whores, the street people, everybody. Because everyone after a while knows who you are. And I was just one of the idiot dancers who was no threat. I didn't deal drugs, I wasn't a whore—which are the basic things that people fight over on the street.

The Natives, shit, they never bothered me. I always had a dollar for 'em or a cigarette. I'd go smoke joints with them in the alley behind the French Quarter.

I didn't know enough to be afraid of people. I wasn't afraid of anybody. I just thought we were all one big, happy family.

But we had hard-core big-city pimps and hookers standing on street corners fighting with each other for space. These girls got ballsy toward the end. They'd wear no clothes underneath fur coats and they'd flash people going by at sixty below. They were nuts. And a lot of 'em were still here for years afterwards, like they didn't have the sense to get out after the business disappeared. And the bars knew who they were and wouldn't let them in. Even the really classy whores couldn't go into certain bars in town. And to me that was my whole life, going to bars. I couldn't imagine not being able to just walk into a bar if I wanted to. I loved the energy. Everybody was real up and happy and partying. We all had lots of money. I loved to dance. I loved to shoot pool. I loved to talk. Between those three I could occupy all my time.

I'd work eight hours at the Bare Affair or the Flame and then I'd go dancing for eight hours. Then I'd eat, go home, sleep. And I was late every day. I got fired a couple of times a month. I was never on time once!

I think the strip-joint scene in Fairbanks is much sicker now. These dancers today might as well work as whores or at least go off where nobody has to watch 'em do it because it's not fun. And what I did was fun! We had lots of couples that were very comfortable in our bar. I didn't do anything to embarrass anybody except myself.

I wasn't that good of a dancer in the beginning either. But I smiled a lot; I was just having fun. And I goofed on people and stuff. But now it's like a bad pornographic movie with no class, style, or fun.

What we did was fun to watch.

I like to dance. I learned from the Las Vegas strippers how to tease. Nowadays in Fairbanks the dancers have taken the tease out of the strip. And when you take the tease out of striptease, what do you have left? A naked body. Naked bodies aren't all that great to look at. That's not entertainment.

Some of our women were *good*. When they went bottomless, it was right at the end of the show, and they'd hit one little thing on their fancy costume, and ping, off it would come, and they'd whip a cape around them and stalk off the stage. That was show business.

This stuff, they walk up there in a G-string, take it off, and that's it. So they don't make any money because the kind of people they attract sit in corners and are not fun. Besides, the pipeline is long over and the fast money is long gone.

At the Bare Affair we had to be fully dressed in long gowns when wandering around the floor talking to customers. And there was no physical contact allowed. No sitting on anybody's lap. The pipeline people were a lot of Texans, Okies, and people from Louisiana that were pretty loud and fun to party with. But the Bare Affair had a rule that you couldn't yell "Yahoo" or you'd get thrown out. We were trying to be more refined.

When I first went on the stage as a bikini dancer at the Flame Lounge in '76, I was freaking out all the time from so many men staring at my body. (We just wore regular bathing suits because stores didn't sell all the sexy lingerie that they sell now.) Later at the Bare Affair I had to go topless after my last song. In the beginning I just flashed while leaving the stage but after a while, it's like everything else, I got used to it. Then guys started asking me how much money it would cost for me to strip completely. So I was mooning for a hundred dollars. Going bottomless was never comfortable for me and I danced with my knees close together, barely moving at all. Mooning for a hundred dollars was pretty tacky now that I think about it.

Some people can't differentiate between the dancer who entertains and the woman who services the men sexually. And a lot of women thought I was very stupid for not taking the money men offered me for sex! But I was so young that I had to draw my boundaries, and that was a boundary that I drew.

I had a whole lot more fun than the whores did, though, because I could meet anybody I wanted and go wherever I wanted. I got to see a

lot of Fairbanks and make friends with all the locals and eventually—
God forbid—become one.

Because I was a dancer on Two Street, I knew all these bizarre people, but they didn't touch me. They laughed at me a lot because I was so
stupid. I would meet women in the bars, and here we were on Second
Avenue in the middle of the pipeline construction frenzy and the bar
packed with people and I would say, "Hi, what do you do for a living?"
And they'd say, "Oh, I work." "Where?" "Well, I'm working now."
"What do you mean you're working now?" And they'd have to spell it
out to me! And finally I'd go, "Oh!" And then, "How can you do a
thing like that?"

For a while I was on a crusade to save all the whores because they
were so young. A couple of them had been born into it. Their parents
had sold them to pimps when they were twelve, thirteen years old. They
seemed like real tough bitches until I started talking to them and looking at them and realizing that they were only fourteen or fifteen years
old. I'd encourage those street girls to tell me about their lives, and I'd
end up crying and feeling so bad. I'd promise I'd get them a job and get
'em out of that.

But they made a lot more money than I did, and they thought I
was a fool for working for two [hundred] twenty-five a week. To me
two twenty-five a week in 1976, God, that was a lot of money! I didn't
need anything from anybody. I wouldn't even take tips in the beginning.
I punched the first guy that tried to tip me. Poor Jim! He's a really nice
man and I got to know him over the years. What he was trying to do
was put a five in my bikini top, but I didn't know that. When he mo-
tioned me over to the side of the stage, I thought he was going to tell me
something. I bent down because the music was so loud, and he grabbed
my top and I nailed him. After that nobody would tip me. I thought that
tipping was disgusting, so I told everybody, "If anybody tries to touch
me . . ." So I lost some money there, but I didn't care because with two
twenty-five a week, I didn't need their money.

Anyway most of the pipeline men were family people, fellas with
sisters. Each of us dancers had her own types of people that liked us.
Men were always saying about me, "God, doesn't she remind you of so
and so that lived next door to Ma?" So I made my money from the people who liked me because they thought I looked like the girl next door.

My job was to sit and party with the men. I'd sit at one table for a
while and laugh and talk and tell jokes and have a couple of beers and
then I'd go sit at the next table. That was my job, to keep moving—or

I'd get in trouble. If the owner thought I was having too much fun in one place, he'd fire me. And hire me back the next day. He was a temperamental guy, a real heavy drinker, and so was I. Some days I'd listen to him 'cause he was the boss, and some days I didn't care. Especially when I had a little money in the bank, then I'd have more guts. So I was probably fired twenty times.

Fairbanks was so small that there were only a couple of places to go, and everybody went there. So I met thousands and thousands of people. Even if they only stopped in Fairbanks once, they all hit the Bare Affair and the Flame because those were the only two places where that kind of person went. Of course, there was a whole group of people that didn't drink. My God, I don't even know where they went. They went home!

I soon realized that the men I met at the Bare Affair were mostly people that just wanted a woman to talk to. Like Klondike Kate in the gold rush, it does take a certain kind of woman to put up with guys that were boring as hell because they had been doing nothing but working and hanging around with men. And reading a lot. Many wanted to discuss books with me, and I enjoyed that part. Other dancers would tell them, "Gretchen will talk to you about that shit."

We made so much money! There were entire sets where all I did was stand there, take the money and say thank you and smile and nod. That's all I'd do for ten minutes was take money. I had my rules for that. They could only put the money in my boot or on my chain—I got that far—or in my hand or I didn't want it. The ones who wanted to put it in my pants or in my top, forget it! So there were people who wouldn't tip me because I wouldn't do that or kiss 'em.

Money was circulating so fast during the pipeline period that some of the same bills I spent came back to me quickly. Someone would tip me and I would tip the cabdriver. He would tip the waiter or pay the babysitter who would give it to her husband who would come to the bar and give it to me. I could tell because people put markings on bills, and the money was no sooner in my hand then I was turning around paying for drinks at the bar and it would be handed to somebody else as change.

I didn't care about money. I thought I was rich because when I went to the Bare Affair, I was making three hundred twenty-five dollars a week. I was nineteen years old, and the most I had ever made was like seventy dollars before taxes. And then I was making anywhere from a hundred to three hundred dollars a day in tips. Sometimes five! Sometimes seven!

And I wouldn't take anything more than a fifty—except when I started going bottomless and people would give me a hundred dollars. But then I got into cocaine and the rest of it is sort of foggy, as I started spending all my money on drugs at work. Before that I saved and went to Seattle and bought my mom things. I was never good at shopping; I always bought stupid stuff I'd never use. But it was neat to think that I could fly to Seattle and do this. . . . People in Seattle used to pick on me and say, "When are you going to get a real job?" I'd answer, "Why should I get a real job when I don't have to work like that?"

People don't like it when you have a lot of vacations and you have so much fun on your job as I did. I loved my job!

But after a year I started being with this guy that hated strip joints, hated the life. He was a woodsman, lived in a cabin outside of town. And I started being sucked into a different side of Alaska, the homesteader side. What a mistake! I never married him, but it was a time when I was challenging all my beliefs. And then I got real confused about what I wanted. And then I knew I wouldn't dance anymore because it had changed overnight.

Maybe the change was mostly in my mind that dancing became so sleazy. But we didn't table dance and we didn't have drink chips. I didn't make any money off the drinks that I drank or anything like that. And that's mostly what the clubs are all about now. Dancers' drinks cost a certain amount of money whether it's just a glass of water. And they now have all these funky rules. You can't sit down with someone. You've got to either be table dancing for him or walking around in your bikini. I know that part is different, but I don't know when it changed. All I know is that I wasn't happy with it anymore. And I had skills as a waiter because I had been a Playboy bunny when I was eighteen in Wisconsin. As soon as I quit dancing I became a waiter again.

Three years ago while I was bartending I married a friend of mine from the pipeline boom. I have been living in Fairbanks continuously ever since, and I have been sober and off drugs for fourteen months. I used to move every six months because I thought, God, if I couldn't move, I'd die.

Staying put is part of my new sobriety, but I have been learning the benefits of living in one place long-term. I have been living in and out of Fairbanks since I was nineteen. I know a lot of people and I like going in the grocery store and sometimes it's just so fun to chat with people I know. The little stuff is starting to mean something to me. When Fred got offered a job in Anchorage, I panicked that we might have to move there. You see, I like living here. I can live here with my past. Everybody in town knows who I am and it doesn't matter. To the people that it matters, I never have to see them anyway. But I remember that when I was in Seattle, there was a constant hypocrisy about my past. People there heard bits and pieces of my life history. "Oh, you're Gretchen," and they would look at me like I was an alien or something. The only ones who didn't do that were a couple of the guys, but then at the same time they always wanted to see my tits. It was like, "Oh, you were a dancer, you must have a great body." They expected me to be something else than what I was.

I just know that I would never live in Seattle ever again. I have tried so many times, and I go down there with high expectations. I go back to the South End and there is so much hatred toward people of other races and people of other kinds. There are a lot of people who hate me because I was a "slut" in high school and I must be a hooker now to have stayed so long up here. They say the bizzarest things to me. They don't know who I am. They want to tell me who I am. And that's weird! They walk right up to me and say these things. They are in my face. They interfere. I have never been able to be peaceful in Seattle with just who and what I am.

In Fairbanks there is not as much pressure to conform. Would Joe Vogler survive anywhere else? I read his letters to the editor all the time. He is a sign of how tolerant people are here. Many absolutely disagree with that guy but no one has shot him or anything. He and his wife just continue writing their letters. People respect them for being as verbal as they are.

I don't want to have to say that I live in a certain neighborhood or drive a certain car or wear certain clothes for people to like me. Fairbanks is a lot more accepting than that. You're allowed to be eccentric, a little bit different, here. In fact, it's expected!

# Mary Shields

*Choosing a Different Life*
*Fairbanks*
*b. 1944*

*Before the coming of modern technology almost everyone who moved to Alaska
had to accept backwoods conditions as part of the northern life-style. Today urban
comforts have largely replaced rural rigors for the majority of Alaskans, but the
state's outdoor culture still encourages people to consider a backwoods lifestyle.
Noted author Mary Shields says that the old Alaska is alive and well. "That
spirit is a freedom to live a different life than you could live Outside. That's why
we're here."*

*Mary Shields arrived in the country in 1965 as a twenty-year-old Camp
Fire Girls counselor. By 1969 she was training her first freight dogs to take her
deep into the wilderness, and in 1974 she was accomplished enough as a musher
to become the first woman to complete the thousand-mile Iditarod race. She now
summers near Fairbanks (where she demonstrates mushing daily for riverboat
tourists) and winters at her bush cabin.*

A T LEAST half of Fairbanks-area mushers are women. The sport ap-
peals to us because we have a feeling of strength to know that we can
get from point A to point B on our own without having to rely on a
stinky, noisy machine.

Plus I simply like to get out into the wilderness as much as I can. I
like being with my dogs. I like to be close to nature and to have a big
chunk of time away from the routines of the city. My favorite adventures
are long trips in March and April, when the days are long and the temperatures (minus twenty to ten above) conducive to travel.

After about ten hours on the trail, about an hour before sunset, we are looking for a campsite out of the wind in a nice grove of spruce so I am nestled in the trees. Near a little overflow or a hole in the ice is perfect so I don't have to melt snow but can get water out of the creek. I look for a place where I will get the sun in the morning to wake me up early. An uphill to start out with the next morning is good because the dogs will be frisky when we first take off. A nice grade going up so that I have a lot of control rather than a treacherous, icy downhill.

The first thing I do when making camp is to snowshoe a platform flat for the five-by-seven canvas-wall tent. Then while the flattened snow is firming up, I unharness the dogs and drag in dead firewood. Spruce boughs and a layer of caribou hides provide insulation under the tent floor. I use my sled and snowshoes to hold out the sides.

After I fire up the Yukon stove, the tent becomes a cozy haven where I have decorated the inside with bright calico pockets for things I need to reach quickly.

After mixing my friends some commercial dog food, fat, and hot water, I make my own dinner of, say, brown rice, frozen vegetables, and salmon. Falling asleep comes very easily.

This life-style is a choice which many of us have made. I do not live near Fairbanks, Alaska, for the sunshine! If I wanted flowers, I would live in Hawaii. Oh, I enjoy the bright, colorful summers but I live here because I like winter best. I love the cold and the frost and the moonlight. On June 21, when everyone else is celebrating the longest day of the year, I am quietly remembering the sound of my sled runners and dogs in the wilderness. I celebrate June 22 because the days start getting a tiny bit darker and shorter. Winter is beginning to come back!

# Willie Smalley, Jr.

*Village Cop*
*Marshall*
*b. 1952*

*In Alaska the Native population was the majority until early in this century. In many bush communities Native ways still prevail. And that is the environment preferred by Willie Smalley, a distinctly non-Eskimo black man and village police safety officer (VPSO) at Marshall, Alaska.*

IT TOOK a while but I am accepted by most of the older people and by those that want to do good things for the village. People along the Yukon River here tend to think that the outside world is against them, but they know that I have two mixed kids, part black and part Yup'ik and Athabaskan, and that contributes to my being accepted.

I was living up in Holy Cross, and a village cop job became available a couple of times. The first few times I didn't even bother applying for it because most of the villages usually look for local hire before they start hiring outside people. And I was still considered an outsider.

I have been working as a village cop for seven and a half years. I try not to show favoritism. That's pretty hard because I have to see the same people every day. Here if I arrest somebody, the way the system is, two or three days later they'll be right back here out on bail. After a while I just expect that to happen and I accept it.

As a VPSO there is a lot of pressure because I'm the first person that gets called if *anything* happens. Even if it's not related to my work. I get called by people wanting some kind of information about civil court matters. VPSOs are not involved with that but with criminal stuff. Or if there are kids up on somebody's building, they want me to tell them to get down. And it kind of wears on me after a while. There's quite a bit of pressure to be the person that if anything happens, the responsibility lands on me no matter what else I have to do.

It's kind of like being a village chief. We don't have a village chief, but we have a president of the traditional council. The traditional elders council is not that active right now and the regular city government pretty much runs everything.

And anything involving safety, I am involved in it. I'm a police officer, safety officer, fire chief, emergency medical technician, and search and rescue man. I'm like one of the old chiefs that did everything. If there is a fire, people start talking about it on the CB and set off the alarm. The village is so small that by the time I get to the fire others will already be there, too. We have all the fire equipment and I know how to use it.

Normally when I am out patrolling I don't carry a gun, only my club, handcuffs, and baton. When we get a gun call, I get my shotgun or my AR-15 and take it with me. I first go into the area to try to find out what the situation is without putting myself in jeopardy. If it's going on at this one particular house, I try to find a good place to observe from before I decide what to do. I try to determine if anybody's in the house, if anybody's been shot, where the suspect is. Then I isolate the area and keep people away. We usually have a couple of officers. Sometimes we have to get volunteers to help out, but we haven't had a situation like that here yet. Because I'm the only village cop here at Marshall now, I usually use my brother for a backup. If I need him, he comes.

When I was working down in Alakanuk I had a rash of suicides. Over a two-year period ten or eleven people from that five-hundred-person village committed suicide. They had a superstition that years ago the shamans, Native witch doctors, had put a curse over the village. When one kid committed suicide, it started snowballing because people believed that the shamans were coming back and taking their young people. People there had strong beliefs in that kind of stuff, so we started suicide prevention workshops, which helped quite a bit, though the suicides continued after I left.

I grew up around superstitions in Florida, where people believed in the bogeyman, witches riding people's back when they are sleeping, all kinds of southern black stories that my parents used to tell us. Ghost stories. I believe that those things don't affect you unless you believe in them.

Alaska has a lot more opportunity than Tampa, Florida, where I came from. And as for being a black person, Alaska is definitely better.

Being in villages, I get stereotyped by  people and there is a certain amount of prejudice in all cultures and I have to deal with that. But I am used to it and so it doesn't bother me.

# Larry Smith

*Something Fishy!*
*Sitka*
*b. 1953*

*The North has always been a colonial or semicolonial zone of extractive indus-tries: fishing, mining, energy, and lumbering. Even today the government occupies about half of the state's economy, and a strong manufacturing sector has yet to emerge.*

*Coloradans Larry and Shelia Smith were bitten by the entrepreneurial bug when Larry's sister, Sharon Gillispie, decided to transform Southeast fish into microwave dinners in 1987. Larry, Shelia, and Sharon hocked everything to create a manufacturing plant in Sitka, at the source of a steady supply of fresh salmon, cod, halibut and, for the Japanese market, sea cucumbers.*

THIS BUSINESS involves secondary processing of seafood. Our goal was to do more of the processing of Alaskan resources in the state to keep some of the dollars here that would normally be going to Seattle pro-ducers. This was such an exciting idea that we just had to leave our other work and give it a try!

It was only a year from the time that we conceived the project to where we were ready to operate. We put in fourteen- to sixteen-hour days, seven days a week. We had to do that in order to keep things going. We invested our own accumulated savings into this business, and it's been tough.

Finding financing to get a business started is always the most diffi-cult thing to do, but it is extremely difficult to do in Alaska because the capital is just not here. And investors in other states are not willing to gamble on sending their money to distant Alaska to have it invested out of their sight.

Finding a supply from fishermen and divers always comes down to price. It's a very simple business relationship. They have a product to sell and we want to buy. Of course, when we sell that product after we process it, the market is pretty firm on a price. So what we can pay fishermen and divers is easy to compute—though they are always looking for more. Don't ever bullshit a fisherman or a sea cucumber diver. You've got to talk to 'em straight or you've lost all credibility. They're down-to-earth and they say what they're thinking. They're gems in that they'd give the shirts off their back, and yet if you ever cross 'em, their whole community of fishermen never talk to you again. When someone gets a bad reputation with the fishermen, that's it!

I really respect the fishermen because it takes a certain amount of guts to get out there when it's blowing forty knots and go fishing for the critters that we need to keep our process going. Especially during the wintertime when it's rough weather and we need some cod. Every year here in Sitka we lose a couple of fishermen during the openings, the short periods when fishing is permitted. When that happens, it brings the danger right to home. So I believe in paying them everything we can for their effort and the risks that they're taking.

We have a lot of people cutting sea cucumbers for piecework wages and every one of them has a story. We had one fella working here who had had a hard time holding down jobs. His wife had just left him and was demanding quite a bit of support from him. And he just loved his work. He would come in every day and say how much he appreciated his job and loved what he was doing. But his performance was just falling off. He had not been producing the last couple of days and Sharon asked if there was some problem. And he said no. And when lunch break came, he just kept working. She said, "You're going to stop for lunch, aren't you?" He said, "No, I don't have a lunch." She said, "You didn't bring one with you?" He said, "No." "Aren't you going to go get one?" "No." She said, "Fred, aren't you hungry?" "Yes." She said, "How long has it been since you've eaten?" And it turned out that his last meal had been a dinner two days previous. He hadn't eaten anything since then because he had no money. It turned out that he had been giving all of his money to his ex-wife. We started to investigate his finances a little bit to find out just how bad it was. He had an apartment that cost more than he was making per month. So we had to work with him and with some agencies to try to find some housing he could afford, and get him on a budget, and work with his ex-wife in the courts, and get to a point where he could have a living and not get lost through the cracks. He finally got a little bit on his feet. He actually got a new vehicle and he got a job prospect up in Craig and he decided to go for that and we wished him well.

We had to help out because without us it just wasn't going to happen. There are all kinds of public programs in the state of Alaska, but so many people's problems get lost in the system. I am critical because we have had many cases here where when it came right down to a person who had an urgent, immediate need to find a place to live or to get some food, they couldn't get that help. All they got was a bunch of bullshit!

I'm sorry if that sounds a little strong, but that's what happens. It just pisses us off every time we get into this.

Here in Alaska neighbors and churches no longer have to take the burden of taking care of people in misfortune because there are state agencies to do it. The only catch is that the state agencies are unresponsive. Plus this Southeast area has an incredible number of hard-luck cases, transients that come to Alaska to make their fortune. They get on the ferry and just see what they can find. Sitka gets overwhelmed! We've been discouraged by our personal dealings with this. But we have been able to help some people and send them on their way when they are ready to leave.

# Molly Smith

*True Gold*
*Douglas*
*b. 1952*

*The Perseverance Theater company in Douglas is Alaskan in several ways. First,
many of its productions are written by Alaskan playwrights or concern Alaskan
subjects. Second, the Perseverance's actors, managers, producers, designers, and
craftsmen are jacks-of-all-trades, the way Alaskans have traditionally been. And
third, as befitting a new state, this theater is a stage for the unexpected, the un-
tried, and the experimental.*

*Perseverance's founder-director Molly Smith has always reached beyond the
Juneau community for inspiration and talent. She and her colleagues like to take
their productions to such communities as fishing villages or logging camps, sometimes by ferryboat or bush plane to perform and teach workshops. At the core of
the theater is an educational center that cross-fertilizes all Alaskan theater.*

*Molly Smith was a nineteen-year-old with a mission when she went Out-
side to learn theater. When she returned to Alaska seven years later with fifty
battered theater seats, she was determined to fill them with an audience. She and
her husband, Bill Ray (Senator Bill Ray's son), and her friends Kate Bowns,
Jack Cannon, and Joe Ross inspired each other to create and develop the Perseverance.*

I CAN NEVER prejudge what is going to happen in our theater. I can
never control the audience. It's a real sickness to think that the artist
can do that. Human nature is not controllable. Sometimes people walk
out of the show at intermission or during the show. Sometimes I get
phone calls or I am stopped in the grocery store or on the street by people who decide that they don't want to come to the theater again. All

kinds of things. That type of violent response, even though at the time I'm going "Oh, my God," is really necessary because it's all part of a rejuvenation. If we aren't having dialogue with the audience, we are not really doing our job. Sometimes that means confusing people or making them angry.

My family moved here from Yakima, Washington, when I was sixteen. I really hated Juneau when we first flew up because it was rainy and dreary. I was in my senior year in high school and I thought I had just come to the worst place in the world. But then within about six months I met a lot of people I really cared for, including my husband, Bill Ray, whom I met when I was sixteen. And I continued doing theater, which is something I had done all through my teenage years and even before that in elementary school in Washington State.

Then I went to the University of Alaska for a year and a half, traveled in Europe, thought I was going to be in a prelaw degree, and eventually ended up deciding that I should follow my heart instead of my mind. My mind was telling me, "Go for the money." And my heart was pulling me in the direction of theater. When I was in Europe, I decided that what I really wanted to do was start a theater in Juneau. There had been a very active theater base all over the state but few theaters where people were doing it full time. I was interested in creating a full-time theater in which people performed out of the traditions that were here.

And so I was nineteen years old and marched into my teacher's office at the University of Alaska and told him what I was going to do. He said that was very nice, and then I left school because I needed to learn everything I could about theater if I were to do this. Back in Washington, D.C., with my husband (who was at the Naval Academy), I worked in a lot of small grass-roots professional theaters like New Playwrights Theater, Back Alley Theater, down and dirty theaters where you just rolled up your sleeves and did anything and everything. I learned design and box office and I taught in a professional actors' studio. I did a lot of directing.

And then my husband and I brought fifty theater seats back with us in a big truck to Juneau, myself in the hopes of starting a theater. I thought it would take five years, but within six months the Perseverance Theater was born!

Some of the people who started the theater with me are still with it now, but originally it was just five of us sitting around a kitchen table in 1979 arguing about what it was that we were going to do.

I think this community was incredibly responsive. That was one of the really attractive things about doing theater in Alaska. Doing theater back East, people were always saying, "No, no, no." People in Alaska, "Yes, yes, yes!"

That absolutely unblocks you and frees you, very much like the environment around here does because it is large and forgiving (even though it can be dangerous) and your potential is always right out there in front of you. As well as how small and vulnerable and human you are. I've always taken a lot of solace from the natural surroundings and I often get my best ideas from being out in nature.

When I first came back, I started to meet people who seemed right to start a theater with. And the first thing we did was a show at the Little Theater called *The Miracle Worker.* After it had closed, a number of people had said, "What's next?" I felt what was next was let's start the theater. But what to do it on?

While taking a walk in the woods with my sister I remembered that a man named Richard from the Office on Aging had said, "Why don't you do something on senior citizens and base it on Alaska?" I thought, "Ooh, that's a good idea" because so many people have come here because of the romanticism of Alaska. I felt that I needed to learn more about that if this theater was to spring from the place where its roots had to be.

In retrospect it was a smart decision. At the time it just seemed like a great thing to do.

We named the theater Perseverance both for the idea of persevering and because it is the name of a particularly rich gold mine here. So I interviewed about thirty-five pioneers of the area. People from all the different cultures and social classes in Juneau. And then a writer put it together into a readers' theater piece. Then we cast the best storytellers including Cecilia Kunz from the Juneau Native village; Mike Zamora, a gold miner from the Filipino community; Mamie Jensen, whose family used to run a little drugstore here in Douglas; Les Parker, who was a gold miner and whose parents had come up during the gold rush. I mean it was just fabulous stories. We had bear tales, Tlingit stories about the beginning of man and how everything has life and how everything has eyes. There were stories about the great fires in Douglas. About the gold rush. There were funny stories and sad stories—it ran the gamut—but that thing took off like a rocket. The first night we only set up fifty chairs so that any audience that came in would feel as if the place was full. The next night we went to seventy-five, and the third night one hundred. Pretty soon we were up to two hundred, there was a line around the block, and we extended that run in the church social hall.

As soon as that show was over we talked about how we really needed a home because a theater without a place is no place 'cause you're just totally nomadic.

This building was built a hundred years ago and it felt warm and small and right to us. The space upstairs used to be a bar with the best pool table in town, and now it was a liquor store. We built the new theater in eighteen days. Our upstairs tenants will never forgive us, but we opened in the summer with *Pure Gold* and then with a full season.

Ever since we have always had at least one show a year written by an Alaskan playwright or about a contemporary Alaskan theme. Like a show called *In Two Worlds* by Earl Atchak who is a twenty four-year-old Yup'ik Eskimo seal hunter from Chevak. *In Two Worlds* is about subsistence issues from the point of view of the seal hunter. Earl comes out of an oral tradition, so it has been a big move for him to write things down.

Our seasons are wildly eclectic because we try to reach out and touch many parts of the community. I like the cross-section of people in our audiences. Often in big cities it's white middle to upper class, well educated. Here it's active people that come to the theater, the same people that you'd see down at a ball game or out fishing. That is very attractive to me because as an artist I want to talk to lots of people instead of just one stratum of society.

For a performance of the *Odyssey* in 1989, a group of six kids came all on skateboards and left their skateboards at the box office door all lined up. I loved it! If we can affect people in that way, that they're going to come on their skateboards, that's pretty good.

I think the theater is going through a remarkable change right now as we become much more focused artistically. We have hired a group of full-time artists from all parts of Alaska and have started an intern program. Normally we had drawn only from this Southeast region.

We are always interested in bringing in people from different cultures around the state. That is what makes the place pop! We did a project several years ago called *Yup'ik Antigone,* which was *Antigone* from the point of view of a Yup'ik Eskimo woman. The play was all in the Yup'ik language and with Yup'ik actors. That project toured the world.

More and more of our work mixes cultures. We are not really interested in traditional works, in preservation. We are much more interested in the new. Combining and drawing from many cultures. But one of my best memories of our theater came from *Yup'ik Antigone,* a play in which Dave Hunsaker had combined two cultures that he felt were closely aligned, the Eskimo culture and the ancient Greek culture.

Sometimes theater can become so much its own world that there isn't a reference into the real world. But this new play became an amazing example of life and the stage mixing.

When the cast was in New York performing *Yup'ik Antigone* at La Mama Theater, the show opened to rave reviews in places like the *New York Times*. The place was packed. And the actors received a phone call from their village at Toksook Bay that two elders were dying. And the decision was made to leave.

I remember Debbie Baley, our producing director, called and said, "My God, what are we going to do?" And of course, the decision was to do what the performers needed to do out of their own culture.

Of course, within a white culture that would never happen. Within the Yup'ik culture it had to happen. When theater becomes isolated from the real world, it becomes deadly theater. But this was a great example of theater rooted in the real world. This theater company went home for reasons of death, which is very much the struggle that Antigone goes through within that play about her decision to do everything she can to bury her brother. And so *Yup'ik Antigone* became a legend in New York as "the show that didn't go on."

# Bill Spear

## Sticking It to 'Em
## Juneau
## b. 1943

*As an undergraduate at Georgetown University's School of Foreign Service from 1961 to 1965, Bill Spear was a Nebraskan in a college full of Easterners; he was also unusual because of his constant preoccupation with drawing and art. Three decades later Bill has passed through a successful legal career only to return to art. Today his finely-detailed cloisonne pins, which are handcrafted in Taiwan and sell in museum shops across the country, depict Alaskan motifs as well as historical and scientific subjects of wider interest. Bill travels frequently Outside promoting his work.*

*Bill Spear's self-identity is Alaskan, even though he often rebels against living in Southeast. He is a person who cares deeply about the troubles facing Alaska. Despite his sometimes devil-may-care persona (he dressed for Fred Bahovic's hundredth-birthday parade as a giant skunk cabbage), he is like one of his own pins, sharp edged and thoughtful.*

I THINK PEOPLE'S perceptions of Alaska are mostly wrong. True, in Alaska if you are willing to live in the Bush outside villages, you can still do what you want within the limitations of nature. But other than that, this is basically a socialist state. Except for a few of us, everybody works for the government or has a contract with the government. And it is very difficult to break into the system. Alaska needs *perestroika* as much as Russia does!

I find traces of the old North more in the Yukon, where I go play hockey. The Yukon is more like Alaska of the fifties and sixties. It's a northern culture, not an Alaskan culture. The gas station attendant is just as important as the attorney general because in winter when your car is stuck somewhere . . . The Yukon is just much more egalitarian, not that I'm egalitarian in every sense. But everybody there has a worth and a sense of belonging in the community that I don't see much of in today's Alaska.

A sense of personal worth is what Alaska ought to be about. But that type of personal pride has often been under attack here. During the pipeline construction period I was working in the Labor Department and witnessed tremendous bureaucratic arrogance and social manipulation. When the pipeline construction started, the big feather in our caps was to see how many villagers we could get out on the pipeline. Well, it was disastrous to take the best twenty members of a village of two to four hundred people out of that community and put them on the pipeline with Local 798, the International Welders who were like the Hell's Angels of the labor movement. Those Natives were degraded in every possible way and exposed to alcohol. Their whole sense of worth was destroyed. When they returned home with plenty of money, they began to feel really stupid about living in a traditional sod house instead of in one of the houses they saw on TV. The bureaucratic white community had arrogantly disturbed village Alaska irrevocably. I'm not in favor of a human museum, but I don't believe in the arrogance of saying that the way we live is right and that if people cannot live up to our standards, their ways are bad. But that is the message we've sent. As a result people are dying horrible deaths because of alcohol and social disruption.

I was part of it, sure, but I did the best I could from 1968 to 1981. I flew up in 1968 and landed in Juneau on a beautiful, glorious day—as only Juneau can have. There was a salmon derby with lots of huge fish being hauled in. I thought, "My God, this place is wonderful! I hope nobody finds out about it or it will be like California."

So I moved up. I brought my wife and dog, but as soon as I got up here it rained for about a year and a half. We had two of the worst winters in memory back to back. In fact, I didn't even leave town for three years 'cause in those days Alaska didn't have any oil money and things were still kind of speculative about the future. At that time the attorney general's office had only eight of us and now they have about eight in a room. But the legal work was always very exciting. I was always in over my head. The eight of us were taking on all the major oil companies in the world. But that petered out and I lost interest in the overly litigious legal system—an institution which is self-perpetuating at the cost of everyone else. There were more lawyers than I felt were justified. I did not want to be part of the problem but part of a solution. I had always doodled and drawn and in 1981 I started turning my paintings into pins.

All my pins together were like one big art act. Their actual drawing was not that original a deal, and my only claim to being an artist is that by sending these little objects all over the world I am letting people make up their own little stories about them. And the fact that the pins are very durable and will be around in the future to create a certain amount of curiosity. And keep reflecting off of each other and other things for a long time.

Today many people are intimidated and afraid to go to a museum for fear of having the wrong reaction. And that's not what art is. It should be part of our culture, but it has been stolen from us by a bunch of people trying to make money. So my whole thing was started from an antigallery impetus, but ironically the same thing happens to my pins as happens to paintings. Some of them are now worth three or four hundred dollars because of their limited numbers. I mean I try to make as many as everybody wants. People always ask me, "Is it a limited edition?" And I might make three or four hundred of them and they think, "Oh, it's not a limited edition." And yet even the rarest coin was made in quantity.

So I'll make as many as I can and as long as my enamelers stick with me. But the whole idea of *selling* paintings is antithetical to me. Give 'em away! Making a living at art is a form of prostitution. At first you start painting for your friends and then you start painting for money. If people like the purple ones, you keep painting the purple ones.

In this country you're supposed to approach art like it's some kind of sacred deal. By my pins being a popular broadside item I am trying to bring art back to where it belongs, into the hands of the people.

There are some decent painters in Alaska but most of the stuff here is kitsch. Drawing a wolf or a puffin may be your cup of tea but I don't think it's art. I am pretty hard-nosed about art. I don't call my pins art, either. Art is supposed to be up there with religion and philosophy as one of the most uniquely human things we do. A lot of Alaskans make money drawing and carving because tourists come up here and have to take something back home and will take almost anything. Juneau is better than Anchorage and we definitely have a group of serious artists in town, but no one would move here because of our great art movement. I think that if Juneau developed a good school system, we would get a huge influx of writers and artists.

That's what Alaska is ideally suited for. It is a great place to paint and write. I don't know how anybody can paint in New York City.

I speak my mind about everything, so I suppose that makes me eccentric. That's one thing that Alaska used to be noted for and which was healthy in the way that we think of the British as being a little eccentric. People who are independent and didn't accept the standard way of doing things. And the more I get away from having to answer to anyone (which this business has allowed me to do), the more eccentric I can afford to be. You can't afford to shoot your mouth off if you are working for somebody who doesn't like what you are saying. It's nice to get out of that and sacrifice a bit of material well-being to be in control of your own life. That's worth a lot of money!

I'm pretty depressed about Alaska. Events happen so quickly anymore that they are impossible to stop. I am most concerned right now about clear-cutting in the Tongass, which I think is a travesty. Alcoholism in the Bush is one of the saddest stories I can think of in the United States. And I just feel like public employees have a stranglehold on the state and are not going to let go. I think we'll have to run out of oil completely before they will ever reduce their numbers.

I remember a huge, angry headline in the *Anchorage Times* in 1970 that the state's budget had for the first time exceeded a hundred million dollars. Now this little town of twenty-five thousand people has a budget of a hundred million dollars. And yet they say we are down to the bone and cannot afford to lay off anybody. I don't know how many billions we get out of the oil business but I know that we don't have assets anywhere near what we get in income. So I am not hopeful about the future.

And because there is money here now, Alaska attracts a different kind of person, people who come here for the money, not for the country.

Alaska's history has been of tides of people coming in. When the tide recedes, it leaves a certain residue on the beach. When I came up, I met the people that had been left over from World War II, the people who had built the highway or been stationed in the Aleutians. They had been waiting for Alaska's many resources to be tapped. Then to their surprise in the late 1960s the residue of the Love Generation headed for the hills in great numbers and just woodshedded for a while. Within five or six years they had captured the governorship and a majority of the House of Representatives.

But then the pipeline came and brought a whole bunch of construction workers. That tide washed away the other one and left a new group of people. Then the state got the money and new people came up to work for the state to get incredible benefits. That tide is still in but its time is rapidly running out.

Should I go out with the tide, too? Particularly in the winter

Juneau is not an easy place to live. But I always seem to choose to stay. And as my friend John Hale says, "If you live here for two years, it just about ruins you for anywhere else." You just have a different way of looking at things. You are a much less formal person and you just aren't willing to put up with people's bullshit is what it boils down to. There is a sense of adventure and independence that I think you develop. There's no way I could sell IBM machines or fit into a law firm down south and go play golf somewhere.

I'm more independent now in what I do. Most of my business is outside the state—including a lot of the creative side. I'm doing drawings about the Southwest desert and about things that don't have much to do with Alaska. But at the minimum I will always maintain a toehold here. I think in twenty years it is going to be the last place left where we can have any chance of not stumbling over somebody else.

# Connie Taylor

## A Helping Hand
### Cordova
### b. 1942

*Constance Taylor, daughter of Berkeley academics, wanted the adventurous life the 1960s offered to footloose young people. She arrived in Alaska with a lot of hope and plenty of gumption. Her jobs included unloading tenders, raising mink, fishing crab, salvaging copper, collecting wild herbs, and selling bags of her smoked herring for twenty-five cents. In 1966 at age twenty-four she began commercial fishing out of Cordova in a twenty-four-foot wooden skiff obtained in trade for two barrels of diesel fuel; she had scavenged her fishing gear from dumps and beaches.*

*That was then. Today you cannot enter the seine fishery without a permit costing in excess of one hundred thousand dollars. And to homestead in Alaska, assuming that you have won a lottery for a site, you must be ready to invest heavily. And, cheechakos, don't try to start a trap line in the backcountry without first boning up on laws, regulations, and landownership.*

*Connie Taylor fished commercially for nineteen years, operated a successful Cordova printing plant and art gallery, refereed fractious meetings of the chamber of commerce, and served on the city council (later winning a lawsuit for having been excluded from secret council meetings). Despite all the changes that have come to Alaska, she is still a strong believer in the North's opportunities.*

WHEN I started fishing in 1966, I was very fortunate to have friends who advised me. And I watched what the other fishermen did and tried to copy the ones who looked successful.

When I started out, I was very green. I fished an area called Coghill, or Port Wells, across Prince William Sound, just east of the mountains from Anchorage. My twelve-year-old brother went out with me for several weeks of his school vacation. We were very inexperienced and we were pulling up our nine-hundred-foot salmon gill net by hand, not with a motorized reel. Folks knew that I was green at it and they kidded me a lot. When I delivered the fish one night at the tender, they told me that the best place to fish was out among the icebergs. And that what I should do to catch a lot of fish was to set the net out right among the icebergs at night. And so I did that and then tried to sleep with the boat bumping the icebergs. It was much too noisy and so we quit; when we pulled up the net, there was nothing in it. I realized I had been sold a bill of goods!

That used to happen to cheechakos before permits became so expensive. There was quite a bit of friendship in the fleet. Helping each other. A lot of joking and fun among people. There's much less of that these days because everybody has so many dollars at stake that there isn't time for anything fun. Fishing is now all "I've gotta make a buck."

When I first started fishing, whenever there was any kind of difficulty, no matter what else you were doing you quit trying to make money and went to the aid of whoever was in trouble. The last summer I fished, in 1986, my boat and another boat got our nets tangled in our propellers and there was about a twenty-knot wind blowing onto the beach. And one of us was washing up on the beach and the other was still offshore a little ways. It was obvious to anyone going by that we were both in some sort of major difficulty but two boats passed right on by, didn't even slow down. That's one of the changes I've seen in the nineteen years I've been fishing.

In the early days when the seasons were still fairly regular for salmon purse seining, you fished from Monday at six A.M. to Friday at nine P.M. And so you had Saturday and Sunday to rest up. We'd frequently sport fish and roast fish on the deck and have a relaxing party with other fishermen. Those were very pleasant weekends, when fishermen shared their experiences and enjoyed a salmon and halibut feed.

I usually salmon purse seined along Knight Island, on the east side of Prince William Sound. One of the most unpleasant trips I made across the sound was returning to Cordova at the end of a season after the oil tankers started running south with oil from the pipeline terminus at Valdez. It was calm when we started across, but it got rougher and rougher until the wind was blowing so hard that we were making practically no headway. We were in the middle of the sound headed east toward Cordova and an oil tanker came in through Hinchinbrook entrance. I could see that they were on a course headed for us. We were going as fast as we could but we weren't moving. The tanker swung around behind us. It was interesting to see how maneuverable they were. They also recognized that I was doing the best I could but wasn't going anywhere.

I much prefer fishing on Prince William Sound to the Copper River flats, where there are no land masses to hide behind when there's a storm. The sound is a beautiful area with lots of islands, so you can nearly always get into a fairly protected spot. And the water is clean and beautiful. After a while, the sound almost gets to be like a street map in your mind. You know where the rocks are.

When you are salmon seine fishing, there are two boats holding the net stretched tight in sort of a U shape. The fish swim into the net and then the two ends of the net are towed together to close the circle. The net is closed at the bottom by pulling in the purse line—much as a drawstring purse is closed. The fish are trapped in a small pocket of the net. A brailer, a huge landing net with a controllable bottom opening, is used to dip (or brail) the fish out of the net and into the vessel's hold.

Once a humpback whale got caught in my gear. The net was stretched very tight and the whale burst through and broke it open and came out of the water just beyond the cork line and rose out of the water with the corks sliding down its back. It swam off unhurt and I was left with a very large hole and with a feeling of amazement at having been that close to a forty-foot critter bigger than my boat.

Then the next week, when we had completely closed the net and it was starting to get slack as the towing pressure was let off, we saw that another whale was inside. So we split the boats apart and pulled the net apart hoping the whale would swim out the opening. Instead it, too, went through the net—another big hole to be mended on the weekend!

The summer before, a fisherman had had his net entangled by a whale and the whale had taken it away. If there is no tension on the net when the whale hits, the whale becomes tangled rather than breaking through. Bad luck for both the whale and the fisherman.

The first time I ever did salmon gill net fishing on the Copper River flats, we were anchored out there waiting through a big storm for two days. Finally when it came time to fish, I didn't know where the boundaries were and so while everyone else was leaving the anchorage and getting ready to put out their nets, I was standing on the back of my boat look-ing puzzled. And Tom Lawrence, Sr., pulled alongside and said, "See the light down there? Don't go below that! See this sign here? Don't go above that!" And so I knew I had two boundaries where I could safely go.

In the late 1960s and early 1970s, I was one of the first women to have a salmon seine boat in Cordova, and I was afraid that maybe a woman couldn't do it, because of the endurance required by the long hours. So for a couple of years I had a man skipper the boat for me. After I watched for a while, I realized I could certainly do as well if not better. After that I skippered the boat myself.

The fellow I admired most in the fishing industry always took off three hours a night and considered that a good night. I never was quite that hard-core. I felt that we needed five hours off every day.

We often fished right through storms because when it's rainy and stormy, frequently there are more fish and less competition. It's exciting to be able to keep fishing even though it is rough, but then there is the added danger. One time just two of us stayed out in the storm and fished. It had been poor fishing most of the day, but just before dark, the fish hit and we both loaded our boats. We were the only two boats unloading that night, one on each side of the tender. The skipper of the tender came over to tell me that the captain of the other vessel said that he had been tempted many times that day to quit but wasn't "going to quit while that woman was still fishing."

And then some days, when it is very hot and very calm, it is hard to be out in the sun all day. That's when you're glad for the evening and the cool and the sight of the snow on the mountains.

There are days when there are very few fish. There are days when there are lots and lots of fish. When a highliner catches a hundred thousand fish, he puts a broom up in his rigging to indicate that he's made a clean sweep. That's an exciting feeling! I've always felt proud of my crews the years we put up a broom. I don't know of any high that's as great as having as many fish as your boat can hold, when you can't catch any more because you have no place to put them.

People helped me along the way, and I feel it is my obligation to help others get a start. I feel strongly about helping kids make money for college by giving them experience on a boat or in the shop. It is rewarding to look back and see somebody to whom you gave even a small opportunity, who turned into something. I think of one fellow named Joe that came up one summer after I got a letter once from a Catholic nun at a school in Sacramento. She said he was her most favorite student and she really hoped that somebody would give him a job in Alaska because that was what he wanted more than anything else, his first summer out of high school. So she wrote to me because my brother-in-law taught at another Catholic school. It was a very distant contact, but I was the only person she knew of in Alaska.

I wrote to Joe and told him that he was welcome to come work for me for a week or two and if we hit it off, I'd give him a job. If not, I'd help him get a job in one of the canneries. So he came up. And he brought a big jar of instant coffee because they had told him that there was no coffee in Alaska. He couldn't live the summer without his coffee. And he had bought a little kit of tools, hammers and screwdrivers and things, so he'd be ready to work. He clearly didn't understand where he was going but with what understanding he had, he had made the best effort to come prepared. Which I thought really spoke well for him.

He worked for me a couple of weeks getting the boat ready. And I felt a real admiration for his willingness to work.

He fished with me for five summers. After the first summer, he operated the second vessel which we named *Roger That*. We communicated by CB radio and *Roger That* was Joe's frequent response to my instructions. Joe graduated from college with some funds to start out in life. That's some twelve years ago now. But I can look back and say, there's a young fellow who because I gave him a hand . . .

Lots of folks gave me a hand like that. I can't think of any single person that gave me a major hand but there were lots of people there when I needed a particular tool or a piece of advice. Or just sometimes a word of encouragement.

I think you can't pay back the specific individual who did something for you but you must pay it back by helping someone else.

Pass it on!

# Drenda Tigner

*Breaking the Cycle*
*Fairbanks*
*b. 1947*

*Drenda Tigner was already an experienced family counselor when she came to Alaska in 1984 to train others to be "teaching parents." The program she embraces is called the Teaching Family Model. It was developed in 1967 at the University of Kansas and imparts family living skills to adolescents. The Teaching Family Model is designed to break the generational cycle of dysfunctional families. Jargon aside, this is an Alaskan story because so many Alaskan families of all races have been debilitated by decades of alcohol abuse and shortsighted government policies.*

*Drenda (pronounced De-ren-da) was born in Oregon and grew up in Pennsylvania. She worked as a family counselor and teacher in Puerto Rico, Michigan, Connecticut, and Kansas before settling in Fairbanks. At Presbyterian Hospitality House she advocates teaching parenting throughout the primary and secondary years.*

SOMEBODY TOLD me that Alaska is the northernmost terminal for all schizophrenics. It does attract people who are runners, who want to give up, who don't want to face the problem, who want to be kids. And people brag about it, saying, "I'm forty-seven and I still haven't grown up." The perpetual adolescent attitude.

Our kids need grownups. They need somebody who says, "Yes, I can understand how you feel but this is the limit." For some reason the kids sense that in me. I try real hard to be honest about issues and not to ever lie to them. And be fair. I let kids slide a little bit if they have been having a bad time and they require a little space, but they still need that

**243**

boundary. They still must know that this is a grownup and she's going to be a grownup no matter what we do. She means it.

I worked as a senior counselor at a drug and alcohol center in Anchorage called Clitheroe. And there I met a wonderful man named Dr. Raymond Dexter. While working as the chaplain on the Alyeska pipeline he traveled and saw most of Alaska. This gave him a special affinity for the people who were spending their last thirty to ninety days of jail time in drug and alcohol treatment at Clitheroe. As the senior counselor, I worked with these incarcerated individuals in addition to a wide variety of other Alaskans—all the Native groups, Caucasians from the pipeline, people who had blown ninety thousand dollars up their noses in three months, women heads of households, et cetera. That's when I started to put my theory together concerning families here in Alaska.

I found that one generation of Natives had TB; many kids were sent Outside to sanitoriums, far from their parents. The next generation was sent to boarding schools. And then the next generation was alcohol and drug affected. So, we have had three generations of families lacking positive parental role models. It's not racial, it's not morals; it is circumstances. Too many Alaskan families have no one to teach them how to be good parents. And too many professionals say the situation is hopeless!

In the old days, even if women had kids when they were fifteen or sixteen, it wasn't a big problem because the grandmother was there to be supportive and nurturing. The grandparents, aunts, and uncles could provide a role model so that younger parents could learn. When one generation was trapped in boarding schools and sanatoriums, there was nobody to teach parenting to the next generation of Native Alaskans. Many other people have moved up from Outside and left their extended families. Some came with the military, some for the pioneer experience, some ran away. They, too, have had few parental role models.

A majority of Native Alaskans has had minimal opportunity to learn parenting skills. Some Native corporations are assuming responsibility for remedying this situation. For instance, Doyon provides tremendous support for families. They do a wonderful job. The Fairbanks Native Association is working for Fairbanks people. Tanana Chiefs Conference provides a wide variety of services.

Programs, however, tend to try to fix things after the problems have developed. For instance, in our program at Presbyterian Hospitality House we work with fifteen adolescents at a time. Maybe thirty-two, thirty-five a year. Well, that's not very many, and we have only minimal support from the church because nationally the church has gotten out of the children's program business.

The state is slowly moving forward in helping younger kids, but they still mainly provide services for dysfunctional adults. What can we do?

It seems to me that somehow we're going to have to begin teaching family dynamics in elementary school if we want to make any real difference. Communities must take responsibility for going into the schools to teach what we mean by traditional parenting because right now some communities deny that multigenerational parenting was part of their pattern. Some say that what I am advocating is not traditional even though three generations ago it was customary for grandparents to live with the young family. If adults are receiving counseling or treatment and we want to stop the cycle of abuse, we must support the whole family.

When these kids come into our program, we treat them as if they are our kids and not delinquents. Our focus is on the teaching rather than on the typical approach of care taking. The goal of our program is to teach the kids the appropriate skills and behaviors that they need in order to make it, to take care of themselves and their real families. We work closely with their teachers in school. We try to get the kids back to their natural families whenever possible. Teaching parents work very closely with the natural families, probably initially going into the home once a week. As the kids get ready to go home we work more and more closely with the families to teach them how to behave and interact.

If, for instance, a mother has been abusing a child out of panic, frustration, or just not knowing another way because she was raised with the "knock 'em up side the head" approach, the teaching parents teach her another way of behaving, at least giving her three other options. "Before you knock the kid in the head, what else can you do? Sit him on a chair for five minutes, give him a maintenance task, or do some exercising together."

Let me give you an example of how successful this can be. Of course, I remember all the graduates of our program that are doing well (and all those that aren't). It's wonderful to think about the kids who were "throwaways" and went on to college. I think of one who had been diagnosed as psychotic because of doing things like sticking fifty pairs of soiled underpants down the chimney. Could he trash a classroom! In fifteen minutes he could go in and just clean the whole place out. Teachers were scared to death of him. And that boy is in college now and wants to work in childcare to pay back the chance that he was given. He went back to live with his abusive mother. She is grateful that her younger children have benefited, too.

We have one girl who had been in and out of fourteen foster homes (twenty-two out-of-home placements and three adoptions). She went from not attending school at all in seventh grade and attending school only three days in eighth grade to now, in the eleventh grade, making a 3.9 grade point average. She is very exciting!

Consistency and teaching *can* make a difference. I am encouraged. The kids (and families) will live up to your expectation. Educational and social services research has documented this over and over. These Alaskan kids are not hopeless!

# Jack and Edie Trambitas

## The Cheechako and the Sourdough
### Juneau
### b. 1919, 1918

*The only person who ever really laid a glove on prizefighter Jack Trambitas was Edith Dora Spaulding of Auke Bay, Alaska. In June 1938 she met the handsome eighteen-year-old army veteran, newly arrived by steerage from the Lower 48. His ways were quite different from those of the boys she had grown up with in her tiny fishing village near Juneau. At first, Edie Spaulding's half-Indian mother didn't trust him. Although Edie's grandfather, John Weydelich, had been the first white to settle at Auke Bay, Edie's mother had seen a lot of Outsiders come and go.*

*Under her mother's influence, Edie resisted Jack's marriage proposal until the night of July 3, 1939, when he gave her an ultimatum: marry him right after his Coliseum Theater fight with Soldier Goode or stop seeing him. Edie eloped with Jack that night.*

**J**ACK: IN September 1923 my stepdad boxed Jack Dempsey for world heavyweight champion in Buffalo, New York, in front of twenty thousand people. Dad lost the decision but he was never knocked down. Through our stepdad, my brother and I had gotten involved in boxing. When Dad was about seven years old, he came over from Romania with his folks. He married Elizabeth Kennedy from Idaho. Portland, Oregon, became his town; he was a longshoreman there. He was a Catholic, a very religious person. It didn't rub off on me. When I was eighteen I became a Presbyterian and my Dad didn't like that, being as he was a strong Catholic. But I figured I'd be a hypocrite if I went on as a Catholic, since I didn't believe in it.

When I was in the peacetime army, my brother and I both done quite a bit of boxing. But I never threw a punch outside the ring. We had a place in Juneau called A Bucket of Blood, where fishermen and miners would go get bombed and get in fights. That's why it was called a bucket of blood!

There were some ham-and-eggers [minor prizefighters who fought for very small purses] who liked to act tough in bars, but my dad told me that when you're sitting on that barstool, you don't know who that guy is alongside of you, so don't be pushy and cocky.

Eventually I made six dollars a day in the mine, but when Edie and I got married July 3, 1939, I had just started working and I wasn't too stakey. Just before the wedding I had to borrow a few bucks from Edie's brother Bill!

My first day in the mine I was a little apprehensive because I heard shots going off and the noise of the trains. Plus there was an underground, locked-in feeling. But I adapted fast because my stepfather explained things to me. He was a contractor in the A J [Alaska-Juneau] mine. I wasn't scared going in there. Some guys, after the first day—they were out!

I was a nipper for two years, hauling drill machines, steel, and blasting powder on a little train for the contractors.

But I was mucking in a ditch when I started in the mine and when I fought Soldier Goode. I needed money and a promoter set up a boxing card for July 3. You only got a small pay for a fight. It was no big deal like it is nowadays. A guy don't have to be too good nowadays to get in a fight and make some money!

I loved to box! That's kind of crazy for a guy to say that, but for me boxing was a lot of fun. I never had prefight jitters. If you don't like it, you're not going to last very long.

Soldier Goode was from the Chilkat Barracks in Haines and the fight took place in the Coliseum Theater in Juneau. They put the ring up on the stage. It was like fighting in a movie house.

Just before the fight with Soldier Goode, Edie and I decided to get married that evening. We decided that after the fight we would go over to Douglas and get married.

I had come to Alaska about a year earlier because my mother was up here nursing and my stepfather was working in the Alaska-Juneau Gold Mine. It was during the Depression and they thought I could get a job in the mine. I met Edie at my mother's Auke Bay house the day I arrived on the boat from Outside. As time went on we got more and more friendly. I saw pictures of her deer hunting with her brother. I figured she was really a gung-ho gal if she went out there hunting and fishing. And on top of that she was one heck of a person. Double so because she stayed with me all these years!

When I came up here, the young Alaskans figured I was some kind of a character. I dressed different. I wore pants that were tight. I smoked T-mades, cigarettes tailor-made by a machine rather than hand rolled. Maybe I was kind of a cocky character, too. I might have had that action!

Edie used to watch me fight in smokers. I think she kinda wanted to see me get punched out a little bit.

Was I nervous in the ring about getting married after the Soldier Goode fight? I had only one thing on my mind when I was boxing, I could not be thinking about love and roses when I was fighting. You don't look at any pretty broads either when you're fighting.

That Soldier Goode was a good boxer. The fight was a crowd pleaser because we both mixed it up with one another. We went after one another for the whole doggone time. We fought like it was life and death!

The fight was a draw and I thought that was a fair decision.

But then Billy McCann and I had to hurry to get dressed and take off for Douglas so I could get married.

The only one that objected was Edie's mother. I came up here and was a stranger to her. Edie was her only daughter. She wasn't very friendly until my daughter was born. As years wore on I guess I grew on her. I called her Ma and we were really close.

*At Jack and Edie's home-built house in Auke Bay a yellowing newspaper account describes the Trambitas–Soldier Goode fight:*
> *An hour after fighting a fast and furious draw with Soldier Goode on the boxing card Saturday night, Nick woke up U.S. commissioner Felix Gray at his home in Douglas to marry Trambitas to Miss Edith Dora Spaulding of Auke Bay. Nick, who wrote his name Jack Nicholas Trambitas on the license application, had for best man another fighter who fought a draw on the Juneau Boxing Club program, Billy McCann, the headliner. Miss Spaulding was attended by Ernestine Tyler.*

*The honeymooners eloped in Edie's brother's fishing boat for three sunny days in the islands off Juneau. Accompanying the couple were Bill and three of his buddies, all of whom feasted on glacier-cooled, hand-cranked ice cream and on strawberries raided from Edie's mother's garden.*

*Edie explains how she whisked Jack from the prize ring to a wedding ring.*

**Edie:** Jack told me that if we didn't get married then, he was going to quit going with me. So I decided I'd better marry him!

I had met him June 10, 1938, down at his mother's next door. We went swimming, boating, bicycling. We liked to hike up to my father's claims on the Spaulding Trail. At first Jack didn't make much of an impression, but then two or three months afterwards I thought, well, he's not too bad! The way he dressed and the way he talked, I thought he was different than the kids I grew up with here. He was big city! And all my girlfriends were crazy after Jack. I had to fight 'em off.

I was nervous during the fight 'cause I thought Jack might have a black eye or something during the wedding. But he didn't. It was a real lively fight but Jack didn't get bruised up or knocked down.

After the fight, Jack's mother took us over the new bridge to Douglas in a 1937 white Plymouth convertible, the only convertible in Juneau at that time. We sat in the rumble seat going over and back and I thought it was real romantic.

All the kids I went to school with were down there at the boat waiting for us July 4 and we had a big party.

Out on the boat there was beautiful weather with light all night long. A moon!

I had wanted a church wedding but we eloped because my mother didn't approve of him. She thought he was too wild. This big-city boy coming up here to Juneau, stealing her daughter away from her!

I didn't understand her view then but I see it now.

My mother inherited my grandfather's fruit and vegetable farm on Auke Bay. My grandfather had been a prospector and then my father prospected until he was married and had a family. Then Dad quit prospecting because he was too busy farming. My father had taken the vegetables he grew to the stores in Juneau and sold them. The road at that time came only as far as the Mendenhall River, and Auke Bay was so isolated that the only way in or out was by boat. My father had to wait for the tide to get across the bar with his boat.

I used to pan gold dust on my father's claims to earn money for my school clothes. And when there was a salmon cannery and a herring cannery in Auke Bay, I used to sell my fish to a fish buyer when I was twelve, thirteen, and fourteen. I used to get two and three cents a pound for the king salmon I caught in Auke Bay. I caught them for school clothes and books. A new bicycle.

I had a rowboat with just a hand line and a reel my brother made and attached to the side of the boat. I didn't even have a pole. It was difficult but I didn't mind it then. I rowed around Auke Bay, caught salmon with herring bait on my hand line, reeled them in, and clubbed them. I gutted my own fish.

My mother caught a lot of fish, too. Her father, John Weydelich, had come to Juneau in 1881. He had been a student at Yale before coming here to be a farmer and a prospector. He married a Tlingit Indian lady. She passed away with rheumatic fever when my mother was only five years old. Both my grandfather and grandmother had already passed away when I was born. There was just my mother and father and the three of us kids in Auke Bay.

I liked what my mother stood for. She was just real friendly and outgoing. She made quilts. And she sewed dolls' clothes for me.

Her name was Dora Spaulding. She was half-Indian but she had never known how to speak Tlingit because she wasn't raised with 'em. My Indian grandmother had passed away when my mother was only five so my grandfather, John Weydelich, sent her out to Washington to school. She was in Washington for fifteen years and then came home when grandfather had a stroke.

I had no relatives except my two brothers and my father and mother. So I never learned the language or the crafts or any of the things that the Indians did.

My mother could bake and sew and still work outside like a man! When she was in her late fifties, she built a house at Auke Bay. Her second husband had a heart problem so he didn't do much of the work. She did all the hard, heavy work.

She was only four feet eleven but she was a strong woman. I sure looked up to her!

# J. D. True

*Derailed by Love*
*Skagway*
*b. 1922*

*Until 1982 J. D. True was a locomotive engineer from Skagway, Alaska, to Whitehorse, Yukon Territory. Now J. D. has a desk job as chief dispatcher of the White Pass & Yukon Route. His book,* Along the White Pass High Iron: Hoghead on the White Pass *is a collection of disasters, such as a derailing J. D. survived when his engine jumped the track in a 1965 washout and plunged two hundred fifty feet into a canyon.*

*Speaking of wrecks, J. D.'s bachelorhood was wrecked at a little cafe up the line in British Columbia. The American train crews used to stop at the Lake Bennett Eating House just north of White Pass. There the shy then-fireman met a friendly waitress named Anna Gabel, and in 1946 the two highballed it to the altar in Skagway.*

IN 1946 I was just a lowly fireman with a scoop shovel, firing steam engines, goin' through Bennett about every day. There was a waitress there and I guess we were attracted to each other. She'd go up to the engine with me when I was through eating. Oh, after a couple of months she got a weekend down in Skagway and I didn't let her leave till I married her!

I was kind of a shy fellow. The train crews claimed they did all the courtin' for me. Well, not altogether but they were all pulling for me!

Her name was Anna Gabel. She was born and raised in Calgary in a Russian-German community. Her parents left Russia right ahead of the revolution. Two sisters and a brother were born in Russia.

I was born and raised in Arkansas. I come from a fair-sized family and there were enough feet under the table back there, and the first chance I had I left to find a home. My aunt and uncle paid my way up here to Skagway and after I got workin' I paid 'em back.

Anna was a fun person. She didn't meet many strangers! I was twenty-three and I got tired of running. When I stopped, she caught me. I didn't have to persuade her. She was quite willing. She made it easy for me, being shy that I was.

**Anna Gabel True:** I worked at the Bennett Eating House as a waitress. That restaurant had been going since the Klondike rush and was still exactly the same. Meals were served family style in the dining room. When the trains stopped at Bennett, all the passengers came in and were seated. The food was on the table in bowls and everybody helped themselves. There were three waitresses and myself and two cooks. We had beef, potatoes, veggies. Blueberry pie was the special.

The train came through Bennett every day. And we girls didn't have a lot to do, so we each picked up a person that we thought we could capture. J. D. True was more shy than anybody I had ever known. But the older engineers on the railroad spoke very well of him and I was impressed. I thought, "This man would make a good father to my children, should I have any." But all I really knew about him personally was only what he ate and drank. In those days he ate *everything* in sight!

After I had been serving J. D. at lunch about three months, a Presbyterian picnic came up from Skagway and they were in Bennett all day. And J. D. was the fireman on this picnic train. After the picnic he helped to clean up the tables, the dishes, and the silver so we could go and have fun visiting, drinking coffee, and riding in a rowboat.

Next day J. D. wrote and said he couldn't make it through again for a while. Mind you, we hadn't actually talked a whole lot at the picnic— just visited a little—so I was very surprised that he had written. Really! I still remember how funny it seemed when Jasper Sullivan, a young baggage boy, the brother of Larry Sullivan the conductor, delivered the letter.

But J. D. explained that on his way home from the picnic the grate shaker handle had broken while he was pulling on it and that he had fallen out of the engine. So he wouldn't be around for a couple of days because he was shaken up.

Later on he surprised me again by asking if I would come down to Skagway and stay at his aunt's house. He said, "My aunt would like to have you stay with her."

So Aunt Etta met me at the depot and J. D.'s uncle Harry loaned him the car and we took a drive and on this drive J. D. said to me, "Ah, would you marry me?"

I said, "Maybe."

He said, "Well, it's now or never."

I said, "Well, in that case, all right, we'll get married." Actually that was our first real date.

So we married in three days. Yes, it was sudden! That's what I said! I had only known J. D. during his half-hour, forty-five-minute lunch stops at the Eating House. I think the train crews and Bennett people railroaded us into this thing. I'm sure they said, "J. D., why don't you ask Anna to marry you?" Or "I think you ought to go after that girl." Then they told me, "I think you ought to go after that man."

Basically the train crew lied to both of us. They told J. D. I was rich and they told me J. D. had a big ranch. I thought, "Boy, I'll go for that ranch."

You've got to understand these people up here. They're practical jokers!

I had come down on Friday and we got married Sunday. Then Monday I went back to Whitehorse, riding with J. D. in the engine, where he was shoveling coal into the boiler. Well, everybody gets off a coal burner *black*. I was probably the blackest bride you ever saw!

Returned to Bennett the next day and went back to work at the Bennett Eating House. And J. D. continued to make his half-hour visits for lunch, same as before for two weeks.

The crew got a little upset. They didn't like that, so they decided I'd better move in with J. D. at Skagway. So I came down to Skagway and I've been here ever since.

The first night I was living here, the boys got one of those huge round saws and a big hammer and they all come down to our little house and banged that saw and anything that would make noise. That shivaree vibrated through the whole valley!

# Tishu Ulen

## Dancing through the Night
## Wiseman
## 1905–1991

*Tishu Ulen was a Kobuk Inupiat Eskimo and a dancer with an infectious love of life. Her coast-dwelling parents had followed the caribou herds eastward across Alaska and had settled in the Koyukuk area when gold was discovered there. In the article "Tishu's World" in* Up the Koyukuk, Alaska Geographic, *Tishu remembers:*

> *The gold camp of Wiseman was an exciting place to live when I was young. Everyone turned out for the dances, and miners and trappers came from miles around. The dancing season started with Thanksgiving, followed by Christmas and New Year's, then Washington's birthday and Saint Patrick's Day, which was the last dance until the Fourth of July. . . . When I was a schoolgirl in Coldfoot, we used to drive the eleven miles by dog sled in the moonlight to dance in Wiseman. I sometimes danced from eight P.M. until time to hitch up the dogs and head back to Coldfoot at eight A.M. There were waltzes, two-steps, schottisches, and square dances. The Eskimos would do their own dances two or three times in the evening. The white people would get up and try the Eskimo dancing for fun. We danced to an old wind-up Victrola or an old piano in the Pioneers' Hall, Igloo #8. Big Jim would beat his drum. The only break from dancing was a midnight lunch at the roadhouse. Those of us girls who had danced all night were pretty tired when we got back to Coldfoot. The women had it harder than the men because there weren't enough of them to go around, and they didn't get many chances to rest between dances.*

*Tishu Ulen's most famous dancing partner was Dr. Robert Marshall, explorer of*

*Alaska's Brooks Range and leading proponent of the growing wilderness move-*
*ment. In 1930 Marshall made Wiseman his base while he explored the region*
*for a book called* Arctic Village. *Tishu recalled how she and her chums went out*
*to the airfield the day he first arrived to see what all the excitement was about.*

> *My girlfriends and I put shoepacs on and walked out there. It*
> *was quite wet. And Bob Marshall had a lot of equipment like tripods*
> *and picture-taking everything. We got there and we women helped to*
> *pack in his lighter stuff. We were kidding one another [in Eskimo]*
> *and paying no attention to him, [saying to each other], "If you can*
> *pack that, you must have weak brains and a strong back!" Nobody*
> *else was around. He was standing back wondering why we were so*
> *happy and so peaceful. He wondered about it, so he decided to write*
> *that book* Arctic Village *about Wiseman. He used to use a little*
> *tiny pencil to take shorthand notes about us. And I told the girls,*
> *"Don't talk. He's writing everything down." So we chased him and*
> *if we had caught him, we would have taken that pencil away from*
> *him because we were a bunch of strong girls!*
>
> *Another time we did catch him when the teacher was making*
> *taffy. She didn't make it good. The more you pulled, the softer it got.*
> *Real soft, all over your hands. We got ahold of Bob and we rubbed*
> *it in his curly hair and his beard. The schoolteacher had to boil hot*
> *water to take all that off.*
>
> *We had a lot of fun! We had some very good old-time dances.*
> *We taught all them young folks how to dance that visited Wiseman.*
> *One night Bob Marshall was sitting on the side of the hall like he*
> *wanted to get up and dance. So we pulled him up and started teach-*
> *ing him. He got pretty good.*
>
> *We taught him how to speak Eskimo, too. Yes, he knew a lot*
> *of words. He stayed there a whole year with us before returning back*
> *East. He was nice, a very educated guy.*

*Dancing was not Tishu's only talent. She was also quite a good hand with a dog*
*team. In the following story from* Up the Koyukuk *Tishu Ulen tells about*
*mushing along her trap line out of Wiseman.*

OLD-TIME ESKIMO women didn't usually hunt or trap. I guess I took after my father. I did quite a bit of hunting and made good money trapping for many years. In fact, I sent my son out to high school from my trapping money. I would get lynx, fox, wolverine, and wolf pelts. A St. Louis fur buyer usually took my furs, but I did make a lynx coat for my son and often kept wolf pelts for ruffs and parkys. Of course, I also had to keep my snarelines going for dog food, and for rabbit stew from time to time.

I used five dogs for my trapline. In the fall of the year we'd cut the dogs' toenails to keep their feet from getting sore and swollen. Then we'd start hardening them every day with a little work. I used to take my dogs up to Big Lake for two or three weeks of trout fishing in the fall. The thirty-mile trip took about eight hours by trail from Wiseman. The rest of the winter, while trapping, I ran my dogs about twenty miles a day.

My trapline started about six miles from Wiseman and ran up Jennie Creek. I would check my traps every five days. I left at six A.M. and would get back about four P.M., taking advantage of as much daylight as possible. I was never afraid to be out there alone.

My team ate well when they were working. I fed them each half a rabbit in the morning and cooked food late in the afternoon. I would cook oats and melt tallow, which was poured over the oats. The hard, rendered beef tallow came in fifty-pound cans from the store. To have a good team you have to feed it well. In the summer the dogs ate lighter, but they needed a lot of water. They seemed to be happy when winter came because they liked to get on the trail and pull. Each dog had its own box house built two feet off the ground with shelter underneath for summer. Inside each house was plenty of fresh, dry hay gathered in the fall. All dogs were fastened to their houses by a five-foot chain.

I often traveled between Wiseman and Bettles in one day with a fast trail. There was a roadhouse at Coldfoot and another at Roy King's fox farm. I always carried my own dog food, and the dogs ate snow for water. I used to take a shortcut across the hills rather than following the winding river all the way. That trail is still there and can be seen from the air.

I was proud of my team. Two of the dogs had some Saint Bernard in them. They had huge long legs. Their dispositions were so good they could eat together and never growl. Three of my dogs lived to be fourteen years old, and could still run. It all depends on how you take care of them.

Lippy, my leader, was smart and fast. Silver-gray and beautiful, she was a one-person dog, probably because she was part wolf. She watched me all the time. She would mate with only one dog and was deathly afraid of wolves. Because I had raised her, she trusted me to handle her pups, but no one else could touch them. Those pups were always in demand because of the wolf strain. I never knew a dog so quick to respond. If I wanted her to take out on a fast run, all I had to do was tap the sled and she'd go for miles.

I guess Lippy was special to me because she saved our lives once. She was leading six dogs across the ice at Big Lake one spring. I was driving with Florence and Benny in the sled. Suddenly I saw the water start bubbling up, and the ice began to sag. I was too frightened to say anything. But I grabbed my fishpole and hit the sled. Lippy took off like a shot just before the ice caved in. We would have sunk in that icy water and couldn't have lasted long. When we got to shore, I just held Lippy and talked to her for a long time. I told her how much I loved her, and she knew it.

Later Lippy got distemper when Bobby Jones brought in a dog from Fairbanks. I lost her three puppies, and Lippy never got well. For a year I fed her by hand. During the summer she seemed to get worse, and my husband said she was suffering. Finally I had to give her up though I wanted to keep her always. When I came home to her empty box, I felt terrible.

# Joe Vogler

*An Independent Streak*
*Woodchopper*
*b. 1913*

*Joe Vogler's father was born in a Kansas dugout in 1879 and later became a farmer. Kansas is also where Wally Hickel and his father were sharecroppers. The Dustbowl eventually drove both Joe Vogler and Wally Hickel to Alaska. Their paths crossed dramatically in 1990. That September, after the primary, Hickel defected from the GOP to become the Alaskan Independence Party standard-bearer for governor. The coup focused attention not only upon entrepreneur-politician Hickel but also upon placer miner–developer Vogler. The two Kansans had more than their prairie background in common. Both fervently believe in a nine-teenth-century "Go west, young man" vision of opportunity and freedom.*

*Joe Vogler was known statewide as the founder of the Alaskan Independence Party (dead as a frozen battery in early 1990) and the miner whose errant Caterpillar had run afoul of U.S. Park Service regulations in the Woodchopper area of the Yukon-Charley Preserve. The party had won headlines in the mid-1970s for its separatist fireworks while the Cat caper won Joe acclaim as a folk hero among antigovernment types.*

*Though Joe Vogler has a 1934 Kansas law degree, his legal work has been limited mostly to fulminations on the Bill of Rights and the Declaration of Independence. He came into the country in 1942 when territorial Alaska's population, including Natives, was only about thirty thousand and when vast areas were still unmapped. Today, more than three decades after statehood, Joe's Alaska has changed almost beyond recognition. Now searching for colors in a creek is less accepted than deciphering columns in a report. Knowing survival skills is less important than whom you know.*

*The new ways are not for Joe Vogler. He believes in a sovereign Alaska where government exists mainly to aid in the conversion of the public domain to private wealth. Just as his family homesteaded in Kansas, Joe has homesteaded twice in Alaska. He has mined gold, developed land, and reminded late-twentieth-century Alaskans of nineteenth-century verities. His greatest moment, the 1990 victory of the Alaskan Independence Party, came like the flash of unexpected colors in a pay streak.*


I GOT UP here March 28 of '42 to work at Kodiak for Siems Drake Bridge and Dredging Company of Seattle. I came here by accident—actually the FBI told me to get off and stay off Dow Chemical's plant at Freeport, Texas, my first day of work there; they said I wasn't a fit American to work at Dow because I had called Roosevelt a dirty rotten son of a bitch and a Communist traitor for setting up Pearl Harbor and killing 3,300 Americans and wrecking half our Pacific fleet, and that's how I ended up in Alaska—but isn't everything in life an accident? You turn a corner to the right instead of to the left and something happens and that determines the entire course of your life. Alaska has been good to me. When I was a boy I never dreamed I'd ever get up here. In 1942 when I came to Alaska, it was the prettiest place I had ever seen. Old Woman's Mountain there in Kodiak, we went bear hunting over on Afognak Island when I worked for the engineers. The part that I liked about it was that the country was still open to do things, even in wartime. There was no rationing up here. You could get ammunition and rubber tires and everything else. You could go ahead and do about anything you wanted.

I had always had dreams about placer mining and as soon as I got here, why I was in the hills one way or another. When I came to Fairbanks in September '43, why that put me right in the heart of the placer mining district. I was working at Ladd Field and I met many of the miners because the mines had been closed down. Gus Votila, mined out here on Goldstream, Miscovich. Frank Miller had come in here in 1904. John Hajdukovich, he came here in 1905. So I knew a lot of men that had stampeded at the turn of the century. They were an independent sort who believed in *doing things*. They were men who had relied upon themselves. They were self-reliant, honest, helpful, but above all, they were able to take care of themselves. They didn't expect a grant or a damn permit.

See, you didn't even have to file your assessment work or prove up. You just lived on the ground. You were there and in possession and the government rewarded you for that. When I came here, the United

States government was encouraging the settlement of its land. I home-steaded twice. The government was entirely different than today. They were helpful instead of being this bunch of regulators, keeping it for a park. Actually this environmental movement is a religious movement . . . They are a bunch of damned pantheists!

But when I came into the country, the old-timers had a helpful at-titude about telling me about this or that. They weren't greedy. They were a different people. America was still advancing and still encourag-ing people to spread out across the land. Alaska was as open and free-handed as could be. Look what happens here yet. If somebody burns out, the people get together and help them rebuild.

The first time I went placer mining was in '51, up on Homestake Creek, a tributary of Charity Creek, about seventy miles up the Steese Highway. Stampeders had been in there in 1900, before they came to Fairbanks. A thousand men spent the winter of 1900 on Faith Creek and there's holes all over hell from their digging and prospecting. And, of course, when Fairbanks was struck in 1902, why they stampeded there. See, this country was alive with people looking for something to do. There had been panics in the States and people were hard up and will-ing to go out and do something. Government encouraged them. That was the part that I enjoyed about Alaska when I came here.

I want homesteading to continue. I wouldn't allow the federal gov-ernment to own one acre of land. Our Constitution never foresaw the American government owning any for parks or anything else except "forts, magazines, arsenals, dockyards, and other needful government buildings and the central seat of government." Where did they get any authority for national parks? They have none. They dreamed it up out of thin air! They are thieves!

The destiny of Alaska is to hold dear the Constitution and the Declaration of Independence while America goes Communist. We'll join with western Canada when Canada breaks up. We'll be a new nation. Our future lies ahead. America is a decadent nation whose industrial might has gone to hell. Our destiny is to keep the dream of America alive. The United States doesn't want that dream anymore.

Alaska has a destiny and it is not as a state of the United States of America. It is impossible for us to survive under the American flag be-cause of their colonialistic attitude. We need to be able to utilize some of our resources here for secondary value-added jobs. We've got to. If all we are doing is providing raw materials, that is a colony of the worst sort. That isn't the America I was taught to believe in.

We started the independence movement in the spring of 1973. I started the Alaskan Independence Party and ran for governor in '74 as a means of spreading the idea. The idea took hold like wildfire. If we had had the money . . . We were living in a house trailer then and the phone almost came off the wall from all the calls. But by 1990 our party was down to just a handful of friends . . . until Wally Hickel joined us to become our governor.

First, a prominent Anchorage attorney, Edgar Paul Boyko, said that we might have the opportunity to nominate a candidate, so I got copies of the laws from the elections office. Then the news media kept calling me to ask if Wally Hickel was going to run on the ticket. I called Wally twice and he said, "It depends on what Jack Coghill does, Joe."

So I made six copies of the statutes and I called everybody that was left of the party. Our secretary, Rosalyn Stowell, couldn't make it, so I let Frenchy De Roche, he was the vice chairman, I let him keep the minutes and type 'em up on his computer. And Martin Ott. And Dee Roberts, the parliamentarian. And my wife. And that was all there was left of the party.

And we had our meeting on a Saturday night and the party authorized me to nominate Jack and Wally by petition, if John Lindauer and Jerry Ward, our candidates, dropped out. Mrs. Lindauer had cancer and it took John's heart and his money. He was in one debate where he couldn't even remember the questions. He had to be asked each question several times because his wife's illness had just taken the heart right out of the guy.

So I dictated the nominating petition and we nominated Jack and Wally. Then nothing happened for a few days.

On the night of Monday the 18th, I got a call late at night from a lady who had attended a meeting at a banker's home in Anchorage. And she said in nice words that all hell had broken loose because the Republican nominee, Arliss Sturgelewski, had alienated all of her supporters. Then the next morning, September 19, Lindauer called me and said that he and Jerry Ward were going to withdraw, but if Wally and Jack didn't come over to our party, why to go ahead and renominate him and Jerry Ward again. So I had that petition in my pocket, too.

About ten o'clock the same day I got a call from Wally's office and we worked out a press release to the effect that I was asking Wally to run on our ticket not as a Republican or Democrat or member of the Alaskan Independence Party but as an Alaskan. I said I would leave it up to Wally Hickel if he wanted to run as a member of our party. I said I know you don't push Wally Hickel. I wouldn't try it. He's either got to come willingly of his own accord or he won't come.

So we issued that press release. Then I waited. About the middle of that same afternoon I hadn't heard from anybody so I called Wally's office at the Captain Cook and they said, "Nothing yet." Finally at five minutes of four o'clock I got a call that the governor would be on the phone soon. I waited and he said, "Joe, it's go. File the nomination."

Jack Coghill came on the line and said, "I'm going to go down and withdraw. Good-bye."

Well, I had nine miles to go and it was after four o'clock and the deadline to file was five o'clock.

I got there and I filed the papers at four twenty-six. Thirty-four minutes to spare!

And that's how it all happened. There were no promises made. The only thing under the table was the legs. I said that Wally Hickel was not required to join us in supporting independence for Alaska. I said that I had that much faith in Wally Hickel. I had never discussed a damn thing with him! There were no promises made and Alaskan independence was not discussed.

Patriotism—you do a hell of a lot of thinking before you renounce allegiance to America. But that is what it is coming to. There is no dual allegiance possible because when the chips are down, you will betray one or the other. You can't go a split path; you can only take one fork. And this is what we're coming down to. Our destiny is with the Orient. We're the land bridge, we're the jumping-off point for tomorrow. The world's greatest mass of untouched wealth lies in Siberia and we're the key to it. Our Native people speak the same kind of language and are related. Hell, the Russian people are about the same hardy type of people that are here. I'd like to see Siberia in the wintertime when it gets ninety-four below. I saw seventy-two once and I thought that was hell. But those people have to be something. They are our kind of people!

I have arranged to be buried at Dawson City in the Yukon because I wouldn't want the damned American flag over me. I'm not an American anymore. They are a criminal, colonialistic power. You can bring me back here when the *Alaskan* flag is flying over Alaska. I pledge my efforts, effects, honor, and life to Alaska. To hell with America!

# Lee Wallace

*The Apprentice and the Master Carver*
*Saxman*
*b. 1952*

*Not long ago at Hydaburg in Southeast Alaska, five young men went out in a skiff and did not return. Though their families searched high and low, no trace of the youths was ever found. But exactly a year after their disappearance five killer whales came up to the village creek and floated beside the beach with their dorsal fins showing. Local elders interpreted this to mean that the five youths had been taken in by the killer whales.*

*That is the kind of event that apprentice carver Lee Wallace wishes to commemorate on a totem pole, especially since no new totem poles have been raised in Hydaburg since his grandfather's time. (John Wallace was not only the founder of Hydaburg but also the last great Haida carver of Southeast Alaska.)*

*Southeast Alaska Native art has been experiencing a revival as formerly practical objects are created anew for their artistic, cultural, and monetary value. Some examples are spruce root basketry, cedar bark basketry, raven's tail weaving, Chilkat weaving, silver engraving, beading and regalia making, moccasin making, and drum making. And carvers produce both two dimensional bas reliefs and three dimensional paddles, rattles, totem poles, masks, and spoons. The key, according to Lee Wallace, is to maintain the integrity of the art by retaining traditional design elements such as the colors, ovoids, U shapes, and motifs of the Brown Bear, Killer Whale, Raven, and other clans. "I'm picking up where my grandfather left off," says Lee, "and I hope to pass it on to my children, nephews, or grandchildren."*

I FEEL A real closeness with the wood. When I was looking for a log for this project, I went out in the woods looking for the right tree. Then to see something like this tree come down, that's about six hundred years old, just watching it come down with all its power and force, and knowing how long it's been a living creature in this world, and knowing that the Creator created the red cedar for us to use!

I have a lot of feelings about what our own Native people are doing right now clear-cutting their private lands for exportation to Japan. There's an island over here where the Haidas first migrated from the Queen Charlottes, and it is just stripped bare! I'm really sad to see that happen. How would my grandfather think about that? How would the rest of our ancestors feel about that? Because the Creator gave us these trees.

My family history in carving goes back about four generations of master Haida carvers. My father's generation was the one that quit.

My father is full-blood Haida; my mother is Tlingit-Tsimshian. So matrilineally I'm really Tlingit. But all my artistic heritage comes from the Haidas and that's the only reason why I'm pursuing it. If there wasn't any family history of art, I probably wouldn't be pursuing it at all. It was always passed down. My father learned from his father but chose not to pursue it. Today he comes out once in a while and sharpens my tools. He doesn't have the strength in his hands to work anymore, but he encourages me.

The missionaries came up and did a mind trip on my grandfather. They looked at totem poles as idols. So they told him, "Quit your carving; destroy your idols that you have carved." He ended up cutting down his own art. Some became fence posts and some were split up to be used in boardwalks. To me that had to be a real hard thing to do, to create something and then destroy it.

But he finally came around years later and he went back to his carving.

Christianity has done that all across the world. Just because Native people are different and have different beliefs. And a lot of times the beliefs are not different at all. I see a lot of parallels between Native beliefs and Christianity, but missionaries took things like totem poles out of context and did not look at their true meaning.

I apprenticed first with Nathan Jackson. Nathan had twenty years of experience behind him and he was selective about who he wanted to take under his wing, and I certainly am, too. I don't want to waste my efforts on someone that doesn't have the heart and commitment for it. I worked at it and loved it and felt that this is what I should be doing. I've done all kinds of things under the sun, but I know now that this is what I was meant to do. Just like my grandfather and great-grandfather.

In totemic work there is often a dividing line between the master's side and the apprentice's side and the apprentice copies what the master is doing. I learned that way when I and another apprentice worked in Fairbanks for a master carver, and the other apprentice was somehow inhibited, awestruck by this master. But I never did feel that way. This other individual asked me, "Lee, when is he going to let me do something major?" I said, "The only thing holding you back is yourself. Just do it!"

My start when I moved back here three years ago was building a traditional long house. They had grant money from Princess Tours to build it and they needed some laborers to do the adz work. I had never done any adz work before but I said that I was interested in the art and it would be a good start for me. So they hired about six of us to do the adzing. Elbow adz doing the texturing of the wood. Nathan at the time was working in the shed also, doing some artwork. He'd come along and watch us and he'd talk to the different guys. But when he came to me, he wouldn't say anything to me at all. He didn't give me pointers or say I was doing great or doing bum. He never said anything to me! And I'd go home and tell my wife, "Nathan came by and I noticed he talked to other guys about their techniques and he'd come up and watch me and just watch, and not say a thing. Am I doing so bad that there's no help for me or am I doing okay?"

I didn't know. And that went on for days.

Then I showed him some of my early artwork. "Here's a frontlet I did," and he'd just look at my dance headgear and say, "Hmmm." There I was wanting some response from an expert and all he did was, "Hmmm." Again I was thinking, is it so bad he doesn't want to critique me or am I doing okay?

That was in 1987 and Nathan had already gotten the bid to do some of the artwork for the new long house at Saxman. There was an outside screen that they hadn't commissioned yet which I wanted to do, but they ended up giving Nathan the whole job. I was adzing away one day and he said, "I hear you're interested in doing some art. How would you like to work with me?" I was elated. I said, "Oh, yeah, I'd love to!" At that time he was working on the house posts, so that's how I started working with him. I'd watch and then he'd give me a little section to work on.

We finished up the house posts and he said, "I've got some more work to do on the inside and outside screens; let's keep on doing it." I said, "You bet!"

So I ended up with a lot of experience working hands-on because

I had the drive and the high interest. Working with Nathan has been very gratifying!

*Nathan Jackson himself began carving while laid up in a hospital with tuberculosis after having been in the service. But the core of his approach to craftsmanship came from his grandfather.*

When I was being raised as a fisherman, my grandfather used to show me how to mend a net. He'd cut the net and he'd say, "Here's where you start," as he was cutting it all out. And he'd cut down to the end [and say,] "And here's where you end up and here is the kind of knot that you tie here," and he'd demonstrate it a few times and say, "You measure it this way and go back and forth and you come out right at the end. Now try it!"

I had only seen it once but I tried it, nervous that he was watching. And then he'd get disgusted and take it away from me. And so I had to try it, not in his presence. I experimented to see what I could do. Then I came back and I said, "All right, here's a net with a big hole in it, and here's where to start, and here's the kind of knot to tie to begin with." And I started tying each one of those knots until I got down to the bottom. I said, "And here's the kind of knot to tie at the end."

And that proved to him that I could do it, that I had experimented on my own, and that I could help him mend the nets. He couldn't hardly see at all; he was about seventy-five years old.

I was able to learn that by watching and experimenting by myself.

I was kind of shamed in that because the Native traditional way of doing things falls a little bit on the negative side. In other words, "You'll never make it. You'll never amount to anything."

So I didn't say anything to Lee Wallace as far as instructing him. I just let him go ahead.

Now Lee has become a genuine carver.

# Marleita Davis Wallace

*Metlakatla Hostage*
*Wrangell*
*b. 1908*

*Marleita Wallace is part of the first generation of children that grew up in the new town of Metlakatla. A schismatic Scottish-born lay minister named Father William Duncan had decamped there from British Columbia in 1887 with several hundred of his Tsimshian followers and had founded a sawmill and salmon cannery. Marleita's father, boatbuilder Rod Davis, and grandfather, John Davis, Sr., were the economic and religious leaders whose Presbyterianism was a counterforce to Father Duncan's cult in the tidy village of lumbermen, fishermen, and fish traps. Metlakatla is today Alaska's only official Indian reservation and still the only place where commercial fish traps are legal.*

*The village was new in Marleita Davis Wallace's time, but it provided most of the youngsters with the traditions of their Tlingit and Tsimshian grandparents. For instance, Marleita's grandmother and her woman helper (originally described by Marleita as a slave because her work, at least initially, seems to have been characterized by involuntary servitude) melted deer heart tallow and spruce pitch into a creamy paste to use as a skin lotion for the teenage girls to prevent pimples. The girls had to remain isolated on an island with the mixture on their faces for three days. "Finally Grandma took the mask off," says Marleita, "and I washed in spring water. My skin was so beautiful—just like peaches, so smooth and creamy and clean—that I couldn't help but love it! Today girls don't even know what I am talking about when I say, 'Did you go with your grandmother to get your face fixed?'"*

*Growing up under her grandmother's tutelage, Marleita was torn away from home at the age of nine and relocated by the federal government to the Chemawa Indian School near Salem, Oregon. She is very resentful of having been held "hostage" there to insure, she says, the good behavior of her family.*

*After many years in Hollywood and New York City, Marleita Wallace now sews Eskimo dolls for tourists at her home in Wrangell.*


I WAS BORN in 1908 at Saxman south of Ketchikan. I'm half Tsimshian and half Tlingit. My father, Rod Davis, was Tsimshian from Nass River, British Columbia. He was twelve years old when they moved over from old Metlakatla.

I didn't grow up at the new Metlakatla, though. I grew up in Chemawa, Oregon, at the industrial training school. I was a hostage from the time I was nine years old! The federal government went around to the villages and picked out the parents that showed initiative, progress. Father was the son of a chief and a chief in his own right, and the government only took the children of leaders. When we were first recruited, I was the only girl taken from Metlakatla. About four or five boys came, too, whose fathers were also very active in our town council.

It wasn't hard for me to go under army discipline because I had learned how to talk to our family's workers. The same thing, in responding to an officer. You knew how to take the order that he gave and you knew how to give orders, too. I had grown up with two "workers"—a brother and sister. They didn't want to be separated, so we just incorporated them right into our family. They knew their place on their side of our big house, we kids learned how to ask them for what we wanted.

In our family we learned how to walk, too, which is something I don't see anybody teaching anymore. Grandfather taught us girls and boys how to walk. If Grandfather wasn't there, we went under practice with Grandmother.

So it wasn't too difficult for me to accept Chemawa except that we were all lonely little children. Some of the others really were belligerent about it, especially because Chemawa was under the War Department right up until 1934 and we were all raised army style on the campus. Girls all had to look alike in skirts and middy blouses and those government shoes, stogies. And the boys had regulation uniforms. It was very interesting to meet Natives from all over the United States, but we didn't really have time for that because we had to mind the rules and regulations or our demerits piled up and, boy, that hurt!

There were a thousand students on the half-girls, half-boys campus. And we didn't walk, we paraded and marched to a cadence. (When I'm not feeling so crippled, I still do it automatically without thinking, and I march away from whomever I'm with because of habit.) And we had to stand straight or we got a demerit.

I lived in two different worlds, the first learning the white culture nine months of the year at Chemawa, Oregon, and the second learning Tsimshian traditions with my old-timers at Metlakatla, Alaska. When I came home in the summer to work in the canneries, I went right back into Native clothes and food with the grandparents. The first thing I looked for was dried salmon and grease. We didn't cook in our homes because that was against our tradition. So we had a food house in the back with an old-fashioned iron stove about four feet high. The side opened for roasting salmon in there. Or dried salmon was stood up near an open fire on sticks and roasted it until it bubbled on the back. Then we broke off pieces of roasted salmon and ate them with boiled potatoes and with hooligan [eulachon] grease from Nass River in B.C. (We never ate roasted smoked salmon straight because it was rough on our stomachs.) So just as soon as we got home from Chemawa, that's what we went for. We didn't really care for anything else. When we got that, we were happy and could cope with the world.

Once we had our treat of salmon, then our souls were satisfied. We called it soul food because at Chemawa we had been eating roast beef and gravy and mashed potatoes and white foods produced by the boys at the school's big farm.

Metlakatla was a lovely little town. My first memory is of its beautiful clean boardwalks. My father voluntarily built and repaired them because he had the first mill, the first everything. And he made the boardwalks with wide boards set so loosely together that the sun used to shine right through. And underneath the big boardwalks he had the most beautiful rocks you ever saw. The water ran over them and kept them clean and the sun shone through the boards and reflected on those clean pebbles while we were underneath there. We children used those underwalks as sanctuaries. I used to love to run up and down those boardwalks just to hear them play like a piano. By the way, every one of us Davis girls had to play piano and sing in our church choir!

In those early days there was a lot of contact between the Alaskan and B.C. sides because people still had living relatives over there. Father used to take the whole fleet over to old Metlakatla, and we'd celebrate Queen Victoria's birthday the week before the American Fourth of July. Groups of people traveled in a small armada with our town band playing on the decks of the gas fishing boats. That music sounded so good! Everybody had fun over there visiting relatives and joining dances, boat races, and street parades. Then for the Fourth of July our B.C.

friends and relatives came to visit us! It was good, clean fun growing up.

Wednesday was baking day in our house and in almost every home. You could smell fresh bread being made in different homes all over that little, tiny town. There were only about eight hundred of us when I was living there.

Our father was the mayor and we were the up-and-coming family. Girls wore little blue skirts and white blouses and sometimes jumpers. We were raised strict by two grandfathers who read the Bible. (Grandfather Rev. Edward Marsden was also the choirmaster and we had to sing in his choir.) Our grandparents on both sides were church people, and we were fully occupied with Bible reading, cantata singing, and everything related to church. We had to do that almost all the year round. Even while working in the cannery I had to join the choir.

I have an old piano here and when I get tired of everything else, that's where I go. I love the old music. Through those church hymns I can still hear my family singing.

We were not even allowed to play with the neighbor children because my parents were afraid that we would get away from our church. Well, the whole town was religious, but it was split and the neighbors were in Father Duncan's church. That's where we had started, too. My birth certificate says that I was baptized in Father Duncan's church. But then my father had his father's half-brother become a Presbyterian minister so that we could set up a new church. When I was little, I can remember real well my grandpa Mars. My father's father's half brother was the first ordained Native minister in Alaska. And it cost our family a lot of money and time to have grandpa's brother, who wanted to be a minister in the Presbyterian church, go back to Boston and stay there until he became ordained.

Father Duncan had come from British Columbia because he and his church wanted freedom of religion. But when they got here, they wouldn't let people live the religion they really wanted to. The town split and there was shooting. Oh yes, oh yes. Shooting and grumping and growling—right up to this day.

Each morning every one of us Davis children got a gentle talking to from Grandmother about how to behave. Before we went to school, Grandma would line us up, the oldest one down to my brother who was a little bitty one, and she had inspection. Our fingernails, face, and ears had to be clean before we went to school. Everything. And at that time the girls had to wear beautiful, wide bows in our hair. They were washed and ironed for the next day. And our hair was braided just a little bit and the ribbon was put on.

While we were lined up standing there we thought we were going to get away with everything, but we still had to learn a new hymn. And not just one stanza. We learned one hymn a week. And at the end of the week, all of us had to sing it exactly the way it was written.

And then just before we went to school, she'd say, "Open." She wanted to inspect our teeth, to see if we had brushed them. Grandpa used to make charcoal sticks and that's what they polished our teeth with every day inside and out. Later on we brushed with a powder that came in a blue can.

When we had all passed inspection, we were allowed to go to school. We lived about a block away and we had a pet duck that used to waddle up to school with us, then turn around and come back home. Dogs didn't bother him because he was mean. And if you chased him, he'd turn around and chase you. So we had a royal escort, even though we weren't allowed pets at school.

Sunday was the one day in the week when we did not do any work. No cooking. Father had us attend the Presbyterian church where Grandfather Marsden preached. The first two pews there belonged to the Davises because we had built the church mostly with our money and time, leading the community effort, because Father had the big carpenter shop and we had several uncles who were still bachelors and could work on the church. Grandpa was still alive then when they built the church, and they built the big town hall, which is still being used today as the David Leask Hall.

But I went back to Father Duncan's big church every chance I got because I liked the music and because my best friend, Lillian Hudson Buchert, was still in the other church as their organist. I loved to push the bellows, which were in the back of the organ, to power the instrument. Every Thursday night was prayer night up at the big church. Lillian was little like me, and she had to stretch all over to use her feet and her hands. She'd say, "Get back there quick!" So I'd run back and I'd pump. And sometimes we laughed so hard that we ran out of air for the organ. The people kept right on singing and we'd just pump hard to catch up with them again.

When I came home from boarding school each summer, I felt that I was going back fifty years anyway. I enjoyed it because my grandparents in Saxman and Metlakatla were still living. I had two sets of wonderful grandparents that took care of us. We hardly ever saw our father because he was so busy or our mother because her role as a young, strong person was to oversee the house and raise, preserve, and prepare food. So the aunts, the uncles, the workers, and the grandparents were traditionally in charge of raising the children. Each person had a station in life. Grandfathers and uncles took over the boys while mothers eventually became grandmothers and saw to raising the girls.

So thirty-five years ago, when I first came back to live up here from New York City, I was really appalled because the grandparents had nothing to do. The children were independent and told their elders, "You mind your own business."

I had expected things to be the same as they used to be, but I found the families all busted like popcorn. Most of the children were into drinking and living on their own. They had no supervision, and they gradually got so that they just lived together because that was safer for them. They helped each other, which was good in a way, but what a sad, uprooted way to grow up, wasting your time and energy instead of acquiring a trade or an education. They seem to try to kill their own roots.

It is sad but today's children have lost the grandparents, so there's nobody really to help. The parents grew up on the streets by themselves and cannot help their children. But we must try to change the parents if we are to save the children.

When I used to return to Metlakatla for the summer, I partly returned to the traditional ways but I had to work in the cannery, too, because I had to earn money for my own clothes and whatever I needed for winter. Coming home each summer, there was one thing that really hurt. I could hear people talking but I could not understand them. My mother spoke a different language, Tlingit. My father spoke a different language, Tsimshian. And the grandparents spoke what my father spoke. And the government people spoke only English. If the federal teacher himself caught you talking Native, they don't care who you are, they'll drag you in by your hair and take brown soap and scrub your tongue out with a brush. And that hurt. After they did it to me, if I saw them coming a block away, off I went!

Eventually there were no more grandparents left to greet me after my return from Chemawa. Then I didn't care anymore about returning because I could see it was the very end of the old ways. My grandparents all passed on while I was in school. When the second set of grandparents died, I felt it was a clean-cut break with the past. So I didn't wish to go back to new Metlakatla anymore.

It was lonely.

# Kelley Weaverling

*Oil Spill Wildlife Rescue*
*Cordova*
*b. 1946*

*One of the most televised aspects of the Exxon Valdez oil spill on March 24, 1989, was the wildlife rescue effort. About two hundred fifty people, fifty vessels, and numerous aircraft were mobilized to bring oiled birds and animals out of the wilds for emergency care. The man in charge of this flotilla was Kelley Weaverling, a Californian who has lived beside Prince William Sound since 1976. Because of his years guiding kayak trips throughout the area, Kelley was a natural choice for admiral of this ragtag fleet. Eventually the wildlife crisis propelled Kelley into politics. Although he had considered himself an environmentalist before the oil spill, he felt compelled by the catastrophe to leave the sidelines and jump into the fray. In 1991 he was elected mayor of Cordova.*

THEY CALLED me at our bookstore–coffee shop in Cordova on the twenty-eighth of March. We collected our first oiled bird on the thirtieth during our initial reconnaissance trip. Nobody knows for sure, but we guess that as many as three hundred thousand birds were lost during the oil spill.

Lots and lots of my special places were ruined. Like the place where I met my wife, Susan Ogle, in 1977. There's a lot of trade and barter in Alaska and that's how we met. We were both artists, making our living in Anchorage during the wintertime in graphic arts. At an office party I traded her one of my guided kayak trips for some artwork for my new brochure. But that early spring shakedown trip, the first one of the season, when I was trying to remember what it is like to guide people, was not particularly conducive to romance. It was very rainy and very cold, early in the spring with snow still on the beach. And there were a lot of people. Actually Susan and I were thrown together in one tent because we had to deal with a couple of hypothermic bear hunters who came up to where we were camped real wet and hypothermic. So the bear hunters got my tent and I had to share Susan's tent. That's when and how we fell in love!

So the oil spill was very personal, you bet! You hear about break-ins and vandalism and you think it's bad. But when it happens to your house . . . I had been on almost every beach that was hit by the spill.

As far as I can tell, Exxon's total plan for wildlife was to make two phone calls. One to SeaWorld and one to the international birds rescue center. The International Bird Rescue and Research Center out of Berkeley has been doing this sort of activity for many years. They're kind of like the Red Adair of the bird world. When there's a spill, they're called out, and they're real good at what they do. It was just that the logistics, collection and delivery, in this remote and harsh environment were beyond their experience. That's why they called me.

After I had sketched out a plan over the telephone, I went next-door to Cordova District Fishermen United (CDFU) and got three fishing vessels and their skippers and some crew members. I made some phone calls to some friends of mine in Anchorage who were real familiar with Prince William Sound and had them meet me the next morning at seven in Valdez. I motored all night long to get there on time.

In Valdez we made contact with the bird rescue people. We collected one more vessel and went out into the spill to figure out the best way to collect and deliver these birds.

We found out how big an area one small strike force could deal with, and then I went back to Cordova and drew up a plan to cover the impacted area. I estimated the number of boats and personnel that would be required and I had it okayed by the bird rescue center. And then I began dispatching vessels.

At first the oil spill transcended all the existing problems, and everything else was out the window. It was beautiful to see the community coalesce instantly in the face of a large disaster like this. But it was only later, when Exxon came and VECO, that the community began to split again when some people began to benefit more than others.

My own motivation was that I had been interested in the out-of-doors all of my life. As a young boy, I had related to nature largely as a physical challenge, looking for difficult climbing routes. But just through being in that environment, my awareness increased to other aspects, to the interrelatedness of the environment out there.

I was born and raised in California. I came to Alaska largely to get away from the world at large. To find a place to hide out and to live in a community which was real and not a tourist town. Just before I came here, I had spent the previous four years wandering around Europe, climbing in the summertime around Zermatt and Chamonix and skiing in the wintertime. Then my wife and I operated a summer-long kayak guide service in Prince William Sound from 1976 until 1980. In 1980 we decided that we didn't care to guide kayak trips anymore because we just liked going out kayaking by ourselves.

So we arranged our lives in such a way that in April of each year we packed all our belongings in cardboard boxes, bought four months' worth of food, cached the food, and stayed out from the first of May until the end of August. From 1981 until 1987.

Three or four months continuous out in the sound. We became very familiar with the area and documented all our travels. All the beaches and wildlife.

Many of the orcas out there I recognize as individuals. I have known some of them longer than I have known a lot of my friends here in Alaska.

That's why the oil spill affected me so much. But out on the rescue everybody cried two or three times a day. You couldn't help it. You just got overcome. It was horrible beyond description. But we had to keep on. If we didn't do it, who would?

# Orville Wheat

*Daisy the Lifesaver*
*Juneau*
*b. 1909*

*In 1909 Orville Wheat was born in Seattle's Dago Gulch, an ethnic neighbor-hood of truck farmers. His grandfather was a motorman on the electric trolleys. When Orville was seven, his mother died, and his insolvent father sent him to an orphange on Mercer Island, which had a strict regimen of uniforms and marching. In the eighth grade, Orville managed to escape by swimming from Mercer Island to Seattle, pushing a log ahead of him with his clothes piled on top of it. In 1925 he got a job firing boilers for the Pacific Steamship Company and sailed from Seattle to Skagway. As a sixteen-year-old fireman in the "black gang," so named for their sooty, greasy appearance, Orville loved steamers but he jumped ship in Juneau because he was fascinated by Alaska. Then began several years of work-ing at sawmills, dairies, and the docks, doing, he says, "a little bit of everything." After putting in twenty-five years as a longshoreman and fifteen years as a com-mercial fisherman, he ended up as a janitorial contractor for the public schools of Juneau.*

*Orville married a Native woman at the start of World War II. His wife, Daisy, was a cool-headed, practical person whose resourcefulness more than once came to Orville's rescue.*

M Y WIFE'S name was Daisy Scott. She was born on Chatham Straits at the Chatham cannery, where her mother worked. Her mother, Lily Scott Edwards, was from the Eagle tribe and Killer Whale clan in Angoon. Her father was Sam Scott.

When I first met Daisy she was working as a janitor at the grade school next to Juneau's Indian village. I don't think she had gone to more than the fourth grade there because she couldn't afford to attend.

When we got married in Juneau just before Pearl Harbor Day, there was a lot of discrimination against Natives. Yes, there was! For instance, we longshoremen used to eat at a lunchroom about a block from the Alaska Dock, where we worked, and we had quite a few Native fellas in our union. Pretty soon one day in 1939 the White Spot Cafe had a sign, "No Natives Allowed." Well, we didn't believe in that discrimination, and if any longshoremen went in there after that, he was blackballed from the union!

Nobody dared discriminate against Daisy—even though she was a full Tlingit Indian—or they would have gotten a handful of knuckles from me!

She was well liked by the white people she worked with. She never drank, never smoked. *I* did! I sometimes made a big slob of myself. One day when I was drinking, she turned to me and she said, "I don't drink and you shouldn't either or we'll split the sheets!" I liked her enough I quit drinking cold turkey. It was hard to do. The boys used to say, "Come and have a drink with us when we get through work." I said, "I've made other arrangements."

I had met Daisy when a longshoreman named Joe Scott took me down one night to meet his mother in the Indian village. She worked in the canneries and had a two-room shack with four or five kids and an old bedridden lady. Daisy Scott was Joe's sister. I was over playing cards with them several times. Pretty soon Daisy and I just naturally fell in together and hit it off.

Daisy was sixteen and I was twice as old, thirty-two. We were attracted to each other but I had to get her mother's consent. Finally a Salvation Army major in full uniform married us in Juneau just before Pearl Harbor. Our honeymoon was spent working.

I was twenty-five years on the Juneau waterfront as a longshoreman loading everything by hand. But by 1943 I figured that there was no future in being a longshoreman 'cause I could never save any money. Well, Charles Switzer was more of a father to me than my real father. I worked for him off and on for seven years at his dairy outside Juneau. He had been very good to me and eventually he staked me to a boat. It wasn't a big boat, only twenty-six foot, but it was big enough for my wife and me and our little boy, Tucker.

Daisy and I fished out of Petersburg, Ketchikan, and Wrangell. We hand lined for halibut and black cod. If we got a big halibut, we had to pull it in to shallow water to land it. But we made a living—at least until one day when the fishing almost did me in.

In 1943 or '44 we were dogfishing out of Ketchikan and getting ten dollars for a can of dogfish livers. They were using the vitamin A out of that so flyers could see better at nighttime.

Daisy and I went to try Kaasan Bay in our second boat, the *Keet II*. Keet means killer whale in Tlinget. At Kaasan Bay at Skowl Arm there had been an old saltery where they had salted gray cod down and put them in barrels. So we decided to try for dogfish by that abandoned saltery.

Anyway, we got in there in the evening and dropped the hook. We baited the gear up, three skates to put out by hand. A skate is a hundred-foot line with a hundred hooks on it. We always baited with bought her ring to start with and later with gray cod we had chopped up.

The next morning we set this doggone gear out. My wife was steering the boat and I put out an anchor with a buoy line and a flag. Then I started putting these hooks out, one at a time, flipping them off with a stick. One of them got hung up. I grabbed for it and the hook grabbed me in the hand and took me over the side.

I didn't even have a chance to holler.

My wife was driving the boat forward but she looked back and she could just see my head going under the water. So she started backing the boat up.

I was going down with the anchor. I could see all the nice dogfish swimming around there and it was really exciting.

I had hip boots on, but I had always heard that you always had to buy them big enough that if they ever started filling full of water, they would not be too tight to kick off. So the first thing I did was kick my boots off.

I knew I was in bad trouble going down. I had taken a big gulp of air, and my face felt like it was swelling up like a balloon. So I just got my hand between my knees and I twisted the hook, just like taking a dogfish off. I didn't feel any pain because I was more than anxious to get a little fresh air.

I pulled that hook out and let it go. And, zoom, up I went! When I got to the surface, my face was about as big around as a whale.

I swam back to the boat. My wife helped me aboard and the wind started blowing. My hand was bleeding and I was afraid of getting fish poison from it. Daisy poured a bottle of Merthiolate on my hand, and I just felt like jumping overboard again. Boy, that hurt!

I just cut the gear loose. I said, to hell with it. I says, "Let's go back to Ketchikan." We started out in big waves and had to find an anchorage to stop for the night. We saw the landing light of another boat down a narrow channel. I had never been through that channel before, so I took my time, and when I tied up alongside that fisherman, he asked, "How did you get in here?" "I came through there," I said. He said, "God was with you, boy, because that's nothing but pinnacle rocks." The next morning that channel looked like a bunch of shark's teeth sticking out of the water!

But the weather had calmed down a bit and we went to Ketchikan and the doctor looked at my hand. "You're going to lose all of your nerves in there but you're not going to have any infection. It looks good to me and there's no use putting any stitches in it." That Merthiolate did the work, but boy, it hurt for a while.

I hadn't panicked because guys had always told me, "Whatever you do, don't lose your head." I was pretty calm, until afterward when the reaction set in.

Daisy was smart, that gal. Oh, if it hadn't been for her, we wouldn't have went to work for the school district after that and bought a home in Douglas. When I bought the property, it cost about three thousand dollars. Right down there near the dock in Douglas.

Before I got married, people told me it wouldn't last thirty days. And if I hadn't quit drinking, I wouldn't have had a wife. And if it hadn't been for her, we wouldn't have had a home and a janitor business for eleven years in Juneau with contracts for quite a few state buildings. She pounded a little brains into my head and made me think for myself. I had been used to being by myself, on the go all the time, from one place to another. Meeting her was the best thing that ever happened in my life!

And if she hadn't of backed that boat and started hauling up the gear, I would have been gone. The anchor was still going down when I got the hook out of my hand!

# Glossary

**AFN:** Alaska Federation of Natives.
**Aleut:** Native people of the Alaska Peninsula and the Aleutian Islands.
**ANCSA:** Alaska Native Claims Settlement Act (1971).
**ANILCA:** Alaska National Interest Lands Conservation Act (1980).
**ANB:** Alaska Native Brotherhood.
**Athabaskan:** Native people of Interior Alaska.
**Blue ticket:** A ticket out of town given by the police to undesirables.
**[The] Bush:** Any area outside the road system.
**Breakup:** The thawing of rivers and streams in spring.
**Bush pilot:** An air taxi operator who services roadless communities.
**Cheechako:** A greenhorn, often pronounced cheechaker.
**Chilkat blanket:** Southeast Alaska dancing blankets spun from mountain goat wool.
**Chilkoot Trail:** One of the routes out of Skagway to Bennett Lake, used during the Klondike rush in 1897–98.
**Chinook:** A kind of salmon; a warm, southerly winter wind.
**Cleanup:** When miners finally extract all the gold from that summer's workings.
**Coming into the country:** Arriving in an area.
**Coppers:** Large, heavy, keyhole-shaped Tlingit money pieces, also called *tinnehs.*
**Cruises:** The vacation of choice for "the nearly dead and the newlywed."
**Doyon, Limited:** One of the twelve regional corporations formed under ANCSA in 1971. Headquartered in Fairbanks, Doyon relates to a vast area of the Interior.
**Driving the line:** Trucking the Dalton Highway haul road between Fairbanks and Prudhoe Bay.
**Eulachon oil:** Oil rendered from candlefish and traditionally used for preserving berries, dipping dried fish, and frying "Indian doughnuts."
**Freeze-up:** When winter reclaims its grip on the country.
**Gee:** Right (as opposed to "haw" for left) in dog mushing commands.
**Gill netting:** Fishing with a net that catches salmon by the gills.

**Gurdy:** A winch used for pulling in fishing gear.

**Jackpot:** A predicament.

**Hanging iron:** Putting chains on truck tires for winter driving.

**Haw:** Left command in dog mushing.

**Highliner:** A commercial fishing boat that catches its capacity of fish and mounts a broom in its rigging to announce that it has made a clean sweep.

**Hooligan:** Smelt or candlefish that are dip netted and rendered into "eulachon" or "ooligan" oil, especially in Southeast.

**Ice fog:** Frozen vapor (often of polluted air) that has been trapped by a temperature inversion.

**Iditarod Trail:** An historic dog freighting route from Seward to Nome, popularized in 1973 as an 1,100-mile sled dog race from Anchorage to Nome.

**Leader:** The sled dog team's initial or lead dog, responsible for pace and finding direction.

**Muktuk:** Edible layer of blubber found in whales.

**Mushing:** Operating dog teams for freight, transportation, or recreation.

**Muskeg:** Boglike, low-growing vegetation.

**Native corporations:** Twelve regional native businesses created under the 1971 Alaska Native Claims Settlement Act to manage lands and funds appropriated by the federal government as compensation for lands taken from Alaska's Natives by the government.

**Natives:** Descendants of the aboriginal inhabitants of Alaska.

**Oogruk:** A bearded seal.

**Outside:** Anywhere beyond Alaska (but usually meaning the Lower 48.)

**Parka:** A pullover jacket descended from the original Eskimo skin-sewn garment, often pronounced "parky."

**Permafrost:** Arctic subsurface ground that is permanently frozen.

**Pigooruk:** Small hill on the tundra.

**Pioneer Homes:** Six state-operated residences for low income, senior Alaskans. The Sitka Pioneers' Home, established in 1913, was the first for "indigent prospectors and others who have spent their years in Alaska."

**Plug-in:** An electrical heater for preheating vehicle engines in winter.

**Potlatch:** A Southeast Indian dancing and gift-giving celebration.

**Seine net:** A large, small-mesh fishing net that closes around entire schools of fish. This net is used by a seine vessel and positioned by a smaller boat, a seine skiff.

**Skaqua:** Skagway's north wind.

**Skate:**  A long line studded with fish hooks used in deep-sea halibut fishing.

**[The] Slope:**  The Arctic plains north of the Brooks Range.

**Sourdough:**  A person seasoned to the ways of the North; also, a flour, water, and yeast starter for pancakes, biscuits, and bread.

**Speed mushing:**  Dog sled racing over a relatively short distance.

**Taku:**  Hurricanelike winds from the Juneau-Douglas icefields.

**Termination dust:**  The first snow of the season (thus terminating the year's search for placer gold).

**Tlingit:**  One of the Native groupings of Southeast Alaska.

**Totem:**  A carved wooden monument, typical of Southeast Alaska. The major types are heraldic, mortuary, storytelling, memorial, and potlatch poles.

**Tsimshian:**  Native people of Annette Island in Southeast Alaska.

**Tsunami:**  A tidal bore capable of massive, sudden shoreline destruction. The best-known accompanied the Good Friday earthquake of 1964.

**Tundra:**  An arctic environment characterized by wet, seasonally frozen soils and peats, strong winds, and a ground cover of lichens, mosses, flowers, and miniature trees.

**Widow maker:**  A tree or hanging branch braced against another tree. It can be dislodged by wind or logging, killing the faller.

**Williwaw:**  Sudden gusts which spill over a mountain into a relatively protected area.

# Index